REFLECTIONS
IN THE
MIRROR

REFLECTIONS IN THE MIRROR

A LITERARY COLLECTION OF SELECTED POETRY 2014-2019

GARY BATEMAN

Copyright © 2021 Gary Bateman

Paperback: 978-1-63767-162-7
eBook: 978-1-63767-163-4
Library of Congress Control Number: 2021905316

All rights reserved. No part of this publication may be reproduced, distributed, or transmitted in any form or by any electronic or mechanical means, without the prior written permission of the publisher, except in the case of brief quotations embodied in critical reviews and certain other noncommercial uses permitted by copyright law.

Ordering Information:

BookTrail Agency
8838 Sleepy Hollow Rd.
Kansas City, MO 64114

Printed in the United States of America

Book Dedication

For my wife Ingrid—always my love and true inspiration

Acknowledgements

Special Thanks to my very talented fellow poets and colleagues: Anne-Lise Andresen, Ingrid Krukenberg-Bateman, Donna Loughman, Michael Clarke, and Liam McDaid for their collegial efforts on the various co-authored poems we had worked on together that are now part of this book

Exordium

Reflections in the Mirror is my second book of poetry that I wrote for release to the general reading public. This new collection of selected poetry gave me the distinct opportunity to undertake a more diverse and in-depth selection of poetic themes and formats than I was able to accomplish before. I sincerely hope you will find my latest poetic presentations here in the classic world of *Ars Poetica* to be interesting, stimulating, and intellectually engaging. Poetry, as the true expressive art it is, speaks to a greater and all-encompassing spirit which represents a profound sense of enlightenment for mankind and contributes to our shared common humanity.

Poetry should leave the reader with a sense of fascination and wonder. It should also serve as a source and an intellectual repertoire for a deeper, personal inner-reflection. After all, poetry is a truly wondrous medium for contemplating and expressing a multifaceted variety of themes, ideas, myths, personalities, drama, tragedies, and thoughts that help to shape and reflect the complex essence of our continuing human endeavor. For me, poetry's inflective nature and its relevance to our modern world are unquestioned. And, as a writer, I see poetry in both a metaphorical and symbolic sense as a type of mystical enchanted mirror which reflects the very soul of mankind.

I have one final thought worth sharing with YOU, "The Reader," as you embark on your journey in reading and reflecting on the poetry that I have set forth in this book:

"A mirror may reflect much more than any mortal shall ever really see, whilst revealing timely images of the past, present, and future yet to be."

Enjoy the book!

Gary Bateman
Schöningen, Germany

October 2020

Contents

CHAPTER ONE
First Visions, Enchanted Thoughts, Shibboleths, and Magical Reflections

A Broken Heart.. 3
A Cold Dark Yellow Unhallowed Moon 4
A Dream... 6
A Most Irish Fairy Tale – Merry Christmas to All 7
A Poet's View on Words 10
A World on Fire 11
All Hallows' Eve Black Mass Incantation 13
Always a Dream 14
An Ode to Fine Drinking 16
Be Courageous Above All 18
Being 19
Black Cat Hath Green Eyes Most Evil 20
Black Witch... 21
Boring 23
Burning Flesh – The Devil's Own 24
Can't Make It Without You Baby 26
Complexus-Syntaxus-Maximus....................................... 27
Cosmic Dust 28
Cupid's Golden Bow... 29
Death 31
Death of a Knight... 32
Diamonds Forever My Love in This World 33
Dreaming of Nature's True Love So Rare........................ 35
Eden Wishes Us to Dream Again..................................... 37
Edge of the Forest... 39
Enchanted Vision of Love So Pure................................... 40
Eternal Soul.. 41
Evergreen in Winter Cold... 42

Frank Sinatra – You're The One 43
Halloween Eve. 44
Hate 45
Heinrich Heine Revisited. 46
I Be, I Sing 48
I Know YOU from My Dream 49
Joe Shit The Ragman. 51
Jukebox Gigolo 53
King Vlad 55
King Vlad Redux – Second Cold War 57
Leprechaun in My Bottle. 59
Life 60
Love 61
Mirror of the Soul 62
Moon Light . . . Moon Night. 63
My Christmas Dream 64
My Heart Skips a Beat My Love 65
My Window 66
New Year's Baby 2015. 68
No Fear My Dear Friend 70
Not Missing Love's Beat. 71
On Meeting You Most Beautiful Now. 72
Our Love and Passion Always Forever 74
Our Passions on Fire My Darling. 76
Pearl Dreams of Rare Love 78
poisonously enchanted mushrooms so luscious rare 80
Prufrock's Eternal Footman 82
Rainbow. 83
Rapunzel 84
rising from out of this cold frozen wasteland. 85
Santa's Favorite – Rudolph The Red-Nosed Reindeer 86
Sending Waves Touching Beautiful Always. 87
Sonnet to a Very Fine Poetess. 88
Spill Ink 89
Star Light . . . Star Night 90
Teardrops. 91
The Evil Jack O'Lantern 93
The Future. 94
The Grim Reaper Cometh. 95

The Noble Language	96
The Nocturnal Delight of Mephistopheles	97
The Past	101
The Present	102
The Radiance of Our Love So True	103
The Sorcerer	104
The Unholy Ones	106
Thinking of You	107
This One's for You Bartender	109
Time Flies	110
Unrequited Love	111
we our souls will spend our time repenting	112
What Our Dreams Are Made Of	114
When Our Eternal Poetry Muse Beckons	115
Where are you Fred Astaire?	117
With You Forever My Love	118
Without Your Love	119
Would You Dance This Last Dance with Me	120
You Never Told Me	122
Your Beauty Is	123
Your Kiss	124
Your Look of Precious Love	125
Zapfhahn	126

CHAPTER TWO

Enchanted Moments, Mortal Passions, Shades of Evil, and Cosmic Destiny and Realism

A Brave Soul Goes Home	131
A Leprechaun's Christmas Dream	132
A Leprechaun's Christmas Magic	134
A Most Beautiful Symphony of Love	135
A Person's Worth and Measure	136
A Progressive Shadow	137
A Rainbow's Magic	139
A Spider's View	140
A Spirit Leaves the Body Seeking Eternity	142
A Teardrop Falls	143
A Time of Bliss	144

A Tree	145
A Winter's Night	147
A Withered Rose	148
Almighty Lord God	149
An Autumn Portrait of Beauty	150
An Echo Through Time	151
Angel Eyes Loving You Forever	152
Animal of the Night	153
Autumn's Promise	155
Blood Red Moon	156
Bryant's Necropolis Conceit	158
Celtic Dreams	159
Christmas Love	161
Chronicler of Events and Emotions	162
Count Dracula's Love	164
Creative Process	165
Dance through your life	166
Despair	167
Destiny and Fate	168
Dream with Me Always My Love	169
Enchantment	170
Frankenstein's Monster	171
God's Christmas Angel	172
God's Return Ticket	173
Goethe's Emissary	177
Halloween Eve's Double Tanka	178
Halloween Treat	179
Halloween's Evil Visage Cometh	180
Heart of Eternal Beauty	182
How Shall I Say I Love You	183
I Shall Feel Your Touch Always	185
Ich weiss schon, was du meinst	187
In the Dark Night Sky	189
Intelligence	190
Into Eternity's Arms	191
Je Suis Charlie – Afterthought	192
Joy	194
Keats – Romantic Humanist	195
King Vlad the Greatest	196

Le Mot Juste	197
Looking So Deeply into Your Heavenly Eyes	198
Lord Byron – Genius Unchained	199
Love is	200
Love Star Night	201
love you can paint all colors of the sky azure	202
Love's Import	203
Love's in the Stars	204
Love's that Magical Wonder	205
Love's the Soul's Fire	206
Lucifer	207
Medusa's Love	208
Moments in God's Cosmic Time	209
Mother Nature Cries	210
Mother Nature's Little Prince	211
My Heart is Yours My Love	213
On Valentine's Day My Love	214
Our Cosmic Existence	215
Our Destiny	216
Our Earthly Appetites	217
Our Excursion is a Pathway	218
Our Two Stars Sparkle as One Soul	219
Our Winter Love	220
Paracelsus	221
Paradise Lost	222
Paris November 13th Makes Me Weep – Afterthought	223
Past Ghosts	225
Peace, Love, and God's Greatest Gift	226
Prufrock's Symbolic World	228
Rapture	229
Santa Claus	230
Sentiments of Love	231
Shelley – Romantic Visionary	232
Smiling Spitting Deadly Sins	233
Solitude	235
Starlight	237
Striking Deeply a Painful Reminder	239
Stupidity	241
Sunshine Radiance	242

That Spring Love in Your Eyes.................................. 243
That Sweetest Starlight and Heavenly Embrace................... 244
The Evil Enchantress with the Greenest of Eyes 245
The Evil Hands of Tyranny...................................... 246
The Final Dance 247
The Fire in My Soul is Real.................................... 248
The Frozen Ghost... 249
The Might Have Been 250
The Moon, The Swan, The Rose 251
The Never Will... 252
The Power of Love 254
The Reaper's Return 256
The Stars at Night... 257
The Sweetest Starlight and Heavenly Embrace 258
The Tides of Our Passion 259
The Walk of Love... 260
The Warmth of Our True Love 262
Theatrum Mundi 263
Tilting at Simplicity.. 265
To Be, To Feel, To Love, To Live, To Die 267
Valentine's Magic 269
Valentine's Unicorn 270
What Kind of People Are We?.................................... 271
What Our Angels on High Meant 275
What the Heavenly Angels Above Speak Of 276
You Told Me Never Again My Love................................ 277
Your Beautiful Heart Doth Beat................................. 278
Your Touch Means So Much....................................... 279
Your Warmest Embrace My Love 280
Zephyr's Magic 281

CHAPTER THREE
Alchemic Notions, Beyond the Veil, Moments of Love, Life's Realities, and Spiritual Epiphanies

A Love So True... 285
Ancient Shadows Awaken into God's Light 286
As Liquid Fire Melts... 288
Autumn's Kiss.. 289

Believe in Angels	290
Fickle	291
God's Holy Whisper of Love	292
Hobbyhorse	293
Love's Alchemy is Eternal	294
Meretricious Spirit	295
Our Human Nature	296
Phantom Slippers of Thoughts	297
Poetic Encryption Like Ancient Egyptian	298
Sailing Beyond My Dreams	303
The Bewitching Call of the Siren	305
The Christmas Spirit	306
The Demon's Shrill Cry of Dread and Horror	307
The End	310
The Magic of Christmas Divine	312
The Master of Nuances	313
The Old Dark House	314
The Soul's Path	318
The Unknown	320
This Fury-Fiery Moment of Hot Sensual Love	321
Trickster Extraordinaire	322
Turbidity	323
Winds of a Frozen Wasteland	325
Your Satin Silk Touch	326

CHAPTER FOUR
Soulful Thoughts, Human Realism, Rays of Light, and Shades of Darkness

A Bohemian Maze of True Evil	329
A Parable of Love's Spell	332
A Psychedelic Whistle Plays a Rhythm into the Darkness	333
A tiny little star lights the way	335
Angel in the Clouds	336
Death and Forlorn Time in the Shadows of True Evil	337
Death Comes	338
Deep in Our Hearts	341
Demagoguery	342
Dreams Divine	343

Erkenntnis	344
Fall of Man	345
Fires of Noise	346
For Our Love So True	348
Irish Nectar of the Sun Goddess	349
It's Your Time	350
Just a tree	352
My Supreme Goddess Thou Art	354
My wish for you	355
Narcissism	356
Now is Our Moment of Forever Love	357
Poetry and the Soul	358
Racism	359
Radio Music	360
The Butterfly and the Caterpillar	361
The Curve of Time	362
The dark blue night of sorrow	363
The Demon's Poet	364
The Devil's Black Eyes	365
The Full Moon Makes Faces Tonight	366
The Hole Deep in One's Own Heart	367
The Holy Dust of Creation's Seed Sown	368
The light of a candle	369
The Oneness of All	370
The Pied Piper from New York City	371
The Strange Parable of Umpti	378
Visions from Beyond	379
When You Truly Love Someone	380
With One's Life	381

CHAPTER FIVE

Messages of Love, Imagism, Notions of Infinity and Metaphysics, Mythology, and Personal Courage

A Heavenly Spirit	385
A Most Courageous American President for the Ages	386
A Most Holy Vision Speaks in Mystical Tomes	389
A Pocket Full of Stardust and Dreams	391
A Reverie of Childhood	392

A Russian Mystic Outré	393
A Spider's Web	394
A True American Hero for the Ages	396
About Fear	398
About That Certain Thing Called Nonsense	399
An Old Copper Vase – A First View	400
An Old Copper Vase – A Second View	402
Angels Speak of His True Love	403
Ars Poetica	404
Being Nowhere	406
Bewitchment	407
Caitiff	408
Champagne in Heaven	409
Charon – The Eternal Ferryman	410
Cherish Your Life Always	411
Dark Shadows	412
Deepest Memories and Thoughts	414
Despicable	416
Don't Talk About It — Write About It!	417
Dreams of Moonbeams	419
Empyrean Rapture	420
Evil, Guns, Cowardice, Stupidity, and Fear	421
Fear Not	423
Finding Yourself	424
First Love's Indelible Memory Pure	425
Forever Love	426
Forlorn Love – A Red Rose Dead	427
From the Great Abe Lincoln to that Lying Ape Trump	428
Frowsy	430
God's Heartfelt Passion	431
Going Somewhere	432
Happiness	433
Hate's Fury	434
Heavenly Hallucinations of Love's Divine Destiny	435
Heaven's Music	436
Human Desire	437
In Love's Time	438
In My Heart and Soul	439
In Vino Veritas, But Whiskey is Better	440

Infinity Beckons	441
Jackaroozapoo — You Don't Say?	442
King Lear's Voice	444
Life Cradles Us to Our Grave	445
Lolita's Conceit	446
Louise Imogen Guiney – Poetess and Writer	447
Love Always	449
Love is that Eternal Magic in Your Eyes	450
Love's Dilemma	451
Love's End	453
Love's Magic	454
Love's Power	455
Love's Rapture	456
Love's Spirit Enchants Our Souls Entire	457
Love's Spirit Speaks to Us	458
Luciferin Flies	459
Lucky in Love's Embrace	460
Magnanimous	461
Mankind's Spiritual Evolution and Beyond	462
Martians Who Walk Among Us	464
me and you	465
Mimesis Master	466
My Broken Heart Shall Never Now Last Forever	467
My Heart's Spirit and Love	468
Nefarious Spirit	469
Nightmares Shall Follow Us	470
On Being Soulful	471
On My Way to Work	473
Only a Mensch	475
Our Dreams from Times Before	476
Our Final Dance with Death	477
Paronomasia	478
Persephone's Flower	479
Phasmophobia	480
Poetry and the Occult	481
Reflections in the Mirror	482
Sadness	483
Sailing Away Under a Silver Moon Forever	484
Soul Essence	485

Soul Ghosts	486
Souls of the Dead	488
Stardust, Love and Dreams	489
Strife	490
Synchronicity and its Prophecy	491
Täuschung	493
Tender Emotions	494
Tenebrae – The World's Shadow	495
That Ancient Darkside of All-Hallows' Eve Past	498
That Heart on Your Sleeve	500
That Thief in the Night	501
The Ancient Mariner's Fate	502
The Body Finds its Rest	503
The Circus Fat Man	505
The Clock	507
The Cosmos	508
The Curse of the Dead Sea	509
The Darkness of Cold Oceans Dwelling Deepest	511
The Devil Cometh Tonight	512
The Ghosts in Those Dark Woods	513
The Grimace of the Human Race	520
The Journey to the Cosmic Beyond	522
The Kiss of a Christmas Elf	524
The Last Dance of the Autumn Leaves	526
The Last Red Rose of Autumn – First Portrait	527
The Last Red Rose of Autumn – Second Portrait	528
The Little Children are Crying	529
The Magic of Love's First Moment	532
The Magical Epiphany of an Old Rusted Can	533
The Metaphor of Time	535
The Mind's Cornfield	537
The Moon	538
The People from Those Shithole Countries	539
The Pilgrim's Ghost of a Thousand Heavenly Dreams	541
The Sacred Heart	542
The Silence of the Butterfly	543
The Strawberry Moon	545
The Wedding Clock's Wish	546
Thinking Out of the Box	547

Thoughts On Infinity 548
Triskaidekaphobia 549
Turning Inside Out. 551
Twilight Whispers. 553
Two Words – A Glimpse 554
Two Words – First Glimpse Redux 560
Two Words – Second Glimpse Redux 566
Two Words – Third Glimpse Redux 572
Two Words – Fourth Glimpse Redux 578
Vincent Willem van Gogh 585
Whatever We is We are 586
When It's Time to Pay The Piper 587
Whiskey Lips So Sublime 588
Wild Roses in Ice 589

CHAPTER SIX
"The Light of the Moths"

The Light of the Moths 595

CHAPTER ONE

Selected Poetry
(2014)

First Visions
Enchanted Thoughts
Shibboleths
and
Magical Reflections

A Broken Heart

I have a broken heart so sad with sorrow,
My love's full of such anguish and fear;
My soul's afire with pain for the morrow.

My heart seeks such a palliative yarrow,
My thoughts are shattered, no longer clear;
I have a broken heart so sad with sorrow.

My desire's gone, a victim of a much harrow,
My emotions are awry and bring no cheer;
My soul's afire with pain for the morrow.

Your anger strikes my heart like a poison arrow,
Your evil intent revealed with no sugary veneer;
I have a broken heart so sad with sorrow.

I live my life now with no surcease of sorrow,
Your former love declarations ring now so queer;
My soul's afire with pain for the morrow.

My spirit's in tatters from your hateful harrow,
And your face now haunts me with a nasty leer;
I have a broken heart so sad with sorrow.
My soul's afire with pain for the morrow.

November 14, 2014
(Villanelle)

A Cold Dark Yellow Unhallowed Moon

A cold dark yellow unhallowed moon smiles beguilingly
Into the pitch-black starless and cold empty night sky
Suckling upon the very blood and the true-life force of
Pure innocence, light, and eternal goodness . . . .

Fear stirs eerily in the forlorn sound of a foghorn that's now
Blowing and crying a sad echo haunting far in the distance as
It warns of the imminent arrival of a malevolent Hellspawn
Force of absolute unmitigated evil . . . The Phantom Vampire!

As the Phantom Vampire materializes from nowhere in the
Darkest shade of night, blanketed in the thickest of fog and
The coldest of night air . . . One can sense with an utter fear
And foreboding, shivering sounds touching from the shadows
As creeping, softly-cold fingers down the spine with walking
Fingers crawling inside a prism of frozen ice and in a mist
Of souls crying in the presence of demons while a yearning
Lust of one blanket covering the sky's face painted showing
Hell's very own hideous face—an exquisite evil and a spirit
Drunken and moaning in an eternal fiery abyss of palpable
Suffering and howling, sounding their own lust for pain, as
A great darkness grips those who walk this troubled Earth
Without any joy, casting happiness to the lepers always and
Forever chained to the deadly darkness and eating out hope
In the very end . . . .

From this spider's web and a nest of dark perpetual evil,
The Phantom Vampire transforms himself from an ethereal
Form to his human form, that's quite frightening indeed for
Any human being who gazes at his grim countenance and
His most fiery red-eyes as they glare intently whenever he
Encounters an unsuspecting soul . . . and the sight of his
Hideous, razor-sharp canine teeth bring on a convulsive
Fear in the hearts and minds of his intended victims . . . .

The Phantom Vampire's ritual on the foggy nights of the
"Cold Dark Yellow Unhallowed Moon" is to drink the blood
Of as many young and innocent people as he can—whilst he
Destroys their lives and torments their souls in a terrible and
An unending existence of evil and debauchery as minions of
The Undead....

As a servant of Lucifer himself, the Phantom Vampire's
Principal charge is that of a "Soul Seeker"— and seeking
Them he does quite successfully while destroying lives....
This unending process is interrupted only by the dawn of the
Next day's morning, as the bright rays of sunlight begin to warm
The Earth and to purify and to sanctify the power and purpose of
Our Almighty Lord God....

As a priest... a man of the cloth in this bucolic Irish village
Along the seacoast, I hold my head in shame and revulsion
At the evil escapades rendered by the Phantom Vampire
During his nocturnal visits to feed on the blood and souls
Of our innocent people....

I always turn and talk to God while earnestly praying for their
Blind souls through their gossamer eyelids and seeking the
Lord's divine protection and delivery from this most dark and
Wretched evil... May the bright sunlight show them the road
To a true happiness during the *Feast of All Souls* and to the
Gates of Salvation....

With no fear and a most clear purpose in mind, and with the
Divine support of Almighty God in Heaven, I shall be the one
Who fulfills God's charge in driving that long, wooden stake,
Blessed with Holy Water and Angel's Dust—through that nasty,
Evil-dead putrid heart of the Phantom Vampire!

November 6, 2014
(Free Verse)

Author's Note: A Collaborated Poem with Liam McDaid.

A Dream

At a moment in my life—long, long ago,
I had a dream of an ethereal existence,
Transcending the mortal bounds of my
Own earthly existence.

What a sublime notion worthy of thought;
To be an "Entity" beyond our mortal existence.

My thoughts are there, each and every day;
Moving outside of "Everydayness."

What a moment to behold whilst gazing
Into the vortex of life: past, present, future.

Who will be my Sage? my Guide?
Questions pervade my Soul, my Being.

When I awaken will I remember or
Continue living as a one-dimensional person?

My dream world should be my reality.
My real world should be not—or is this so?

September 28, 2014
(Free Verse)

A Most Irish Fairy Tale – Merry Christmas to All

It's not just Santa Claus who we perchance meet during this very cold time in December right before Christmas. There is "Carolina," and she's the beauty of a wondrous winter that is picture-perfect, and reflects a magical image that bespeaks an aura of true joy and majestic moments of mirthful activity replete with an undeniable spirit of happiness, jollity, celebration, and fun.

With luscious, long-locks of beautiful black hair that flows far down her back, Carolina, at once, captures the immediate attention of all who meet her during the Christmas season and are enchanted by the nature of who she is, as a true fairy princess. With her bright, blue eyes and a truly incandescent glow that's radiant now for all to see, she's dressed in a sparkling white robe that is made of an angelic content with a glossy coat arrayed with both pearls and diamonds.

During her evening stroll through the forest out in the deep woods, Carolina walks quietly in the night's fresh snow accompanied by two deer, a fox, a rabbit, a moose, and several reindeer who always join her during her walks in and around the forest. As a real fairy princess, Carolina possesses the delightful ability, and God-given talent to speak the languages of the various animals in the forest. This reality is known only to the forest animals and to no one else.

As the "Fairy Maiden of this Enchanted Forest," Carolina keeps a careful watch on the evening horizon whilst the snow falls now apace, in the hope and wish for a marvelous and joyous Christmas. During Carolina's evening walk, the ground is frosted-frozen-hard and now radiates a shining, silver sheen that reflects readily in the evening mist until the next morning when the very first early rays of the enraptured sunlight begin their breaking and peeking through the thick morning mist. The image of this whole event is truly so divine and fabulous to behold as the annual "Spirit of Christmas" now comes alive again for all to see.

The forest animals join in now and begin dancing joyfully whilst creating a melodic sound that resonates with a dash of vim, vigor, and a bewitching alacrity throughout the forest entire. And then, out of nowhere, all of Santa's Reindeer appear together in their resplendent glory: Dasher, Dancer, Prancer, Vixen, Comet, Cupid, Donner, Blitzen, and Rudolph, with his "Red Nose" so beautiful, and oh, so bright! And the sounds the reindeer make, stay in the minds of the little children—just like sweet-sounding little voices wonderful so in dreams, singing special celestial tunes as a bright light appears magically on the horizon whilst planes from all over the world begin landing with such precious cargo like loads of neatly written letters to Santa Claus from little children throughout the world.

And with this most joyous moment at hand, Santa Claus begins to call his elfin helpers into quick action whilst the "Irish Leprechauns" do all of the heavy work as they are much tougher. But all the while, the "Old Fighting Irish Spirit" in the leprechauns does reflect a softer side too, as they drink a few cups of some very fine and stout, old fiery Irish dew to keep themselves warm and smiling like the very wee "Little Devil" in them who is mischievous and all, yet so content and so happy to be a part of such a delightful yearly moment and event that's full of real memories and truest joy for all of the "Little Children of the World."

As the merry leprechauns do all their work in helping Santa's elves, they do so with a jolly spring in their steps, whilst almost bouncing on the very tips of their Irish green toes much like little jumping springs that are full of boundless wonder, energy, happiness, and fun.

And then, day after day, as the letters keep arriving at the North Pole, Santa's elves and the leprechauns there begin working busily in the North Pole toy factory whilst Santa checks the letters of all boys and girls through a magical window, that when he shakes it with both of his hands, he sees through a fairy mist in a glowing glass bubble—all of the Christmas treats—whilst calling together all of his reindeer, for it's time now to leave!

With the sound of hooves on the snow Santa now readies his sleigh, and he's very quick to start whilst all of his helpers are loading up gifts for the children. And then, he flicks the reins of his sleigh and the bells start ringing, and in a flash of magic dust and in a "Great Spirit," he sings with a booming voice to the ground below as he waves and wishes Mrs. Claus a very fond and loving farewell, and off he goes in a bright flash of light, with a merry Ho! Ho! Ho! . . . Ho! Ho! Ho! that echoes melodiously, as it resonates now in the far distance for all to hear!

At each chimney, Santa slides down quickly—A Big Surprise!—whilst eating some of the food laid out for him. He then brings back some of the food to share it with his loyal reindeer after the night is over. And now, Santa feels both fat and plump from eating so much on his mystical trip, and heads home now to the North Pole whilst smiling so contently at the children bounding with such joy and happiness, and there's ringing in his ears, filling them with cheerful sounds, as he relishes the children's images with such sweet and golden smiles! He wishes now everyone a Very Merry Christmas, and then falls asleep after Mrs. Claus makes him a really nice cup of hot chocolate.

With this, Santa's very tired, but easing his weary bones like this each year makes him love his job even more whilst feeling the magical delight that his efforts and those of Mrs. Claus, his elfin helpers, the leprechauns, and the fairy tale fun of his reindeer—bring to all children in the world during the Christmas season!

Merry Christmas to All! Merry Christmas to All! Merry Christmas to All!

"I shall be back again next year," says our old, dear friend Santa Claus with a mirthful twinkle in his eyes and that most enchanting and playful smile of his!

May God Bless all of you and keep you always!

December 9, 2014
(Free Verse)

Author's Note: A Collaborated Poem with Anne-Lise Andresen and Liam McDaid.

A Poet's View on Words

Words are the sublime mystical fabric and common medium of all poetry.
Words portray what the poet sees, senses, feels, imagines, and dreams.
The very magic of poetry comes to life from a deliberate woven process
Of words blended into thoughts, metaphors, beliefs, situations, and emotions.

There is a saying in the original Latin: *"Verba sunt indices animi,"*
Which when rendered in English is: "Words are the indices of the mind."
Words, in the poetic sense, form the ethereal undergirding for these indices
And beckon all poets to think deeply and precisely about their thoughts.

As poets develop and expand the precious word treasures of their minds,
They begin to sense over time a deeper understanding of the human psyche,
And a greater appreciation for the complex circumstances affecting people,
Which shape the human endeavor—good, bad, happy, sad, glad or indifferent.

Words then form the symbolic arrows in the poet's quiver to be employed
With thoughtful care, devout meaning and intent, and an enchanted vision.
We as poets should strive for nothing less as we reflect on our poetic visions,
For these can be realized in: "Words are the indices of the 'poetic' mind."

September 23, 2014
(Quatrain)

A World on Fire

We live today in a world of great tumult
And of rising uncertainty and anxiety
Which pervade the world stage like a cancer

Despite soaring technological advances
Our environment and our home Earth
Are bearing an unimaginable burden

People are wondering what must be done
To right these wrongs and adjust our course
Before we turn the corner to "No Return"

Tyranny, Poverty, Disease, and War
Are still with us today since the beginning
Of time and are mankind's greatest shame

God may be with us intellectually
But mankind must be self-reliant
To survive an inattentive, distant deity

People see answers to these enigmas
Sounds are made, echoes are heard
But nothing comes back in response

Frustration reigns supreme for many
Fear and anxiety multiply all concerns
There can never be easy answers

Tyranny still reigns alive in many countries
As the actions of tin-eared dictators abound
And are on ample display for all to see

Poverty is still a shameful, terrible curse
Which afflicts the most unfortunate
And is paid lip service by the wealthy

Disease is a scourge still in our world
And still felt by those most in need
And never enough is done to change this

War is the ultimate insult to mankind
And its wide-felt swath and affliction
Plagues yet our modern, enlightened world

What to make of all these challenges
Is not easy for any of us to digest
And let alone understand why

Yet understand, comprehend we must
If we want a better world for all to live in
A Sisyphean task at its very best

Man still holds the key to make change
Positive and real for our troubled Earth
But can it ever be really so in the end

October 16, 2014
(Tercet)

All Hallows' Eve Black Mass Incantation

We Pray In The Name of Our Father Lucifer,
Which wert in Heaven:

Boil, Boil plague-ridden rats and toads in oil,
With a pair of gleaming snake eyes too.
Mix in fresh hen's blood and a rabbit's paw,
With a touch of horse dung and a lizard's tail too.
Add six cups of Vitriol and a tablespoon of Goldwater.
Stew, Stew this Stygian alchemic brew for near six hours
During Vespers for Our Midnight Black Mass on All Hallows' Eve.
Serve this unholy sustenance to Our Coven at midnight,
As we pray in Lucifer's name for his guidance in defeating
Jehovah's holy forces of eternal goodness and the light.
We do this in the name of Lucifer—The Dark One.
We seek forever darkness, degradation, evil, and negation
As Our Coven has the power of "His Power" as granted
By His Unholiness as the full moon's shadow crosses over
The face of the Earth.

October 5, 2014
(Narrative Incantation)

Author's Note: An earlier version of this special Black Mass incantation appeared in my epic narrative medieval witch's tale, "Rosalia – The Evil Black Witch of the Harz," that was in Part II of my first book of poetry, Conversations with My Muse, which was published in 2015.

Always a Dream

A little fairy princess one day sits resting on a most beautiful sunflower,
And magically, she begins stretching her wings for an anticipatory flight,
Whilst capturing a wondrous, majestic vision of the brightest flying colors,
Of one gentle and soothing rainbow promise—a shining and a light to delight;
As the ground begins to tremble and crumble now underneath her tiny feet,
She takes flight on her splendid little wings—quite magnificent to behold . . .
Through the colors of the mist and veil of magic she sees a bright light shining,
And it all becomes clear—as she sees gold, and even more gold on the horizon
Radiantly gleaming in front of her very eyes and charming her senses entire.

Then a most curious little green man with curved ears pointing heavenwards
And possessing remarkably strange, and yet, soft mesmerizing green eyes,
Presents himself both kindly and boldly to the little fairy princess in person;
He jumps right in the pot alongside her, dancing a jig to his heart's content,
And the princess shines all colors of love and warmth over him under the mist
Of a most dazzling and enchanting dream to behold and cherish now forever.

With this the little green man reveals his true nature to his new-found princess,
And with a most proud alacrity bearing a quaint princely nature, he declares:

"Me Darlin' little princess so near and so dear to Me own little heart,"
"You must know I'm your Leprechaun always obedient from this very start,"
"At this moment, most precious Me knows you've captured Me little heart,"
"And with this you've captured too Me overflown' Pot of Gold now in part,"
"With Me undying love and devotion to you always carried in Me little heart."

With this the Leprechaun and his little fairy princess danced a mystical old
Irish jig together whilst singin' and laughin' both so gently and contentedly;
All the while his soft-green eyes and her sensual eyes azure locked now in
A most romantic gaze and affection when they began kissing one another,
And brushing inside and both sharing heartfelt fluttering emotions and a
Swelling with a deep beauty and a most passionate love in Heaven born.

With the genuine passion-felt affection and the romantic kisses exchanged,
The Leprechaun and his little fairy princess began to transform themselves
Right before each other's very eyes, and Behold!!—in a quick moment, the

Leprechaun became a most handsome and sweet-loving young prince, and
His little fairy princess, in a flash of bright light, lost her wings and changed
Into a most radiant and quite beautiful young princess with long-flowing,
Beautiful black hair, and a very lovely smile as resplendent and sweet as
Any angel in Heaven above.

And now, the handsome young prince and his beautiful young princess were
An elegant and most wonderful couple to behold and cherish—kind, smiling,
And so deeply in love.

The young prince with his Irish blessings began sparklin' and sprinklin' star dust
All over his young princess and they both lived happily ever after with a profound
Passion and love, emotion and devotion, kindness and charity, vision and purpose,
Forever to their end on this Earth and later in Heaven by the Almighty Lord God.

October 29, 2014
(Narrative)

Author's Note: A Collaborated Poem with Liam McDaid.

An Ode to Fine Drinking

(Something on the Lighter Side)

With alcohol coursing through my veins,
I sense and feel the best of my pains.

With double resolve to amend my aims,
I can't believe I really want to.

Oh Alcohol! Oh Alcohol! Oh Alcohol!
You are the balm and bane
to my existence;
and yet, if I must choose,
I choose the balm to my existence.

As I tear through the shadows of my life,
I know that thou art with me,
every time I pour a glass of fine red wine,
or a stout shot glass of Irish whiskey,
I marvel at the sound and tenor of this fine alcohol
as it moves in waves and slaps the inside of the glass of choice.
The sound it makes is indeed notable and quite pleasant.

As they say in the German:

"Das macht ein gutes Geräusch."
-or-
"Das macht ein guter Klang."

With alcohol coursing through my veins,
melancholy is never one of my pains.
This emotion is not allowed
nor will I ever be cowed,
and depressed—as some suggest:
to slump, to sulk, and to sit in the corner
crying over what might have been.

When drinking and thinking and being, and—
with alcohol coursing through my veins,
I do indeed savor the sound of fine alcohol being poured
to quite rightly ensure that I shall never be bored.

As they say in the German:

"Das macht ein gutes Geräusch."
-or-
"Das macht ein guter Klang."

August 24, 2014
(Ode)

Be Courageous Above All

Be Courageous Above All in everything
You do and become involved in since the
Inverse of doing this is often anathema
To leaning forward and getting things
Done and becoming a viable and vibrant
Force in your own life which is so vital
Since we all have just this one chance
Within our mortal coil known as "life"
To make things happen and to make a
Difference and so the message must be
Why wait because the positive impact
You have on yourself can have that
Wonderful alchemic by-product on
Others you know and interact with
In our finite cosmos of the majestic
Human Endeavor and so standup for
Your beliefs and ideas but always be
Polite and gracious to others since
These attributes go a very long way
In helping one to get things done and
In achieving goals both big and small
And so—Be Courageous Above All
Since you only live once with your
Current Soul Body on this most finite
Mortal Earth Plane! (And don't forget
To laugh at yourself from time to time!)

December 12, 2014
(Didactic)

Being

The discussion point—
I Be, I Am, I Exist.
Being is presence.
Philosophers rejoice, yes . . .
The mortal plane is confirmed!

November 12, 2014
(Tanka)

Black Cat Hath Green Eyes Most Evil

Black Cat hath the coldest green eyes of a most hideous evil,
That chilleth my blood and causeth me the greatest upheaval.
Darkness doth pervade this creature's vile and gruesome gaze,
That giveth me unbridled terror, leaveth my soul in an utter haze.
Lucifer himself giveth this evil black demon animal its dark life,
Only to bring me a terrifying malediction of a most evil strife.
Black Cat with its visage and promise of an eternal damnation,
Seeketh for me now its vilest of intention and darkest tarnation.
I pray then, Dear Lord God, that thee save my life and eternal soul,
And deliver them now on All Hallows' Eve most sound and whole!

October 8, 2014
(Rhyme)

Black Witch

Born and raised as a little child in a Witches' coven,
the Black Witch was indeed a very precocious child
whose hell-spawned soul was seared in Hell's oven,
and like Medusa herself was a creature gone wild.

The Black Witch had a craggy, malevolent demeanor
and at a glance was stark, sinister, menacing and unholy,
with jet black snake-like hair making her even meaner;
she was a reincarnated spirit dispelling all things good and holy.

The Black Witch was imbued with uncanny, unearthly powers
and had dark probing eyes and exceptional sensory perception,
and a bulbous, bile-ridden black wart was prominent among her powers,
and protruded close to the tip of her nose from the time of her conception.

She used the bile, putrid liquid extracted from her black wart to capture
and poison and corrupt the life essence of her victims—if they resisted;
she acutely honed her pagan skills in the Black Arts to the highest rapture
whilst using her Gorgon-grimaced face to strike fear in all who resisted.

As the most favored disciple and mistress of the Dark One,
the Black Witch possessed a withering and wicked mesmerizing gaze
that was used masterfully to corrupt and control souls for the Dark One,
and for dooming her victims forever to a land with an impenetrable haze.

The Black Witch brewed alchemic poisonous potions to a hideous effect,
using them to startle, stun and paralyze her victims with unending fear
whilst unmercifully taunting and tormenting them with equal evil effect,
and using Witchcraft to destroy once innocent souls and to harvest fear.

Intoning "Our Father, which wert in Heaven," the Black Witch
began her Black Mass sessions with spirited evil and debauchery,
conjuring terrifying dreams and consigning victims to a black pitch
all the while laughing and reveling in all the evil and debauchery.

The Black Witch delighted in being "The Devil's Concubine" by name, for her liaisons with Lucifer made her omnipotent and devoutly unholy. Her unbridled sense of power and invincibility was the Black Witch's aim, for this fed her conviction to do vicious and evil things, and to be unholy.

To know the Black Witch was to realize a gorgonesque damnation forever whilst she pursued the unholy glorification of her master—Lucifer. The Black Witch was granted the power of all hell-spawned demons forever to support and consummate her unholy activities in the name of Lucifer.

August 19, 2014
(Quatrain)

Boring

Don't be such a bore
Spark your soul bravely alive
Your life then will soar

September 28, 2014
(Senryu)

Burning Flesh – The Devil's Own

Things begin turning around and very
slowly they take a nasty foreboding twist
as Hell's Dragon has not breathed yet
a deep burning fire melting red his eyes
dripping blood upon fury and destruction
pumping inside the uncontrollable fire
equal to that of a thousand steamboats
and only he sleeps in the dark dungeons.

Chained and suffering in utter Hellfire
chained in untold torment and anguish
unleashed he would burn your heart no less
in a flash—whilst scorching all to nothingness
fried black from the deepest ashes falling
cold silently sleeping with wings on fire and
chained to love's weakness as the dark fables say:
Do Not Call Upon This Beast—He's The Devil's Own!

Hell's Dragon stirs inside with tongues of flames
lashing with the pains of hate to strike all now
leaving hottest cinders and funeral pyres a plenty
it's now the Devil's very moment to unleash His Evil,
His Demon Dragon upon the saintly and the pure
and the precious doing their good works and all
and unsuspecting of the malevolence awaiting them.

The Devil enters afresh the earthly plane once more
and releases His Dragon to inflict harm and to upset
God's celestial equation of peace, harmony, and light—
bringing death, destruction, and retribution to all in
its flight path whilst breathing out the harshest and
cruelest and hottest flames of fiery perfidy in the
name of Lucifer who laughs boisterously at God and
all the while not knowing the coming angelic answer.

The Almighty Lord God works in the most mysterious of ways and He will not let his Fallen Angel have His way by murdering innocents through His Dragon proxy only too willing to serve His Master and to bring horrible and hideous death to all of mankind who fall within its flight path and intention to inflict the most treacherous and dastardly plan of unmitigated death and horror ever to be unleashed.

The angelic answer of the Almighty Lord God comes swiftly now as the Archangels, Michael and Gabriel, with their Band of Angels, enter the earthly plane to confront the horrid Hellfire vengeance of The Devil and His Dragon as they reap and sow their evil upon mankind, and with a sudden determined fury, Michael does fatally smite The Devil's Dragon whilst lopping off its head and sending its evil soul back to the depths of Hell as Gabriel banishes entire the demon forces waving his wand!

With all this, Lucifer knows with all due certainty that He must return and rejoin His evil minions who lurk in the infernal regions of the Earth, knowing that he's lost once more to the Almighty Lord God in another struggle of Good versus Evil and has now been deprived of his most prized and valued pawn of death and destruction—His very own Dragon whose blackened soul suffers now forever in the depths of Hell, and can never be reincarnated again in its bodily form!

November 28, 2014
(Free Verse)

Author's Note: A Collaborated Poem with Liam McDaid.

Can't Make It Without You Baby

I can't make it without you Baby—
When I hold you in my arms,
I feel so good like a man
Whose favorite dream is fulfilled.

I can't imagine living otherwise—
When we caress each other,
I know that our love is real
And that no other can ever be.

I can't live without—
Your touch ... Your feeling ... Your laughter ... Your love.
To me dearest one you are all-consuming
And will always forever be a part of my soul and my existence.

I can't make it without you Baby—
When I hold you in my arms,
I feel so good like a man
Whose favorite dream is fulfilled.

Like a man whose favorite dream is fulfilled.

September 30, 2014
(Lyric)

Complexus-Syntaxus-Maximus

Complexity-Syntaxity
Ezra Weston Loomis Pound
Flamboyant expression
Poetic modernity new.

Seeking no *rifacimento*
Onomatopoeia
Confusing readers so
Intricate verses make us blue.

November 22, 2014
(Double Dactyl)

Cosmic Dust

Since time immemorial across the infinite Universe—
Traces of my vapor, my trails, my footprints, my being
Light up the skies of innumerable planets etching themselves
Indelibly in the consciousness of the stars and making visible
Impressions in the cold continuum of deepest dark space.

I'm the merest of particle matter—in reality, an iota of infinity
Continuing its travel through time and space and all dimensions
Visiting the vast frontiers of the Universe whilst leaving minute
Traces of my very own Cosmic DNA.

I'm part of the Universe's great existential family—
My quest is to travel, to arrive, to be one with everything I touch,
And to savor a continuous divine purpose.

What unbounding possibilities there are as I traverse the farthest
Outreaches of infinite dark space on the "Flight Paths of Eternity."

And sometimes, I'm a part of rainbows that kiss the Face of God.

March 24, 2014
(Free Verse)

Cupid's Golden Bow

Cupid's golden bow and arrow in hand
always hits the target to the tightest degree

Shedding his green skin like the chameleon he is
the frog began drowning non-stop smiling as
he fell deeper into ocean colors of all shades of a pearl
in a deep pool of beauty bathing so bright he felt
an electric bolt filled with deep undercurrents
stirring sparks fly in the first kiss with all
feeling and close intention and emotion

As stirring sparks fly in the first kiss and bring dazzling
amazing golden warm struck straight on his green lips
he's—oh, so gallant . . . and . . . oh, so wonderful

His heart's on fire with burning passion pure
underneath the stars sailing into deep space
inside floating thoughts of his first love mate
desiring his affectionate smiles, laughs, and grins
singing in the mind's eye grace of lovely swans in flight

Traveling in space and time over the Milky Way as jewels
sparkle like stars bringing soft doting to the soul's eyes
floating to you bouncing on waves steaming sensual hot
seductive lashes move with us as we join our souls as one
as lovers with tender wooing and woven passion pure
softly we kiss my dear love as my desire lays with you

I need your love to take me to the edge of the night
dancing in my dreams deeply while turning this world
upside down into a paradise ball with all bells and whistles
I've dreamed of and wished for my entire amphibian life

Cupid's golden bow and arrow in hand
always hits the target tight and perfect
Always! Always! Always! Always!
And even a Frog in love like me knows he will find his princess

October 16, 2014
(Free Verse)

Author's Note: A Collaborated Poem with Liam McDaid.

Death

Marks the end of life—
Transformation now begins.
The soul exits the Earth's plane . . .
A new journey's underway . . .
Heaven's the destination!

November 12, 2014
(Tanka)

Death of a Knight

Blood surges bright-red through the deep gash in his armor,
while the brave Knight writhes in pain and cries in anguish.

The battle is over now, and the Knight drops hard to the ground,
knowing that his life force is ebbing away and his strength wanes.

With the battle finished the Knight begins his final fight with Death
as part of the inevitable destiny, glory, and result that follows life.

The Knight's life blood now slows to a quiet trickle like blood tears,
while key moments in his life flash before his eyes lightening quick.

The Knight finds final solace in his love of family, friends, and country;
this is a moment of sadness as his body tightens slowly in Death's grip.

His blood now seeps into the ground itself as his breathing grows shallow,
and twilight moves to darkness in the Knight's final conscious thoughts.

The Knight murmurs: "fighting, war, and duty to my king and country
have been my life's purpose, but now I take leave of this mortal coil."

With that, Death now takes the Knight's mortal body, and God's holy
angels carry his soul into the everlasting peace and eternity of Heaven.

Amen ... Amen ... Amen ... Amen ... in Almighty God's name.
Deus est qui regit omnia ... Deus miseratur ... Deus vobiscum.

September 9, 2014
(Couplet)

Diamonds Forever My Love in This World

Diamonds forever sparkle deeply as a treasured jewel
Dawning and revealing pure in a fresh breath of light
Shining on warm gentle bonds inside one's very heart

Tears just beating drums with sounds splashing gently
Young and beautiful as with a coldness of clouds above
Golden shattering silver reflections in a most azure sky

Falling rain inside believing in a dream of pure redemption
Sadness now looms heavy in a kingdom of one-eyed dwarfs
Who live daily without any hope, love, and surcease of sorrow

Water falls down over a fountain of divine beauty in a land
Of magical fairies imbued with supernatural powers of good
Bringing healing to those afflicted and ignored by humans

Everlasting happiness inside beauty cries joy and happiness
For joy will skip in every single beat of a person's heart and
Happiness abounds with naked electric and alchemic powers

And not to have love is completely devastating to one's soul
For without it men and women are robbed of happiness and
Miss the rapture and joy coming from shared emotions pure

Beauty and ugliness, hope and despair, joy and sadness—all
Pervade the human endeavor in pairs of obvious dichotomies
Reflecting warm and cold winds of continuous contradiction

Dreams My Love are a way to play on the better nature of
Our human psyche as we all seek to find calmer waterfalls
With magical properties and reflections to make us all one

Diamonds Forever My Love bring smiles and fulfillment in this
World and in our personal world too with each of us struggling
For meaning, love, hope, desire, and happiness here on Earth

A new tomorrow arises from the ashes of the Phoenix as it again
Takes its flight high into the sky making our imaginations soar in
Finding those warm gentle bonds inside our hearts making us one

December 30, 2014
(Tercet)

Author's Note: A Collaborated Poem with Liam McDaid.

Dreaming of Nature's True Love So Rare

Standing as I look across sweeping thoughts and hopes
I am alone crying into distant faraway hills and valleys
as I dream and see before me a big white puff of smoke

Drifting now low-circling from out of chimney pots high
slowly moving creeps an inner-vision dancing within me
as candy floss moves toward the glen a sweet aroma scent

Scenting turf fires the nostrils smell a wild scent in the air
as the sun melts her warm fingers into one's back soothing
pure in a baby-blue-clear-sky setting of rising high feelings

Upon a cool caressing of an autumn breeze Mother Nature
now arrives with songbirds singing sweet and clearly with
echoes of most beautiful tunes carried so gently into the air

Within a quite stillness silently whispers gasp and cry now
splitting down the middle as a teardrop falls always slowly
in love with this forever dream and to the end comes sighs

Standing on the edge of a very pretty crystal-cool blue pond
whilst watching the magical presence of beautiful fairy elves
I hear their wonderful laughs and see their radiant smiles true

Smelling the wonderful aroma of the pure mountain air now
conjures that assured feeling that all is fresh, crisp, and real
as the flowers, plants, grass, and the bees talk to one another

Dreaming perfect dreams of many beautiful mermaids sitting
and grouped in a green water pool at the waterfall's very edge
I sense and see now their true joy, beauty, laughter, and smiles

This is what Mother Nature's dreams are made of as we sense
and see enchanted visions of an environ with perfect symmetry
and feel the touch of mountain rain and a delicious soft wind

Mother Nature and her magical world of treasures bespeak a radiant beauty which makes all gods of the centuries past and present stand up and applaud so graciously this dreamy vision

November 20, 2014
(Tercet)

Author's Note: A Collaborated Poem with Liam McDaid.

Eden Wishes Us to Dream Again

A rapaciously violent storm roars now with heavy winds howling wolfishly as angry breaths pelt us like rain bullets, whilst hurling and whistling the apples of these certain eyes which can see us dreaming inside of one another as our romantic moans heighten the feelings we have, as our caresses now touch and embrace our souls whilst we see another world where kissing mists exist and are falling down, as we weep inside another magical and majestic dream that shows both of us always together side by side.

A deep sigh of sadness yearns always for a true love's voice as distant tears weep deeply at the pain afflicting both the heart and soul, which are floating and bathing in a wondrously radiant light that shines now from this other world blinded by everything one sees as a joyous reflection of a rainbow's pretty mist, that presents us now with a vision and a bouquet of mystical colors whilst we begin now to sense and feel robust and powerful emotions arousing us from a trance-like state into an active consciousness as we begin to cry happy, to cry sad, and to cry glad as we finally seek out our destiny and fate together, and dream of one another always being by each other's side forever until the end of time.

This is Eden's wish for us as we dare to
dream again and to live our love forever.

October 14, 2014
(Free Verse)

Edge of the Forest

I gaze at the edge of the forest
and wonder of life therein.
My native knowledge tells me
there is much to marvel at.

Whether it's morning, afternoon or evening
Mother Nature's intervening schedule is
continuous, seamless, and wonderful.

The forest displays a sense of beauty
and at any given moment—
a wild desire to be understood and appreciated.

I know that when my days are numbered and short,
I will conjure up in the depth of my consciousness
a past image as a child
standing at the edge of the forest—
eternal in my studied gaze and enchantment of all
that's wonderful and beyond description in
God's World.

September 28, 2014
(Free Verse)

Enchanted Vision of Love So Pure

Enchanting deep forest sparkling magical dew
Vision of beauty takes to clouds in silver lining
Starlight vision dancing with the deep shadows
Rainbow skies set to light mist of cool rain pure
And the warmest thoughts of you my Dear Love!

You are so very beautiful and precious My Darling
Behind the mirror your soul sings soothingly so
Stirring hot emotional feelings and passions afire
How the passion burns the flower of flowers so rare
Regal crowning desires petals touching softly My Love!

Silken lips purse blushing one rose holding bright
Sunshine beams inside warm fingers of light touch
Stroking hair gently halo radiating chords deeply dance
Looking into jewels of a treasure gem shines so exquisitely
Gifted I am to have met your beautiful soul and you My Love!

Over and over my heart skips beats when we caress and kiss
Beams jumping over the moon silver whispers wonderful so
Silently making love to you in every single thought of mine
Hot sexy kissing and so sensual in every inch nibbling softly
Within the deepest love inside loving you forever My Love!

December 25, 2014
(Free Verse)

Author's Note: A Collaborated Poem with Liam McDaid.

Eternal Soul

The soul's forever—
As an eternal spirit.
Leaves this mortal coil...
Again to the spirit world
And home to Heaven's Kingdom!

November 7, 2014
(Tanka)

Evergreen in Winter Cold

These lovely plants, trees, shrubs
Thrive the year around with their
Constant coloring and aura of most
Majestic "Deep Greenness" which
Testifies powerfully to the symbol
Of life that they portend in all of
Mother Nature's varied seasonal
Weather conditions especially in
Winter as the snowflakes fall both
Cold and White the Evergreen is
There with its trademark glory of
Green that signifies continuous life
Renewal as the Cold-White Snow
Falls on the ground and prepares
Our next Earthly Transition into
The new calendar year.

December 9, 2014
(Verse)

Frank Sinatra – You're The One

Frank Sinatra's name still has instant recognition even today.
He was perhaps the greatest singer of the twentieth century
And possessed those famous "Blue Eyes" and that trademark
Voice which thrilled and fascinated audiences worldwide.
For most people, his music was very special and moved their
Spirits along a unique and subtle path that only Sinatra could
Create and hold with his voice while mesmerizing them and
Charming them every step of the way.

Entertaining and enchanting the audiences in America and
Abroad catapulted Frank Sinatra to a special iconic status as
A world-renowned singer, entertainer, and Hollywood actor.
Yet, singing became his common thread and link over decades
And generations to most willing audiences who hungered for
The tenor and pitch of his voice and his fabulous songs with
Most memorable lyrics, and haunting and evocative melodies.

Some legendary songs reflecting his status and long reach with
Audiences worldwide include: *(My Way) (New York, New York)
(Strangers in the Night) (I Get a Kick Out of You) (That's Life)
(I've Got You Under My Skin) (Summer Wind)*. All these songs
And many others were trademark, vintage Sinatra and brought
Audiences to their feet while he serenaded and captivated them
Like a Pied Piper, bringing each listener momentarily along with
Him as an invited guest into his very own special vocal dimension.

Frank Sinatra was part of the Greatest Generation along with other
Famous American entertainers who packed audiences and dazzled
Them with music and dancing, and created an aura of legendary
Perfection seldom seen in today's twenty-first-century world.
Frank Sinatra – You're The One!

November 10, 2014
(Biographical Narrative)

Halloween Eve

Halloween Eve is a time for a most "grave" reflection,
When Ghosts, Goblins, Ghouls show us no affection!

On this Eve the veil between life and death merge as one,
And the wicked spirits laugh so loudly making us all run!

They sing, chant, howl, scream, and dance with much delight,
While we the living wait for dawn praying for no more fright!

Boo! Boo! Boo! Boo! Happy Halloween! Happy Halloween!
Boo! Boo! Boo! Boo! Happy Halloween! Happy Halloween!

October 30, 2014
(Couplet)

Hate

Hate's human folly—
A most tragic emotion,
A sign of despair...
It splits people asunder...
Brings sadness and wounds the soul!

November 19, 2014
(Tanka)

Heinrich Heine Revisited

I can clearly sense your utter despair of *Die Matratzengruft*
as you valiantly carried on your poetic works to the very end.
This did not change your literary accomplishments well-known,
and your courage through the misery and morphine is undeniable.

Your lyrical poetry speaks volumes among all of German literature,
and it was most marvelously set to music by the likes of Schumann,
Schubert, Silcher, Mendelssohn, Brahms, and Strauss—to name a few.
Their melodic tones as applied to your verses then, now live on forever!

Your role in and principal contributions to Romanticism fall in line
with the highest quality of your poetic language and its intention.
Your role in battling early nineteenth-century censorship in Prussia set
you out front of many of your contemporaries who resisted much less.

It's so tragic Herr Heine that your literary resistance so prominent in
challenging Prussian censorship would make you ever so more noted,
and besmirched as the Nazis in 1933 burned your books and those of
other German scholars as a reflection of their insane and twisted beliefs!

It's with great irony indeed that the banning and burning of your works by
the Nazis was parodied further by them as they ignobly quoted and used
your famous line from *Almansor* when you likened that "where books
are burned, in the end people will be burned too." We know what they did!

And so, with both honor and sadness I do understand the very cry of lament
from the confines of your mattress-grave about your final exquisite poetry,
written through writhing pain and tears as you faced the end of your life.
It took great courage to face your end like this while staying true to your Muse!

December 15, 2014
(Quatrain)

AUTHOR'S BACKGROUND NOTES:

Die Matratzengruft from the German means "The Mattress-Grave." (Heinrich Heine was confined to his bed, his "mattress-grave," in 1848 with various illnesses until his eventual death eight years later in 1856.)

Heine poetically referred to his pain predicament in the poem *"Morphine,"* written near the end of his life when he noted in two famous verses: *"Gut ist der Schlaf, der Tod ist besser—freilich / Das beste wäre, nie Geboren sein."* (In English: "Sleep is good, Death is better—of course, / Best of all would be never to have been born.") Source: Peter Branscombe, *Heinrich Heine – Selected Verse* (Baltimore: Penguin Books, Inc. 1967), 244.

Almansor was a play written by Heine in 1821 that had a most famous line in German: *"Das war ein Vorspiel nur, dort wo man Bücher verbrennt, verbrennt man auch am Ende Menschen."* (Rendered in English: "That was but a prelude; where they burn books, they will ultimately burn people as well.") The significance here is that as the Nazis burned the books of Heine and other German artists on the Opernplatz in Berlin in 1933, they actually celebrated this event by "engraving" Heine's famous words from *Almansor* in the ground at the Opernplatz site. The obvious depravity of this terrible event reflects the innate cruelty, stupidity, and evil of the Nazis as they burned the books and defiled the names and reputations of Heine and other famous German writers. Their actions were monstrous and shameful, and were indicative of mankind's base instincts at their very worst. Moreover, despite converting to Protestantism from Judaism in 1825, Heine's Jewish origins played a continuing presence in his life and were one of the major factors for him being scapegoated by the Nazis later in 1933. And besides, it is obvious that the Nazis were always more interested in burning books, and not in reading them! Should anyone be surprised about this? Think about it! (Source: Heine, *Wikipedia*, see "Universities" and "Legacy.")

I Be, I Sing

Russian chastushka folk poem I be,
When recited quite lively think of me.
My message is clear and not hype,
For when I'm sung, I'm my type.

September 13, 2014
(Chastushka)

I Know YOU from My Dream

Dreaming quite deeply one dark night
I saw your image and most beautiful face
Passionately kissing my soul and spirit . . .
Charming my innermost desires and wishes
Beguiling my inner child, making him smile
Soothing my feelings, capturing my emotions
Mesmerizing me with an unconditional love.

This dream stayed with me on many lonely
Nights for at least a year or so whilst
Leaving me to awaken feeling very happy
But also very sad with only seeing YOU . . .
As a dream and a part of my unconscious self
Yet, I longed and longed so deeply to see
And to meet and to love the real YOU!

And then, one day about two years removed
From my recurring dreams of YOU . . .
I was walking along a beautiful ocean beach,
And watching the waves break and come ashore,
As I felt the warm summer wind touching me
Quite soothingly and enticing me most deliciously,
When I walked literally and directly into YOU!

Upon this event, we both stopped cold in our tracks,
At first surprised, then stunned, and not talking . . .
Then our mutual surprise and astonishment quickly
Gave way to warm smiles, laughter, and some shyness
And then, YOU said to me: "Where have you been?"
Your question said it all to me—then my heart melted,
And I said: "I have always been with you my darling!"

Call it Fate . . . Call it Destiny . . . Call it Karma
Both of us had been dream beings to one another,
And now—we are standing in front of each other
Very real, Very alive, and Very much in love . . .

Reflections in the Mirror

Personifying at once—two giddy, star-struck lovers
Whose very spirits and souls are now united as ONE...
As we embraced passionately and kissed so longingly!

As we embraced, it was as though time itself stood still...
And our mutual dream worlds connected in this real world,
And the effect of this moment of finally finding each other
Was both quite overwhelming and very intoxicating for us,
As our mutual fondness, desire, and love—were all there,
As we kissed passionately and caressed with the deepest desire,
And, as our joyous eye contact and open tears confirmed all!

We sat for several hours on the beach and were entranced in our
Very own world of rapture, devotion, presence, and true passion,
Whilst talking, caressing, kissing, smiling, and laughing—
And learning so much of each other now, so fast, so deeply—
And never ever wanting to leave each other's side now, knowing
Our souls had crossed a millennium or more to find each other again
As we seek to unite our human spirits as one on Earth's cosmic plane.

I never expected to meet my true love, my real soul mate—YOU,
In such an improbable fashion by crossing over deep space and time,
As we found our souls had bonded in love and blended into one spirit,
With our real lives together now filled with an unbridled passion,
With our goals, desires, emotions all cascading together as one,
And now, at night, as we lie together sleeping and dreaming...
Our lives, our souls, and our love are all real—since I found YOU!

October 28, 2014
(Free Verse)

Joe Shit The Ragman

Joe Shit The Ragman should be an inspiration
to anyone who has dealt with nasty and rude people
and to everyone who has been in difficult and ridiculous situations
with people imbued and enamored with *"stuporvisory authority."*

As a mythical and derisive name and title and character
from the utter depths of colloquial American English usage,
Joe Shit the Ragman has certainly made his proverbial mark
LOUD and CLEAR
in the workaday world of everyman,
and is an oft-repeated name
that has weaved itself ever so gingerly
into the favored fabric of common speech
of many who serve or have served in the American military.

Joe Shit The Ragman is the classic Mr. Nobody
who embodies, at once, idiocy and is viewed as a Total Loser.

Joe Shit The Ragman is also a situational character
who can be readily referred to in stupid or provocative situations; hence:

"Why are you giving this to me to do?" or *"Why are you telling me this?"*

"Do you think I'm stupid?" or *"Oh Boy! This is a dumb thing to do!"*

"You must do this, I'm the Boss!" or *"This decision is totally brainless!"*

"This person is so nasty at work!" or *"Why does he want me to do this?"*

And the expected response: *"Who do you think
I am?"* ... *"Joe Shit the Ragman??!!"*

And so: Remember that "Joe Shit The Ragman," aka: "JSTR"
is an appropriate response to those who need to hear it
in your time of need to confront and to combat:

STUPIDITY…RUDENESS…OBNOXIOUSNESS…MINDLESSNESS.

Need anything else be said???

March 25, 2014
(Free Verse)

Jukebox Gigolo

Old Zack Adams sits a slouch'n so sloppy drunk on a bar-room stool,
Wear'n his cheap-threaded cowboy suit and a stained satin shirt.
All the while a peek'n and a leer'n at women like an old poor fool,
But think'n man tonight—Oh Boy, I'm really gonna hit the pay dirt!

Old Zack in this small Texas town is reputed to be quite a lecherous hoot,
As he raucously and recklessly rolls old-worn quarters into the slot
Of the old bar-room Wurlitzer while snicker'n and smil'n to boot,
And plays his tearful and twangy jerk-water music while smil'n a lot!

Old Zack is this town's "Jukebox Gigolo," a real lover boy—Oh Boy!
He wears his patched cowboy hat and his scuffed silver-studded boots,
Meant to impress young girls and bar-fly floozies who have the Joy!
Of being with this bewildering, withered, weathered man and his boots.

Old Zack has a fad'n recollection of events and a silver mane of hair,
With a cigarette in his hand and cuss'n like a nasty little stable boy,
He downs whiskey shots and tequila seconds like no tomorrow on a dare,
While chas'n whiskey glass ice cubes and the tequila worm—being so coy.

Old Zack while a swigg'n down his whiskey mucho fast and direct,
He has now that blind courage to fight or to love—whichever is first,
While the old Wurlitzer resonates a rueful hick song for a teary effect,
But Old Zack can't move now for this song has him cry'n very loudly!

Old Zack with his nicotine-whiskey breath and his pockmarked face,
Personifies the image of an ideal loser of a man—with problems all,
While fight'n, scream'n, and punch'n others to get some precious space,
As he's a showcas'n his reservoir of macho prowess—with problems all.

Old Zack was young once and not so wild, withered, weathered like now,
And he thought he was a really smart dude—with all right moves and all,
But was really a crazy old man act'n far above his funny-fake smart brow,
And now, a cry'n on his bar-room stool and act'n like a fool before a fall.

Old Zack Adams—alcoholic as he truly is and sly and slick as a Texas fox,
Is not really so good with his women friends nowadays—for his real talent
Is in roll'n those old-worn quarters of his one-by-one into that old Jukebox,
Sing'n—"I'm the Jukebox Gigolo"—"a Drunk and a Delight," that's real talent!

October 7, 2014
(Quatrain)

King Vlad

King Vlad is anything but Democracy's "Man of the Hour."
Rather, *à coup sûr*, he's really Stalin's nasty little boy who
ironically parades *svoboda* and *glasnost* like he really means
them—and actually, in reality, he means them not.

King Vlad's political traditions and pronouncements are
well known among those who are sadly aware of his ugly
tapestry of treachery and deceit—oh, so slovenly woven
for all to see, just like some of his fellow-gangster favorites:
Lenin, Stalin, Beria, Molotov, Brezhnev, and Andropov.

King Vlad is anything but a real-world leader . . .
His "Kind" are an open book for all of us to see and
understand what they are, and what they mean for all
who strive for freedom, openness, decency, and real
compassion in the twenty-first century world order.

King Vlad—just like his Dracula name sake,
is a man without a soul, without a conscience,
who shall never shudder, wince or cry at the
piercing death rattle of a Kalashnikov.

King Vlad is truly no friend of Democracy,
sounding even, at times, not unlike Hitler.
He's a demon leader with innocent blood on his hands,
and is always quick with the old Soviet reply:
Lie . . . Deny . . . Accuse . . . Reject . . . Criticize . . .
all tools of this redoubtable Master of Prevarication.

King Vlad should know that the Heavenly Souls of the
fated Flight MH17, are an inviolable testament to the
"bitter truth," *gorkaya pravda*, surrounding his lies, his
treachery, and his deceit—all pejorative attributes to a
man with the mask of a real monster who had the very
best of Soviet teachers. The very brave souls of MH17
lost their lives to this treachery of King Vlad and his

willing conspirators serving in the Russian military and the security apparatus. The cowardly cover-up of this tragic incident continues to this day. Just ask Malaysia, the Netherlands, and the Ukraine. And don't forget the thoughts and concerns of the very brave families who lost their loved ones who were on that MH17 flight on that fateful and tragic day.

And so, "Generalissimo Stalin," to your departed Ghost, I proffer the following observations about good old "King Vlad," who worships and promotes your glorified memory:

How do you like your nasty little boy now?
He's right up your historical alley, right?

And it's very noteworthy to add that "Putin" has five letters in his last name just like the "Devil."

With all of this said, one can make one's own reasoned judgment, observations, and thoughtful conclusions.

And, I shall only say in closing: До свидания!

August 9, 2014
(Political Verse)

Author's Note: The Russian expression "До свидания" in the Russian Cyrillic Alphabet is the expression for "farewell," "goodbye," or "until we meet again," and is used in everyday Russian conversations. In its transliterated English form version this expression is rendered as "Do svidaniya."

King Vlad Redux – Second Cold War

Vladimir Vladimirovich Putin's grimy fingerprints on current history are for him nothing to gloat about—*au contraire* I say emphatically: His actions bespeak one who's not an architect for peace—not at all, rather a quite deceitful dictator and a harbinger of a Second Cold War.

King Vlad's old Soviet-style actions are clear for all who care to see, and make no mistake about it—he's without remorse and a soul to boot. A Master of Malarkey and an International Bamboozler Supreme, he certainly is, with a menacing image and not one iota of conscience.

King Vlad risks a Second Cold War with his violation of international law concerning the blatant, illegal annexation of the Crimean peninsula. With his brand of new-style Soviet adventurism on the march, the Old Soviet Bear has been resurrected anew—and it's hot on the prowl again!

King Vlad's new spirit of nationalism for Russia is not at all progressive as evidenced by his ongoing war on certain ethnic minorities: Jews, Tartars, Armenians, Gypsies—to include anyone who chooses to resist and protest against his new-age fanaticism rebranded anew in the twenty-first century.

King Vlad's lineage to and proclivity for the old Soviet Union and its star cast of past gangster luminaries: Lenin, Stalin, Beria, Molotov, Brezhnev, and Andropov—to name a few, are quite telling since they reflect the real nature of his psyche and the tragedy he brings now to the world stage.

And lest we forget, the innocent souls of the murdered passengers from flight MH17 in eastern Ukraine who cry out, as do their families, for justice from the criminal thuggery and hooliganism perpetrated by King Vlad in support of proxy groups that do his evil biddings soaked in lies, treachery, and deceit.

King Vlad takes pleasure in fulfilling a fanciful role today of the old Soviet *Bolshoi Nachalnik* (Big Boss), whose historical antecedents from Soviet Big Bosses of past fame, doesn't augur well for future democracy in New Russia, and doesn't align with the precepts of good governance and human rights.

King Vlad's treachery and deception are certainly open for everyone to see as he executes his plan of disrupting the balance of the current world order. We all should be forewarned of the clouds of tyranny and aggression that could be unleashed one day on the European continent and the entire world.

King Vlad, despite very strong objections and economic sanctions imposed by Western leaders and diplomats, understands only one word rendered so poignantly in the German language: *die Macht* (or Power), which lurks ever behind his public mask and psychological makeup as a former KGB officer.

King Vlad's actions reflect his virtues of lying, denying, accusing, rejecting, and criticizing—all poison arrows in his quiver as a Master of Prevarication. His real mask is that of a Monster who had the very best Soviet teachers and wishes to tilt the axis of his New Russia on a collision course with the West.

And so, Generalissimo Stalin . . . how do you like your nasty little boy now?

November 30, 2014
(Political Verse)

Leprechaun in My Bottle

One dark dreary night while happily drinkin' up a big-big storm,
I beheld a tiny green man in my bottle!—not the norm.

He's my tiny green man in my Irish whiskey bottle.
He's my Leprechaun with whom I'd like to drink a pottle.

He's the man with a certain quaint eye twinkle and attitude,
And he has all the fine alcoholic credentials and certitude,

Of one who's done much, seen much, drunk much-much,
And has great insight, insatiable charm, and a very deft touch.

My friend the Leprechaun tells me of his present living situation:
"Medrinks, Methinks, Mesleeps, Medrinks, ah!—My salvation!"

I tell him my ancestry is "Half-Irish" which makes me Celtic,
And he says, "Me good friend Gary, no shame, Me too Celtic!"

My Leprechaun asked me of my present situation with poetry,
And I says—"Medrinks, Methinks, Mewrites, Meloves poetry."

Over time I found I was mimicking more and more my little elf friend,
And he says, "Me brother Gary, no worry, we both be Irish my friend."

I told my Leprechaun that he does indeed have quite an alcoholic ego,
And my little elf quipped, "When we both drink Gary, I'm your alter ego!"

And so, my Leprechaun in my bottle is my good friend—my adviser,
And, I find that as we both drink together my poetry flows all the wiser!

September 9, 2014
(Couplet)

Life

Live Life completely—
Seek always new adventures. Find your destiny...
Emphasize the positive...
Always give your best effort!

November 12, 2014
(Tanka)

Love

Love's most emotive,
And so special to us all.
It's all-consuming...
Capturing the hearts of two...
Binding flesh, blood, soul as one!

November 19, 2014
(Tanka)

Mirror of the Soul

Gazing into a clear lake pool...
I saw a reflection of my life before me.

The gaze and what I saw depicted...
A progression of past life experiences.

I savored the funny and kind moments...
Looked despairingly on the difficult moments.

This gaze into the mirror of my soul...
Astounds and confounds me still today.

And the knowledge that we are all...
Much more than the sum of our parts,
Means so much more to me today.

What I've learned are six things...
Ignorance begets Stupidity,
Knowledge begets Wisdom,
Inspiration begets Creativity,
Light begets Illumination,
Passion begets Vivacity,
Love begets Happiness (but not all the time).

To know yourself...
You must see and sense yourself
In the mirror of your own soul.

September 28, 2014
(Free Verse)

Moon Light . . . Moon Night

We hold hands walking under the bright beam of God's Moon Light,
And stop and kiss so intently in the soft cradle of the dark Moon Night.

The passion and rapture together we feel so on this cold black night,
Is reflected and majestically warmed by the touch of the Moon Light.

I look lovingly into your eyes on this quite special dark Moon Night,
Marveling at the love so reflected in your eyes by the Moon Light.

This is an enchanted sight to behold by All who love the Moon Light,
Reflecting the beauty and meaning while savoring all the Moon Night.

A deep cosmic darkness pervades the canvas of this great Moon Night,
Whilst God's grace and love pleasure us with a most bright Moon Light.

Almighty God in Heaven gently modulates the tone of this Moon Light,
Bringing constant wonder and glory to All on this most dark Moon Night.

My love and I now understand the mystical meaning of this Moon Light,
As we ponder and hold so special God's emotion felt on this Moon Night.

October 19, 2014
(Couplet)

My Christmas Dream

My Christmas Dream is for a
More peaceful and calm world
For all of mankind as the clock
Of the twenty-first century ticks
Away before us and all of us seek
To meet the many daily challenges
And travails of life that impact us
And the planet we all live on since
The Earth is our very home for the
Entire human race, animals, insects,
And all of the varieties of sea creatures
And wondrous plant life that grows
And flourishes as part of God's most
Divine Plan which is certainly worth
Our attention and desire to address
Our shortfalls and shortcomings in
Making sure that the Earth and all of
Mankind are compatible and we can
Meet the destiny and final glory that
God has planned for all of us—Amen.

December 11, 2014
(Verse)

My Heart Skips a Beat My Love

My heart skips a beat my love each and every time
I am with you my dearest sweet and lovely Darling
Since the passions and feelings you stir in me
Touch the very depths of my inner being and soul
And render themselves not to mere words only
Suitable for depiction, exhibition, understanding
Rather to the image and strength of your beauty
And your rapturous desire and feeling as they
Defy rational attempts at any simple description
For you are the most radiant beyond all compare

My heart skips a beat my love when we lie together
Locked in a most enchanting embrace and kissing
So deeply, palpably that we run out of breath and pant
Anxiously at what comes next in our mutual longing
And crescendo as our passions explode and express
Themselves in a most hungry trail of urges and desires
Which makes finding love for us all the more magical
Pairing us together like a couple of star-struck kids
Lost impossibly in moments of hope and imagination
In a timeless world of love, desire, emotion, and oneness

My heart skips a beat my love when we walk so closely
Together while talking, laughing, and living our dreams
Confronting the world and taking on whatever comes
Next as we steer our ship of destiny on a true course
Where our like-thoughts and deep love for each other
Mean something quite special that only Dreamers and
Poets can imagine and set to melody and harmony in perfect
Verses of sheer passion and delight painted onto a canvas
Of unending happiness where Heaven and Earth are one—
As my heart skips a beat my love when we are forever one

November 5, 2014
(Free Verse)

My Window

I look at the sky
from my window

I observe people
from my window

I feel raindrops
from my window

I sense loneliness
from my window

I think deeply gazing
from my window

I cherish love
from my window

I ponder eternity
from my window

I sense the struggle of God and Lucifer
from my window

I cry
from my window

I yell
from my window

I evoke emotion and rage
from my window

I am joyful and sad
from my window

And—I see my soul
from my window

September 26, 2014
(Lyric)

New Year's Baby 2015

The New Year's Baby each year starts out fresh and new, always exciting, the life of the party, and never ever blue. He's a quite active little Cherub who's cute and funny, and he'll be there at the stroke of Midnight to usher in the New Year and to escort Old Man 2014 outside where the unforgiving "Dust Bin of History" awaits his tired old body and his failed attempts to improve mankind's lot. The New Year's Baby shall be a busy little fellow indeed!

The New Year's Baby is now eager and chomping at the bit to get started on January 1st to make his mark in our world during 2015, and brings with him both enthusiasm and hope! The reality for our little Cherub shall be much different than he realizes since certain age-old specters still pervade "Home Earth" today: Tyranny, Poverty, Disease, Famine, and War. And we shall not leave out a couple of new ones at home with us today, as well: Global Warming and Worldwide Pollution.

With these major problems and mankind's "Seven Deadly Sins," along with murder, rape, guns, slavery and nuclear proliferation, and all other types of crime—you'll see and understand why our bright, young, and full of hope New Year's Baby will begin to age so fast over his allotted 12-month tenure here on our Home Earth. Really, all we can do is to wish our Cherub friend our very best and pledge to work with him, world societies, and world governments to make things better on our planet and among our world citizens.

The transition from the Old Year to the New Year is no doubt a time For both celebration and reflection—and in spite of the negatives, as listed, not all is so terrible nor lost, as long as our world community begins to realize that the brightness of the future we hope to have for generations to come is very relevant to the solutions we contemplate, and the decisions we pursue in attempting to improve our situation. The Big FACTOR "X" in this whole equation, lest we forget, is never to forget to turn to Almighty God in our hour of maximum need!

I'm personally not a zealous religious person, but that doesn't mean that I don't believe in the power of divine intervention in the affairs of mankind. The key, I believe, is for everyone on this Earth, to include all nations and people alike, to work hard and commit to make our world a better place. We inherited this world by the beneficence of the Almighty Himself with the hope that Man, in the image of His Maker, would become his Brother's Keeper, but time may not now be on our side, as Mother Nature, of late, has been negatively affected by mankind's destructive behavior here on Earth.

A little faith and prayer to Our Lord God never really hurts, since the stakes facing our world for the survival of mankind are indeed grave. Make no mistake about the challenges I have listed, for they are quite real, and won't be that easy to readily solve as they shall require the concerted effort of everyone as we march forward with our dreams. We have such wondrous tools in our arsenal of modern technology for accomplishing grand and great things! Why not use them for the good of our world and mankind, and strive to make the difficult job of our "Little Cherub New Year's Baby" a tad bit easier?

I now rest my case.

Happy New Year!! Amen!! Amen!! Amen!!

December 31, 2014
(Narrative)

No Fear My Dear Friend

Have no fear my dear friend in this grand life,
For your actions should often be so bold;
Courage is the answer to this life's strife,
And makes our dreams now so precious as gold;
It's with time and thought we know and are told,
Makes us always quite brave, stalwart and spry,
And gives us sweet courage never to cry.

October 10, 2014
(Rhyme Royal)

Not Missing Love's Beat

Not missing love's beat . . . .
Sails to you this golden bright morning rising so high and
Sails waving with light, joy, and promise and a real hope
With one smile gasping breathless always for you my love

You walk with me now hand-in-hand into Eden's paradise
Dancing my heart love on that yellow brick road of dreams
Dying to be with you forever my love as eternity call to us
Dreams inside eternal youth as my heart pounds loudly now

Awaiting the very day to come when I can stand before you
Down on my bended knee whilst holding your hands warmly
And kissing each and every single fingertip of yours fervently
As I shall ask you to be forever and always with me my love

You will be my Queen with dazzling jewels an ocean wide
The other heartbeat echoing as two becomes one complete
Our thirst for love and hot passion are almost unquenchable
And my very psyche is afire with excitement when we caress

Sleeping at night my love brings me into your dream world
Where it's me and you, you and me, together now floating
Through the ether of time as we breathe this rarefied air so
Deliciously and are mesmerized by the depth of our true love

When we awaken from a deep dream trance so joyous for us
We hold one another lovingly and caress so warmly at once as
We kiss passionately, longingly in a most sublime spirit now
Not missing love's beat . . . .

December 24, 2014
(Free Verse)

Author's Note: A Collaborated Poem with Liam McDaid.

On Meeting You Most Beautiful Now

On meeting you most beautiful now with
adoring maiden kisses and loving thoughts
whilst deeply inhaling one warm breath
and a stout sip of the finest auld grog of
a mountain dew breathing a precious pure.

Golden leaves sweetly float in a dancing
twirl with a shining inside vision so sweet
of us walking hand-in-hand on golden sands
as perfect waves unfold into a carpet of blue
to white as romantic thoughts signal our love.

Against the deepest walls warm from a soft light
as silent echoes whisper true as sweetly melting
emotions palpably touch our hearts beating as
one—whilst brewing kisses from peach-colored
clouds mesmerize us with their enchanted beauty.

Silver treasured thoughts of love and happiness
speak volumes to the beautiful dream vision of
a gem of dancing petal flowers and one red rose
that captivate my visions of you dancing in the
very depths of my dreams as I sleep blissfully.

On soft clouds in the bright azure sky above,
at times, I gaze continually skyward on days
when I think of you so bright and so beautiful
and see your lovely face etched in the cerulean
sky and feel the warm passion of your true love.

With the finest of texture and the scent of a most
sensual red rose, I watch as its petals gently land
now on the sweet dew ground and I thank Almighty
God above on meeting you most beautiful now as my
thoughts of love for you touch the depths of my soul.

The indelible nature of our true love and happiness
create certain visions of fire storms of an unbridled
passion and pleasure that eternally speak to us both
of the sweet love and magical enchantment we share
as our hearts beat now as one in God's grace forever.

November 13, 2014
(Quintain)

Author's Note: A Collaborated Poem with Liam McDaid.

Our Love and Passion Always Forever

Since I met you my love, the passion I harbor
for you knows no bounds or limits since our
love is genuine, special, and from the heart—
I'm always so happy to be with you my darling.

Every time I see you and we meet, it's just like
starting over with both of us so glad to see one
another with that hopeless expectation of two
young kids with emotions and passions on fire.

Your kiss and your very touch release an ardent
and burning desire each and every time we caress
and hold one another so rapturously becoming one
at times shedding true tears from Cupid's very arrow.

Our love—so special, so sensual, so real and true
gives us that unique reality of two lives and souls
united as one and always so very confident in our
lives as lovers, best of friends, and soulmates.

When we're together no explanations are ever needed
as we both are most confident as one in what God has
foreseen as our destiny on this Earth and in Heaven
since the power and passion of our love are endless.

My Darling, you and I are very much one of Cupid's
success stories in finding one another, being always
together, and facing what life throws at us each day,
yet always secure in our destiny and love as one.

My Darling, only poets and dreamers can see and
visualize the exquisite beauty of what we share in
our life together and the love we possess which is
worth walking to the very ends of this Earth for.

My Darling, My Love this is indeed our storied walk together through this life and later into that infinite cosmos beyond as two best friends and lovers as ONE in love with a true passion always forever and forever!

November 24, 2014
(Quatrain)

Our Passions on Fire My Darling

A very long time passed between us
Before we met once again
Quite unexpectedly and surprisingly
Exchanging very intense looks
Harboring most hungry urges
Possessing the wildest desires
Feeling rebounding emotions
Charged nerves, electric and cosmic
Greeting happily and nervously
Walking closely together but unsure
Interested and yet afraid of what
Next could happen . . . .

A drink or two or three later at the bar
Then a couple more sitting in the booth
Losing the edge of pent-up tension from before
Us both now quite talkative
Us both now quite oblivious to time
Us both now quite friendlier
Us both now quite guarded still
We now hold hands remembering
Fun times, much laughter, much smiling
Depressing times, much hurt, much unhappiness
Like strangers in the night we really are
But not attracted for the very first time
Ready and wanting to start over again
But not so sure of the "forever" part
Interested and yet afraid of what
Next could happen . . . .

And then—suddenly . . . it magically happened
Just like destiny taking charge at once . . .
Your touch, my touch, our touch, one touch
Emotions exploding, eyes probing, hands feeling
Moving closer, becoming one and one and one
Breathing faint, then excited, and more so

Crying sobbing, laughing smiling, revealing
Our eyes locked and rocked as one in a spiral
Saying I missed you so much . . .
Saying you missed me so much . . .
A burning, yearning desire, and a trembling fire
Our lips meet sweetly, hungrily with much intent
Our desires at fever pitch, ravenous and craving
Igniting our passions now on fire, on fire, on fire

Shutting out the rest of the world—be gone from us
While crying and caressing, kissing openly and deeply
We find each other all over again and again
A giddy feeling of love once lost, yet love found again
Asking why? How come? How could we? Why not?
This time all is forgiven—our bond unbroken
Our love rediscovered; our lives restored
Our personalities mesmerized as one
Our minds in tune, same time and channel
Our emotions most electric and having fun
Our oneness whole and most rewarding
Our love and desire both for an eternity
Our hearts afire . . . our hearts desire
Our passions on fire my darling!

October 22, 2014
(Free Verse)

Pearl Dreams of Rare Love

Break these chains that bind
holding us in the deep ovens
blazing afire for love.

Smiling midday moon
dressed in a baby-blue sky
sparsely scattered clouds dotting.

White mother of pearl
a silver lining treasure
held soft, a beautiful warm babe.

In her finger beams
a light touching inside thoughts
sitting posed at three.

The moon just pops out
in kissing a golden sun
white ivory pearls smiling.

Within daylight thoughts
sweetly I pray in sunlight
shining warm all over you.

Deep ocean salted
with the bluest, warmest waves
luster smiles with sunshine color.

The magic teardrop
forms a silver lining bright
and cries for ivory pearls.

Alchemic water
wondrous, most blue, dark and rare
lies love in the Salt of the Earth.

Mermaids caress hope
encouraging happiness
make all more magical.

Pearl chain links in place
Neptune commands, do it now
with finest gold most smiling.

Bathed best and brightest
white ivory pearls ready
for their concatenation.

Neptune's grandeur finds
all sea creatures in awe now
abounds pearl dreams of rare love.

Pearl Dreams of Rare Love
fourteen linked all so precious
from the ocean's heart and soul.

November 16, 2014
(Tercet)

Author's Note: A Collaborated
Poem with Liam McDaid.

poisonously enchanted mushrooms so luscious rare

one fine sunny morning dazzling golden sunrise
dancing with rays of magical sunshine
dewdrops on silver webs glistening drops
he began whistling and dancing
picking wild mushrooms on the forest floor
to make magic wonder and happenings occur
he begins building and stoking the fire
throwing turf on until red hot
sticks the pot over the flicking flames
stirring emotions inside bubble and steam
throws in a mountain of carrots, peas, herbs
with lots of other sorts of raw veggies
adding a rare drop of mountain spirits . . . .

next freeing a soul adding an alchemic fuel so rare
making himself a most magical and delicious stew
as he cooked, he began devouring more of the stew
then slowly he felt himself floating high, so high
in a bubble, so wonderful and dear and so clear,
picked up by a pocket of air and floating even more
so when . . . .

a lovely fairy princess appears gossamer wings your light
and then appearing again under a radiant rainbow bridge
and with one cherished and most special romantic kiss
he began waltzing with her to a melody so haunting yet pretty
and while lost in this mystical trancelike moment of splendor
the fairy princess stole his heart that was pure gold
and when he came around alone—so alone
an icy cold shiver then ran down his very spine
it was just a silly old leprechaun dream and all he thought as
I see her magic sparkling potions cast on someone else too . . . .

then the big ethereal and mystical bubble of fairy elves burst
now wide open for him and all others to see while the elves
laughed raucously so hard with little warm tears running down
their little rosy cheeks . . . .

the leprechaun pondered . . . next time methinks me be much more
careful with them mushrooms me happily picks on the forest floor
and stick to drinkin' the old mountain forest dew with some lovely
luscious shots of the oldest Irish whiskey with a stout nip o' gin . . . .

December 3, 2014
(Free Verse)

Author's Note: A Collaborated Poem with Liam McDaid.

Prufrock's Eternal Footman

I think this Footman likes to snicker,
and the human situation is the kicker,
when one becomes sicker and sicker,
and it's one's time to die and to cry for one's soul.

Prufrock's point is well-taken and understood for
the Footman is at the end of life's reality and is
the "King of Finality" and doesn't care while seeking
mankind's banal end, since Man is really small potatoes
in the Universe's great and grand pecking order.

I think that I shall not want to meet this Bamboozler,
at least this would be my choice, if I really had one.
I doubt that I, like others, could ever be like Lazarus.
The Footman presents us all with a one-way ticket to
what awaits mankind beyond the pale of death!

And so we all await the end of our finite time as
measured in grains of sand and the clock on the wall;
waiting for the day and time of our final departure,
and hoping not to hear the scornful snicker, snicker,
snicker, snicker of Prufrock's Eternal Footman!

July 17, 2014
(Free Verse)

Rainbow

A rainbow forms and blooms bright after the rain
Finishing its task of wetting, replenishing the Earth,
As part of God's plan to ease Mother Nature's pain
And give our home, our planet a moment's rebirth.

A rainbow is really God's gracious smile at the rain's end,
And when you think about it, it occurs in perfect rhythm
So all can see and marvel at its splendor at a storm's end,
And though its time is fleeting, its image is God's prism.

A rainbow is always God's promise and divine intention,
To help people pause and focus on a dazzling-colored array
Tinted and formed in a picture-perfect image and conception,
To help them relax, reflect on what's important on a given day.

A rainbow is a noble and sublime reflection of God's selection
Of wonderful images from Heaven brought to our mortal plane,
For a moment's majestic gaze at this image of God's conception
So people can seek a moment's happiness and a surcease of pain.

September 2, 2014
(Quatrain)

Rapunzel

Rapunzel rolling down your barriers
dazzling jewels opening sparkling chambers
one begins climbing each curling warm feeling
touching each emotion sweetly
one step a little closer in kissing
each and every memory entering
sharing these thoughts
cherishing every last minute
each minute special
each second heavenly

Rapunzel heart of a rose
your lips sweet blushing
silk satin petals soft lips
blushing as you my love entranced
entering your one tower
letting your hair down smiling
the bath we walk heading forward
none of us really have a clue
but each strand holding
unto a perfect dream

Rapunzel princess of my dreams
thoughts and love intertwined
walking hand-in-hand now
both blessed with passion
both blessed with emotion
both blessed with true love
walking together unafraid
talking caressing holding kissing
arms locked embracing passion
a perfect dream forever

October 13, 2014
(Free Verse)

Author's Note: A Collaborated Poem with Liam McDaid.

rising from out of this cold frozen wasteland

rising from out of this cold frozen wasteland . . .
a blanket white unfolds with pure hope and love
melting snowflakes on such a clear blue ocean
lying on the edge of a world that's very scared

while inside this mindset unfolds a radiant light
a sun shining buttercup of such special rare beauty
in every little thing and precious detail which ever
so sweetly draws me to you my love, my darling

even the sound of your soft voice echoes on
inside with such mellifluous golden whispers
sweetly enhancing the very music you sing
to me which plays magic tricks so enchanting

and hypnotizing my very soul while stealing
my heart away and bringing me under your
spell and the softness of your wonder and love
both so overwhelming and intoxicating so fully

with this our mutual joy and love are so deep and
rare that makes our time together seem so endless
my love for you is so special and so right that I
must pinch myself at times to see if all this is real

and so, rising from out of this cold frozen wasteland . . .
our mutual spirits, souls, and emotions are now ONE
and with my special enchantress, fate and love have put
us now as ONE on the edge of a world that's very scared

December 20, 2014
(Free Verse)

Author's Note: A Collaborated Poem with Liam McDaid.

Santa's Favorite – Rudolph The Red-Nosed Reindeer

Santa Claus has travel worries at the North Pole,
With terrible winter storms brewing there afoot,
He knows Christmas is so close and so he must put
His children first now whom he loves deeply and whole!
And so he must find the red-nosed Rudolph to cajole
Him into guiding his sleigh on Christmas Eve to boot,
For this would bring his kids so much joy—what a hoot!
Rudolph's red nose bright guiding them from the North Pole!

Rudolph leads Santa's reindeer on Christmas Eve night,
While all shout out with joy on this blessed holy night!
Santa's reindeer love Rudolph in equal measure,
For with him they won't be lost—oh what a pleasure!
Rudolph's glowing red nose shines now ever so bright,
As we all with Santa celebrate the Lord's night!

December 12, 2014
(Petrarchan Sonnet)

Sending Waves Touching Beautiful Always

She who sends waves touching beautiful warm and gracious words
Draws bright sunshine smiles in our hearts as they sing in her grace
Flowing from the heart her beauty held in her Quill ready to write
Pure diamond sparkling rainbows as a true friend is a friend indeed

The tidal wave raises fine-soaked sand from the bottom of the ocean
And the waves curl out pearl white reflecting a most picture-perfect
Image that is truly splendid and always sublime to behold and cherish
As Nature's soft wind caresses your aura and inspires your next poem

She who sends these very waves touching beautiful personifies a Muse
So rare, so special—and brings her influence and talents to bear in
Masterfully supporting the efforts of fellow poets and dreamers as they
"Spill Ink" on blank pages late at night crafting their next poetic masterpiece

The very power and wonder of her good works and positive influence are
Always there magnificently arrayed like pure beams of sunshine touching
And dazzling all in her reach quite profoundly with the magic of her thoughts
And the quiet courage of her convictions as the simply wonderful poet she is

November 26, 2014
(Free Verse)

Author's Note: A Collaborated Poem with Liam McDaid. This poem was written by both of us in honor of our dear friend and colleague, Anne-Lise Andresen, for her very fine poetry and her professional encouragement of other fellow poets within our poetry community. Her talent and grace, and her friendship, kindness, and intelligence are truly remarkable and beyond all measure.

Sonnet to a Very Fine Poetess

I know a very fine poet, a dear colleague, who's quite talented and bright,
And has a superb facility with words making them all fit perfect and right.
She has an unrivaled mastery of the poetic art, writing with the best approach,
And has an unparalleled ability to write the finest verse beyond any reproach.

This poet's sense of depth, empathy, and poetic variety is so great to behold,
And she brings compassion and power to her work worth its weight in gold.
With majestic themes and images she invites readers to a special dimension,
While exciting them magically with sublime verses that hold their attention.

This poet communes with Our Poetry Muse seeking her enchanted vision,
And shares all with her readers with enraptured intent and perfect precision.
My friend's poetry reflects the human dynamic with such power and grace,
As she finds the right tone, tenor, and pitch—putting them in proper place.

I'm very proud of my colleague's splendid work and her marvelous poetry,
And I'm glad she's with us and gives us such rear elegance from her poetry!

November 9, 2014
(Shakespearean Sonnet)

Author's Note: This sonnet was written as a special tribute to a fellow poet who shall remain anonymous.

Spill Ink

Spill Ink—the poets' timeless warp and woof
Signifies our mantra beyond reproof;
Late at night as poets struggle to write;
Our Muse enchants poets to such delight;
Poets seek tone and tenor for a splash,
And images and nuance for a dash.
"Spill Ink!" Poets cry seeking perfection!

October 19, 2014
(Septet)

Star Light . . . Star Night

Gazing at the dark sky as arrayed on this cold black night,
We are enraptured by the radiant view of bright Star Light.

This is a wondrous sight to behold by all on this Star Night,
Reflecting now all earthly things gracious, grand, and right.

The cold beckoning darkness of this very special night,
Serves as the cosmic palette for unlimited points of light.

The majestic, magical light reflected on this holy Star Night,
Reveals God's intention with His heavenly-made Star Light!

At once we realize the divine dichotomy between light and night,
On this enchanting eve that's imbued now with God's Star Light.

Almighty God implores all who see His mosaic of Star Light,
To ponder now ever gently the dark beauty of His Star Night.

Oh! Radiant and grand Star Light on this most special Star Night,
We are forever spellbound now by your God-given glorious sight!

September 14, 2014
(Couplet)

Teardrops

Putting down now that sharp sword of truth so gallantly
falling from the darkest clouds above are true dark blue
feelings you draw so warmly now from the ocean deep
curling waves warmly galloping soothing loving kissing
sensual summer wind warm and moist with our first kiss
that love glance we had at the very moment our eyes met

Our emotions floating softly quietly speak volumes to us
upon majestic whispering silent winds we embrace desire
kissing warm golden sands enchanted with an eternal love
as wet freshly salted teardrops reveal our true feelings as
we wash now our inner spirits with love's truth and virtue
as we fulfill always our sincerest wishes now and forever

Most beautiful one I adore you with all my heart and love
in the name of your beauty I find my truest love knowing
always is forever sure and I shall wonder now never more
for sweetly in the end I know our souls shall be with God
and gazing into your eyes so deeply I see love's real intent
as your moist lips arouse our passions and emotions afire

Loving you liberates me freely to tell you of my feelings
if only one could see this soul one would see me whole as
crystals crashing to the ground speak to life's true turmoil
and rising to the occasion with love I shall take that chance
as we cherish every moment fully when together everyday
And I never say goodbye only hello to all I meet in this life

How precious shining is a treasure that's so true in hand as
touching gossamer wings that long for a brush with angels
as we wish in an everlasting memory so pure now with love
devoutly hoping for the best and never less is what we do as
we make our life's passion happen now honest pure and sure
never showing any fear no matter whatever comes our way

Memories of a deepest love so true with our hearts now one wishing a life together that's forever with true heartfelt love embracing each other so warmly now celebrating our love caressing and kissing openly now without any reservation seeking one's fate and following one's destiny with no fear crying teardrops openly and unafraid of what life brings us

October 20, 2014
(Free Verse)

Author's Note: A Collaborated Poem with Liam McDaid.

The Evil Jack O'Lantern

Walking near that Old Dark House under a morose moonlit sky,
I spied a furtive glance at Old Demon Jack's big ugly evil eye.

This Jack O'Lantern is not by any means a friendly and funny face,
For he makes your blood run cold with a leering gruesome grimace.

Whilst looking at people with a distinct Mephistophelian delight,
Both of Old Demon Jack's eyes give us all a quite palpable fright.

This Jack O'Lantern sits perched by the Old Dark House front door,
Waiting for each Halloween to seek its revenge and even the score.

Old Demon Jack's spirit eternally lives on in this undying fruit gourd,
Annually resurrected for Halloween as one of the Devil's own horde.

This Jack O'Lantern is indeed a macabre physical object from Hell's pit,
And Old Demon Jack's spirit lives there possessing souls as He sees fit.

On Halloween beware of the Old Dark House there on Old Hob's Lane,
For Old Demon Jack and The Devil shall cause you forever agony and pain.

Now you know this is not the house on Halloween to make a trick or treat,
For in the end it shall be your final destination and you're The Devil's Treat!

September 25, 2014
(Couplet)

The Future

One's future footprints in the sands of time,
To be enshrined for all to see in time.

A time period of shall and shall be,
Descriptive too of what again shall be.

A future view of such constant motion
Of people, events, passion, and emotion.

A planned assumption that is great or grave,
That a future parade of time must save.

A dream so enchanted for the future,
Not revealed—as one must learn the future.

A future hope for wantonness and wit,
To be resurrected now from Hell's pit.

A vision of future epochs in time,
Now must our poets plan to set in rhyme.

December 27, 2014
(Heroic Couplet)

The Grim Reaper Cometh

As All Hallows' Eve approacheth my thoughts turn now to a darkest dread,
Whilst in old age I harbour the deepest fear of seeing this one's grim head;
Methinks the Grim Reaper cometh this time with his evil scythe in hand,
Which striketh maximum fear in me and maketh him feel quite so grand.

Death and darkness doth pervade this spirit's intent from the great beyond,
And brings one a most chilling fear, if one's destiny be unending Hellspawn;
All Hallows' Eve is the image I conjure now of my most imminent departure,
Whilst I hope for a divine intervention and protection during this departure.

For I shall not want to feel the fear and malediction of the Grim Reaper's gaze,
As he eerily walketh in the deep mist to bring my soul into that darkest of haze;
I pray then, Oh Lord God, to have an Angel escort me on my final trip beyond,
And spare me the Grim Reaper's terrifying visit and his images of Hellspawn.

I ask thy divine power and goodness in protecting my eternal spirit and soul,
And to deliver them to Heaven on All Hallows' Eve quite sound and whole!

Amen! Amen! Amen!

October 25, 2014
(Shakespearean Sonnet)

The Noble Language

Tears from your eyes are so special and true;
They are real emotions from each eye,
And reflect a love so deeply renewed;
Our spirits soar high in the azure sky!

Our heart and soul are ever the tears' source;
Our tears attest to love so rare dearest,
And keep our love so special and on course,
That I must be always with you nearest!

Our tears—the eye's language ever noble;
They draw us together so close and one;
Our love's so special and ever noble,
And our heart and soul together as one!

Love requires we dance together as two,
As Harmony pure brings divine love too!

December 1, 2014
(Shakespearean Sonnet)

The Nocturnal Delight of Mephistopheles

One dark, dreary night whilst working on a poem of hellish, hideous, and horrible fright, I became, at once, quite so fatigued and could barely keep my eyelids open anymore. And then, suddenly falling asleep, darkness came at once enveloping my inner psyche in a most eerie and frightening way, only to find when awakening a sinister, dark presence lurking at my chamber door.

I thought I was dreaming with the furtive appearance of this dark visage before me, when suddenly he began to speak slowly, and to mesmerize me whole with his fiery eyes. As this dark visage spoke to me, I sensed immediately an awful aura of macabre right before me, and my senses were paralyzed, not so much by fear, but by a strange curiosity of this rather grim and menacing eidolon with his fiery eyes.

On my inquiry I found to my shock and surprise that this terrifying wight was the evil "Mephistopheles," here in spirit and body—now whole, who was here to quench his rapturous desire in fulfilling his "Nocturnal Delight," the purported essence of his lurking presence now at my chamber door. "Mephisto" was indeed a most loyal demon who served Lucifer with an ardent intensity.

I couldn't believe my very eyes and ears, the evil Mephisto now standing before me with his fiery eyes of fright, beckoning me toward a world of death, demons, deception, and debauchery. I told him I knew of his fate and association with Faust, and Mephisto replied, with his smiling delight: "Faust was only fiction, a figment of Goethe's imagination, and I can assure you that I'm quite real to you and indeed most unholy." "Thinking of me only in a chimerical sense would be most unwise my young friend!"

With Mephisto's revelation to me, I began to quake and shudder with a most pure fear, for I knew this dream was not a dream, but a real nightmare taunting my very soul. Thinking fast, I then asked: "But why am I here in your presence tonight?" Mephisto replied, "This is the night of my Nocturnal Delight as I've already told you—and I've come now to take your soul!"

With this, I asked pray tell, "Why me, Sir?" "I'm only a struggling young poet." "Why my soul of all things, Sir?" "I'm still learning my craft and mastering my poetic works." To this Mephisto replied, "My Master loves the vim and vigor of your writing young poet." "He admires your passion to learn the Black Arts and your desire to put dark evil ideas in your poetry." "And, he needs a poet just like you!"

His direct reply and intention plunged my spirit into a cold and dark vortex of the vilest evil. I told Mephisto that I did not consciously summon him on this darkest of nights. He replied: "Your concerns matter not to me young poet, for in time you'll become most evil just like me." "And, I'm here now to make you a most wonderful offer—one that you shan't refuse tonight!"

How did this situation move so fast from whence Mephisto graced his presence at my door? My mind now was racing in overdrive and overwrought with images of death, evil, and fear. I had little time left before Mephisto would act to doom my soul making me both a tragic and poor figure. "What do I do?" I pondered to myself, as these events tortured my inner being now leaving me in an absolute state of panic, despair, and utter fear!

The stage was now set, and from out of nowhere . . . Mephisto handed me a missive written in medieval Latin to read. He said, "Young poet, the hour is now late, and I know that you're a scholar who can read this letter for better." "Sign it now you must to decree your fealty, and to commit your mortal soul to My Master—so now take heed and question it not!" And with that very tone and tenor of Mephisto's declaration, my eternal soul was now the vaunted prize to be bartered with to make my life one of pure evil—for the better? I thought not, of course, for this could never be the case!

For a moment, a seeming eternity . . . I dreamt a thousand dreams, died a thousand deaths, and "NO!" was my clear answer to this unholy charlatan and prevaricator of the truth, as he stood close by quiet. "A most unwise decision my young friend," responded Mephisto, whilst seething in anger at my "NO!" And then, Mephisto declared: "I shall take your soul anyway, and bring your life to its final close!"

That was it, my time was up! I knew I must act decisively to save my soul, if not my life! Dropping quickly now to my knees, with my eyes shut, and a small silver crucifix in my hand, I replied, in kind: "Get thee away from me unclean evil spirit in Jesus Christ's name I pray!" "And save my life Almighty Lord God, and deliver my soul from this foul, evil tempter and cleanse my mind of his evil thoughts and vile overtures!"

With that declaration, trembling and shaking, I continued by chanting the Lord's Prayer, when suddenly I heard a sonorous, searing scream and my eyes opened wide to behold Mephisto engulfed in the flames of a holy fire and the fury of heavenly damnation resultant from my impassioned recital of the Lord's Prayer. This final event ended Mephisto's slavish captivation and control of my mind and spirit—so delightful and wonderful to behold!

With this final image in mind—I jolted awake quite suddenly, as if from a very deep dream, and I was sprawled out on my writing desk, with my ink pen nearby, whilst feeling the warm glow of the bright morning sun as it was now peering through the window in my chamber. With this, I now felt safe and very much in the Lord's grace as I looked up from my desk, basking in God's most radiant sunshine that now engulfed my entire room through the window.

For the first time, I paused, and I smiled—and I said: "Thank you Almighty Lord God, Master of the Universe!" "For now I've learned a most powerful lesson about the wages of sin and temptation of thy Fallen Angel." With that, I felt I had truly been saved from the unending darkness and spiritual evil that Mephisto personally represented at the behest of Lucifer himself. And now, I have committed myself to begin writing again, and this time against that perverse and evil Kingdom of Lucifer. I also wanted to spirit into print, pure poetry in praise and celebration of Our Lord God—Our Creator and the supreme omnipotent force of the universe!

But then, I spied one final observation when I glanced at the floor from my writing desk. A small note lay there in the middle of the floor. With that, the initial warmth I had immediately felt, evaporated—and my nerves twitched, and my body contorted—as I stood up from my desk. I picked the note up from the floor with the exquisite blood-red writing on it, just as it had been placed there earlier, and read: "You won this time my little poet friend, but next time I come, Lucifer, My Great Master shall be with me and he shall take your holy soul forever and all eternity into hellfire and damnation from whence there shall be no escape! P.S. I still like your poetry very much! My Best Wishes, Mephisto."

After reading Mephisto's ghastly and threatening note—I stood now in a daze—bewildered and speechless—and, for a moment, most afraid again! But then, I realized that this was just another threat from Mephisto and that this choice was not his to make at all but was mine! I would never let him or his Master take My Holy Soul, for I have now recommitted my true faith and obedience forever to the absolute power and glory, and the loving grace of Almighty God, which from this point on is undeniable and unassailable!

I stand now both as a man and a writer, not in fear, but in a spirit of jubilation for I shall commit the power of my pen and all of my poetic works from this very moment forward toward being one of Almighty Lord God's literary warriors in fighting Lucifer and his evil on Earth. My literary works shall now reflect this unending crusade for light and goodness in our world against the Kingdom of Lucifer! With my heartfelt and passionate declaration here, I chuckled for a moment and wondered if Lucifer would like my poetry now!

Amen! Amen! Amen!

October 11, 2014
(Narrative)

The Past

One's former footprints in the sands of time,
Engraved and set for all to see in kind.

A time period of was and had been,
And descriptive too of what might have been.

A former snapshot of motion frozen,
Of people or an event so chosen.

A historical fact so great or grave,
That the procession of time has so saved.

An enchanted dream one dreamt deep and well,
Which is gone and one now can only tell.

A past moment of wantonness and wit,
Dead now and buried so deep in a pit.

A wondrous procession of epochs in time,
Now bygone for poets to set in rhyme.

December 25, 2014
(Heroic Couplet)

The Present

A fleeting moment in eternal time,
And ever progressive in real time.

One's "now" moment, then in history past,
Now in motion moving to future fast.

My words become history when I write,
No need to worry now—I'll make them right.

As the present is present progressive,
The past then follows now so possessive.

The night stars are past in a mere eye blink,
Their images not part of "present" sync.

A constant portent of events to come,
As we each live "now" in what we'll become.

Give me your hand for this moment is it;
Let's seize now this moment and live in it.

December 26, 2014
(Heroic Couplet)

The Radiance of Our Love So True

The radiance of our love is so true,
From the first time we met my dearest one.
I saw your eyes, felt your joy, and I knew
That no one else but you could be the one.

Our first embrace was so warm and intense,
And we sensed everything felt nice and right,
And we kissed deeply feeling no pretense,
As we strolled on that wondrous starlit night.

Our hearts and souls have melded now as one,
With our emotions afire my dearest!
Our love and life's journey has now begun,
And we must keep us ever so nearest!

We have radiance in our love so true,
And pray to God for his divine love too!

December 29, 2014
(Shakespearean Sonnet)

The Sorcerer

Monseigneur Reygus Hameltus
A defrocked priest and sorcerer of the black arts . . .
An epiphany of evil and a master of debauchery . . .

He looks among his minions with a grim-bearded countenance
and with
a pair of piercing beady eyes with a distinct grimace of utter revulsion.

As the full moon rises and arches in the evening sky . . .
Reygus Hameltus menacingly stands by . . .

He was once a famous, devout, and humble priest of medieval times
and a biblical scholar and factotum of great intellectuality.
His walk and conversion to the dark side
mirrored his frustration with God Himself.

Reygus Hameltus felt that God had deserted him
and no longer cared to listen to him.
With this . . . and losing faith . . .
Hameltus turned to the Devil—the ultimate corrupter of the human soul!

As the full moon rises and arches in the evening sky . . .
Reygus Hameltus menacingly stands by . . .

As Reygus Hameltus assumed his apostleship in the world of evil
every ounce of goodness and spiritual greatness
left his body and soul in good measure.

He raped and murdered, cajoled and lied
and brought deception and reeked destruction
on all who crossed his path and his disciples no less.

As the full moon rises and arches in the evening sky . . .
Reygus Hameltus menacingly stands by . . .

It should be said that all evil one day runs its course
and when the good people of Montserrat fought back and answered in kind
Monseigneur Reygus Hameltus and his most evil witches' coven
suffered the eternal vengeance and wrath of Almighty God
and were banished to the Devil's Kingdom forever—faraway from mankind!

August 13, 2014
(Free Verse)

The Unholy Ones

ISIS is a Black Vortex that has attached itself to and infected the World's Soul . . .

Murder, Rape, Beatings, Beheadings, Destruction, and Terror—
These thugs, criminals and hooligans are the unholiest of the unholy.
The world's painfully aghast and their victims are pawns of this horror.

A truly nefast nest of murderers, thieves, and prevaricators of the lowest kind.
These thugs and their evil cronies lack any iota of human decency and scruples.
How could God tolerate these creatures in our society—such a despicable kind?

Almighty God in Heaven weeps so deeply at their unbridled savagery—
But God is not here today (not yet) to stop their vicious, hideous rampage.
The Civilized World weeps so deeply at their malevolent snickering mockery.

The evil they do and foment and spread is supposedly in God's name,
And how dare they commit such a sacrilege and expect all of us to bow?
To the Civilized World their actions cry out the very worst moral of shame.

It is undeniably tragic that mankind has this horrifying human cancer
In its collective DNA which bodes not well for the human species,
And 72 Virgins await them NOT as they enter the Gates of Hell—The Answer!

Nameless old and young people: men, women, children, innocent babies—
Who are savaged by hunger, disease, injury, and an unrelenting palpable fear,
Form the fodder of the ISIS ritualistic blood sacrifice as they destroy families.

All in the name of a Procrustean philosophy of nihilistic niddering nothingness . . .

August 24, 2014
(Tercet)

Thinking of You

Giving into emotions now wildly
passionate in thought but softly too
thinking realizing meaning always
dreaming during an evening walk
listening to the tone of your heart
conquering my shyness and pity
kissing the lips of nature so golden.

A mounting trail of grief and tears
real and salted in a wound so fresh,
finding beauty so pure and honest,
forgiving all in a moment's flash, and
finding love again so sweet, so pure,
with eyes moist, crying—the soft part
of the soul, running fingers through hair
that's so soft.

I seek your presence in my heart now,
intense in feeling and hopeful in intent,
playful always sweetly kissing your lips,
gazing now deeply into your eyes whilst
touching, holding, feeling happy, smiling
and realizing, just how much you always
mean to me dear one in our time and our
life together.

My love is present and shall be forever true
this soul cherishes all aspects of our love
as golden teardrops form their emotions pure
and dry their splashes as laughter comes as
we live each moment now to its fullest pitch
and saying always "Hi" and never goodbye
a real passionate love most wondrous true.

How precious dear one our love now truly is
with ancient treasures no greater nor grander
and wishing always that everlasting memory
and wanting the best against all odds in life
and seizing every day making all so joyful
and crying, at times, and forgiving always
this makes our spirits and our souls one.

Walking in that sweet summer wind with all
of our cares away and with emotions palpable
and present as we embrace warmly and often
and caress ever so gently in that moist warm
wind whilst kissing most divinely and so often
and finding out about our love and destiny so
true as we cry our teardrops rejoicing in our life.

Angels and happiness pervade our thoughts as
we share the light, the intensity, the feeling, that
consummates our spiritual oneness now whole
as our dreams are fulfilled and passions rewarded,
and our hearts beat magically together always as one
under Mother Nature's beautiful umbrella on this Earth
that's full of love, passion, and the sweetest emotions.

October 20, 2014
(Free Verse)

This One's for You Bartender

Bartender, Bartender... mix me a drink...
and give me one of your alchemic, mystical concoctions.

Bartender, Bartender... tell me what you think...
as you give me your magnificent magic elixir.

Bartender, Bartender... I don't want to think...
but I need that feeling of sublime nothingness.

Bartender, Bartender... I'm in love with her...
but only YOU know the truth of what I can't tell others.

Bartender, Bartender... I'm really not a broken man...
and—believe it or not—I still have faith in my fellow man (sometimes).

Bartender, Bartender... I do love your alcohol...
and your enviable mastery of the alcoholic arts.

Bartender, Bartender... I dislike stupid people (immensely)...
and I avoid them (like the plague) whenever I possibly can.

Bartender, Bartender... my love of poetry is for all eternity...
and my passion for it knows no limits in the human imagination.

Bartender, Bartender... mix me a drink...
and whether one day I meet Jehovah, the Devil, or even Mephisto
please always give me one of your alchemic, mystical concoctions!

August 30, 2014
(Free Verse)

Author's Note: This poem was written as a special tribute to a Bartender friend of mine.

Time Flies

Time flies in this world . . .
It's part of our very lives.
A running meter . . .
Tracks when, how long, how much
And measures what can be done!

November 7, 2014
(Tanka)

Unrequited Love

The love I felt exists no more
I can't believe we're no more
Darling how can this ever be
Don't you even care and see

I sleep at night in such a hopeless torment
My soul inside crying tears of a sad lament
I once felt at the very pinnacle of my life
Now I hang my head only in fear and strife

The feeling, passion, and warmth are now all gone
We had such fun in love and life, now that's gone
My hopes and emotions are awash in this strife
My desires and dreams are gone now in my life

I gave you all my love Darling straight from my heart
And you returned nothing Darling from the very start
My soul now cries so sadly in a most horrible, hellish fire
Knowing my love remains unrequited and my soul on fire

The love I felt exists no more
I can't believe we're no more
Darling how can this ever be
Don't you even care and see

November 1, 2014
(Lyric)

we our souls will spend our time repenting

we our souls will spend our time repenting
but the body of truth always comes to light
in drawing an end to come with true believers
so they can see the many evil faces of the Devil

greed in this world as money takes over always
and as they worship first with the Devil's tools
invading our space all for the sake of the black
liquid-gold tainted hearts in their colors so pure

shame on this world absolutely since mankind
has not learned at all given profound problems
aplenty and stands the testimony of our times
as war fails to resolve anything at death's end

only when family lives are directly affected do
they have the fighting right to protect and live
wherever they choose but we are all controlled
and always told what to do openly or furtively

in a system rolling unto the very end of mankind
there are shut eyes in the face of truth and honesty
and the whole setup is a joke making one laugh as
countries now run amok and history repeats itself

doing the Devil's work at command or by one's own
will, whilst throwing our money around with such a
profligate zeal like they are royalty with a birthright,
all this says so much for the world we live in today

looking at their greed, it's now so clear for all to see that
with food dished out on silver cutlery and others starving,
our priorities have run afoul of charity and common sense
running everything into the ground to support their lies

present catching the past, and past is the future's prologue
Earth soon develops a chasmic breach at depths reaching
a heart's song of unheard powers that possess a most awful
and pronounced quest of more which destroys our souls

in a such a pitiful world that's so desolate and blind there
are pure souls who wish their love will now shine bright,
and that one chance will come to them with the golden sun
but can humankind seize this special golden glory at hand

two paths lie ahead in tomorrow's dawning shadow dark—
the path to the end or to the new beginning for mankind,
we live ever together striving for a peaceful endeavor, and
we live at war forever bordering on the fringe of Hell itself

the way to Armageddon lies open and wants to greet us now,
the way to the golden life of a peaceful bliss is still possible,
yet, at tomorrow's dawn, do we change our path or will we
sing a song of stupidity and choose darkness for our future

We Must Have Peace . . . In Our Time or Perish Forever!

December 4, 2014
(Quatrain)

Author's Note: A Collaborated Poem with Michael Clarke and Liam McDaid.

What Our Dreams Are Made Of

Dearest one I think so very often of our special love,
And thank God above daily for that chance meeting,
For this Darling is what our dreams are made of—
And makes seeing you always such a special greeting!

Dreams are the mystical fabric of poets' ink and verses,
And reflect emotions and tears very special and so rare;
For one's heart and soul weave into these very verses,
While poets ponder passion pure and love so ever rare!

I sense and see the sweet tears from your eyes so true;
Real emotions they show me always my dearest love,
And your thoughts and passion never leave me blue,
For this Darling is what our dreams are made of—

Our love's so real and special as we walk life's path as One,
Knowing our dreams are made of love for two—now One!

December 9, 2014
(Shakespearean Sonnet)

When Our Eternal Poetry Muse Beckons

Poetry is a highly personal endeavor for those who choose to write it, and who want to delve deeply into the recesses and mysteries of the human mind whilst seeking to answer the true inspiration and calling of Our Eternal Poetry Muse.

Why do we write poetry?
This is a most compelling question for all of us who "Spill Ink."

Poetry is a most wonderful magical medium. And, as an art and a methodology in the field of literature, it speaks to and addresses the classical realms of the mysterious, arcane, uncanny, mystical, esoteric, and divine as well as Mother Nature, people, things, and the human dynamic of relationships and problems.

Poetry is my personal endeavor to master the complexity of relating my deepest thoughts and connecting with the reader, developing a memorable and intriguing theme or subject, choosing the right words and composing meaningful verse, finding the best metaphors and the proper tone and balance, and exploring key themes and emotive attributes such as:

Feelings, passions, emotions, light, dark, happiness, sadness, humor, good, evil, intelligence, stupidity, right, wrong, ethereal, ignorance, indifference, politics, war, famine, tyranny, and so forth.

Our Poetry Muse touches each and every one of us at special times when we least expect it: morning, noon, evening, and at midnight.

Our Poetry Muse captivates my thoughts and illuminates my soul whilst compelling me onward to communicate and share with others what I see and perceive, sense and feel, think and understand about themes and subjects as they resonate with me in the depths of my innermost psyche.

I know that I have much to say now in my life as I write poetry, and I find when working with verse, meter, rhyme, tone, metaphors, metonymy, allegory, imagination, etc. — that these particular poetic methodologies, among others, all enliven my efforts and make easier my attempts to mirror my thoughts and views to the reading public.

I want my thoughts and doubts, as my passion abounds, to connect with those deepest elements of my human psyche, in making my written message to be something that has a realistic and varied blend of attributes, feelings, and emotions which may be meaningful and significant, resolute and spirited, full of passion or compassion, humor or sadness, courage or fear, strength or weakness, Heaven or Hell, bliss or misery, or whatever inspires the "Creative Process" for me now as a professional writer and poet.

Our Poetry Muse is there to inspire and help us in bringing passion, meaning, certitude, and direction to our thoughts as we attempt to infuse these attributes into our poetic narratives.

Our Poetry Muse leaves it up to each and every one of us to go one step further beyond Her ethereal influence and inspiration, that is, to invest and infuse at the end of this creative process, our own "Spirit of Free Will" in making those critical and timely decisions that pertain to what our final narrative products and poetic verses shall look like to Our Reading Public.

This is my take, my specialized view on what happens when Our Eternal Poetry Muse tantalizes us and awakens within each of us that undeniable influence, which reflects a "Spirit of Inspiration," and that certain irrepressible desire to "Spill Ink!"

October 3, 2014
(Narrative)

Where are you Fred Astaire?

A man with impeccable charm, sophistication and grace,
Fred Astaire was, at once, both marvelous and enchanting
As the twentieth century's greatest dancer and master artist.
He made his sublime dancing ("Hoofing") seem effortless.

Capturing the American spirit with both panache and verve,
Fred Astaire glided across some quite wonderful movie sets:
Top Hat (1935), Swing Time (1936), Shall We Dance (1937).
All done magnificently and harken back to a different America.

This America, though more old-fashioned, was one of "can-do,"
And it boasted a gutsy bravado even in times of great hardship.
Fred Astaire, with others, was a famous star symbol of the then
"Greatest Generation" that brought peace to a war-torn world.

Fred Astaire, as part of this "Greatest Generation," serenaded his
audiences and dazzled them with dance steps of joy and perfection.
Although he's gone now, his contributions serve as a prologue for
New generations to come and to seize opportunities for greatness.

Where are you Fred Astaire?

September 2, 2014
(Biographical Narrative)

With You Forever My Love

Darling no matter what's coming our way,
We'll be full and content in heart and soul,
As we walk with joined hands day by day,
Our love shall give us so much to extol!

May our love be such a joy on this Earth,
As we seek meaning in our lives daily spent.
We must master our destiny from birth,
To learn what the Angels in Heaven meant!

With faith and love so pure we're happily one,
As we march with hands joined against all strife;
We've learned the reason why for being one,
Is to know that God's part of us in our life!

With our passion as one in Heaven above;
Please know I'm with you forever my love!

December 21, 2014
(Shakespearean Sonnet)

Without Your Love

Without your love my darling—
It's
me against the world,
me against the world,
me against the world.

And when I first met you my love,
at first glance I was smitten
and could never lose sight of you.

Without us together my love—
It's
me against the world,
me against the world,
me against the world.

And when I think of you my darling,
I can smell your scent and see your smile,
and dream, dream, dream all the while
of being in your loving arms again.

And so
Without your love my darling—
It's
me against the world,
me against the world,
me against the world.

A lonely man so desperate for your love!

September 30, 2014
(Lyric)

Would You Dance This Last Dance with Me

Darling—Would you dance this last dance with me?
I thought of this question so intently as I gazed at
You afar tonight across the busy dance floor and
Your very smile and presence shined for all to see.
It would take courage for me to ask for that dance!

Looking at you first glance captivated my very emotions,
And I thought, "How could this be?" "I've not met you!"
Yet, I also saw your most magical and most warm smile,
And roared deeply inside of myself each time I heard your
Funny, wonderful, and most exciting laughter so sweet!

And so, I decided to move closer and closer to you while
Passionately thinking and trying my best to conceal my
Shyness and fear of looking foolish when I spoke to you.
I knew that I had this one chance and didn't want to blow it,
And so I downed some fine alcohol to free up all my words!

All this seemed like an eternity, but finally—there you were,
And my inner voice cheering me on cried, "It's Now or Never!"
With that, our eyes met and locked at once, and I said, "Oh Gee!"
You then smiled so warmly and laughed and touched my hand,
And I knew then and there that you were the ONE in my life!

At first, not talking, but looking at each other I noticed at once
Your most beautiful blue eyes, radiant hair, and luscious red lips.
Your touch, your scent, your smile, and your warmness captured
My heart entire, and then I knew our meeting would entail much
More than just a dance—it could be a dance for the rest of our life!

And so, I thought: "Romeo, it's time to talk, to start charming her!"
But she spoke first, both gently and laughing, putting me at ease,
And I was enchanted at once by her—and her voice had a melodic,
Smooth tone that bewitched me as her eyes mesmerized me entire.
We touched further, embraced, and kissed with so much delight!

As we stood there as ONE locked deeply in our embrace and emotions,
Time stood still for us both as the sensual stirred the spiritual, further
Enriching this splendid moment that we had hoped would go on and on!
After which we talked, walked hand-in-hand, never leaving each other.
The evening grew later, and the music was dying down now—it's time!

With this cue, I gently cupped her hand in mine and kissed her once
More so very warmly while gazing lovingly and deeply into her eyes.
And then, my question finally surfaced and erupted with much delight!
Darling—Would you dance this last dance with me tonight? We did,
And it started a long romance-filled dance for the rest of our life!

November 8, 2014
(Narrative)

You Never Told Me

You never told me you didn't really ever love me,
I can't believe how crass and cruel you could be.
What possessed you my Darlin' to act as such,
When I loved and cared for you—oh, so very much!

Our love was always something quite bold and unique,
Your voice, touch, scent, smile formed this very mystique.
You beguiled me ever with your false expressions of trust,
Only to go elsewhere to satisfy your desires of carnal lust.

I once felt we were on top of the world with a love—oh, so rare,
Only to find out our love's a cruel joke and this I can never bear!
With this my very hopes and dreams burn in a fiery storm of doubt,
And your actions my dear sweet Darlin' only double my redoubt!

Our emotions, passions, joy, and warmth now are nevermore,
As I stare into this frightful chasm of despair I can only abhor!
My soul sadly cries out now in a raging storm of outrage and fury,
And you my Darlin' no longer deserve my love now—only my fury!

I once gave you my true love and boundless passion from my heart,
Only to see you laugh and ridicule my very feelings from the start!
And so now my Darlin' it's your turn to cry and feel unending despair,
As you realize my love and feeling for you are gone and I no more care!

You never told me you didn't really ever love me,
I can't believe how crass and cruel you could be.
What possessed you my Darlin' to act as such,
When I loved and cared for you—oh, so very much!

November 15, 2014
(Lyric)

Your Beauty Is

Your beauty is a most precious flower
Which signifies our love by the hour;
Your eyes twinkle most bright like stars in the night;
Your touch is gentle, exciting, and feels so right;
Your scent is enchanting, and your skin is so soft;
All of these make me think of you darling—so oft!
You are my beauty and my only true love in this life!

October 11, 2014
(Septet)

Your Kiss

Your kiss is so rapturous my sweet love,
Your red lips are like red rubies precious,
A love quite special made in Heaven above,
And ever no doubt much and more precious.

I know that my emotions soar now very high,
As your thoughts pervade my thoughts so true,
You shall never have to ask me when and why,
We share our love passion now so very true.

Your kiss shall always be my special bliss,
Your touch and caress so gentle and warm,
Our eyes gaze softly as we move to kiss,
And our love shall be so sweet and warm.

And by all on this Earth that I value so much,
Nothing compares with your kiss and touch!

October 14, 2014
(Shakespearean Sonnet)

Your Look of Precious Love

Whilst I gaze warmly into your eyes my dearest,
I see deeply your pure angelic soul of love
Reflecting like the radiant flight of a dove,
Charting its flight on so high emotions purest!
Our spirits ascend high in the sky so clearest
To the very boundaries of Heaven my love,
Where the power of brightness is God's best above.
Your look of precious love is always mine dearest!

When we kiss so passionately our lips now melt,
As we caress warmly our emotions are so felt!
Why we do this darling defines our love so dear,
As counts the worth of angels' blessings to be here!
How we truly love each other matters on God's Earth,
As your look of precious love exceeds all gold's worth!

December 5, 2014
(Petrarchan Sonnet)

Zapfhahn

D*er Zapfhahn* has several meanings in the German language:
The Spigot, The Nozzle, The Tap, The Faucet, The Hose.

Without its definite article, the noun "Zapfhahn" is also the name of a local pub located in a small historic German town with discernible vestiges of the Roman Empire near the city of Braunschweig.

My introduction to and earliest experience with this rather colorful establishment dates back to the year 1990, at the outset of the very hectic period of the German reunification. What follows are some of my unique reflections of this very special moment at that time:

Zapfhahn is the ideal place to go to imbibe alcohol of all variations—
and to have intellectual discussions (at rare moments, if possible),
and to have interesting conversations (all the time or so it seems),
and to dodge errant beer bottles speeding through the air (occasionally),
and to sing songs (mostly in German) *apropos* to the crowd gathered.

Zapfhahn is the place to go for those wishing to solve personal, societal and various problems of the world—or at least attempt to engage in this typical and fruitless aspect of human adventure whilst laced with that certain demon called "alcohol."

Zapfhahn, with its unique public medium and its daily influence on those wishing to imbibe alcohol, is the place:
to adjust your attitude,
to fall in love,
to fall out of love,
to get drunk or to get really drunk,
to find redemption (depending on your religion or a lack thereof),
and to just have a good time.

With fun had by all, with the night very late, I simply cannot wait to indulge myself again—Oh, "those famous last words."

And so, Zapfhahn—with your mythic, mystic, and alchemic relation to those grand "Spirits of the Night," I shall surrender my immortal soul now to thee in all due course so that I might see it resurrected later in all of its resplendent glory.

I can only pray and hope so, as I chant, Amen ... Amen ... Amen.

August 29, 2014
(Narrative)

CHAPTER TWO

Selected Poetry
(2015)

Enchanted Moments
Mortal Passions
Shades of Evil
and
Cosmic Destiny
and
Realism

A Brave Soul Goes Home

No mortal power on this common earthly plane,
Can ever call you back as Heaven makes its final gain.

Your mind was one steeped in such numeric certitude,
Possessing a spirit with a most certain pulchritude.

Your life strode a period of only six decades plus two,
But in God's divine plan, He knew so well the real you.

You developed in time a zest for friendship and love,
Which God felt with such passion in Heaven above.

Your life had its great share of such suffering and pain,
But that never dampened your spirit on this mortal plane.

God was most aware always of your charitable nature,
As you helped those in need, all victims of human nature.

Your departure from us was sadly short and unexpected,
But God's plan and wishes for you were always expected.

And so Brave Soul we mourn your loss from our mortal home,
But we take solace in knowing God's called you to His home.

April 27, 2015
(Couplet)

Author's Note: A special tribute to a departed and beloved family member.

A Leprechaun's Christmas Dream

This story is of a spry little elf's most sacred special-ever dream;
His hope to work one day for Santa Claus on his North Pole team.

This tiny green man, a true Leprechaun with a funny and bold way;
Santa first saw this elf as he was flying his sleigh o'er him one day.

Another time fly'n o'er Ireland a day prior to Christmas Eve's time,
Santa again saw this elf—a smil'n and a sing'n in best Irish rhyme!

The Leprechaun's name was "Timothy" with such a cherubic face;
He could down three shots of stout-hard Irish Dew at a rapid pace

Santa wanted such a wonderful Irish helper full of humor and fun,
Who could make kids laugh and smile with every story-told pun!

Timothy's quaint green-eyed twinkle Santa saw, making him smile;
He knew Timothy would always work hard and go that extra mile!

For Timothy being an Irish elf didn't always match his true-self real;
With his magic gifts and Pot of Gold—he would make Santa a deal!

"Methinks Santa, all shall be fun for us with the kids' puns and play!"
"Mewishes to give o'er me Pot of Gold to you, on this blessed day!"

Santa sensed and saw Timothy's true self and his real Heart of Gold,
Now giving o'er his Pot of Gold for needy children—an act so bold!

Timothy came with Santa as his "First Helper" on Christmas Eve night;
Happy all children were seeing Santa's radiant sleigh in the moonlight!

Santa even let Timothy ride on Rudolph, whose red nose shone so bright,
As Santa's sleigh made its sacred, happy journey on this wondrous night!

Timothy's story of his Christmas Dream came true on this star-lit night,
When he became one of Santa's team members on this most divine night!

December 3, 2015
(Couplet)

Author's Note: A Collaborated Poem with Ingrid Krukenberg-Bateman.

A Leprechaun's Christmas Magic

And so, perhaps it's no illusion at all—
When you can feel some magic in a special time;
A special time like Christmas!

There is maybe a magical Leprechaun around,
To show people his mythic "Pot of Gold" which
Lies at the end of God's Divine Rainbow!

Yet there's always another "Pot of Gold" to find too;
One that lies in the very spirit and hearts of the people
Around you especially now at Christmas time!

And so, try your best always to look carefully when
You may sense and feel that this magic is in the air;
And that Leprechaun is guiding you now in kind to
"The Golden Heart of Christmas!"

December 3, 2015
(Free Verse)

Author's Note: A Collaborated Poem
with Ingrid Krukenberg-Bateman.

A Most Beautiful Symphony of Love

Rhythmic tones form a most beautiful symphony of love
A shining star as nature's splendor reflects Heaven's light
It's my destiny to learn a passion and purpose to use now
Even for a moment, I would not change, for you are my love
And love is a blessing, an eternal gift that keeps on giving
Take your wish, shattered dreams—leave this world behind
And we shall seek and find a togetherness with lullabies pure
For each new emotion, my heart shall always find you dearest

Sending warm golden stirring echoes dancing into your dreams
Softly lips whispering so gently in the air as a loving tune sings
As the warm sun lights up our footsteps treading on golden sands
Perfect maiden you are the siren ringing bells for midnight chimes
True precious bride inside the heart you have keys to all the doors
Walk with me hand in hand as the soul breathes and butterflies sigh
Ocean waves crash—kissing salt of the earth as windows flutter free
Safely sitting on the throne as the crown graces a fair maiden queen

Our special music reflects the precious nature of our love dearest
As we share enchanted moments with each other so real and pure
When I take your hand in mine, I feel the magic warmth of passion
When I gaze into your eyes, I sense the depth of our love forever
The delight I share with you dear one defies all human description
And so my love—enjoy the oneness we share as two souls together
As we bask in God's own heavenly light and music in His Universe
Our hearts unite as one in forming a most beautiful symphony of love

June 21, 2015
(Free Verse)

Author's Note: A Collaborated Poem with Anne-Lise Andresen and Liam McDaid.

A Person's Worth and Measure

A person's life is sacred in God's eyes,
For we all know that God tells us no lies.

God views a person's worth and measure,
As something grand and always to treasure.

A person should fear not his or her measure,
Rather strive always to find God's pleasure.

A person's azimuth lies in God's very hands,
And only God knows one's destiny and final plans.

A person who does good works in this life,
Is one who's good and penitent before all strife.

As a person's life nears its final-end days,
God's there to show him or her His holy ways.

A person's worth and measure mean so much;
In God's eyes such values always merit his touch!

June 6, 2015
(Couplet)

A Progressive Shadow

A series of real challenges and troubling world events
In our twenty-first century give us a definite reason and
An urgency to pause and reflect on mankind's situation.

Our world today—more than at any other time in the past,
Is faced with an uncertainty and a palpable anxiety that is
Pervading on the world stage for all of us to sense and see.

These challenges and situational-events are so daunting and
Form a "progressive shadow" engulfing the soul of mankind.
They cry out now for collective action to find real solutions.

Our technological advances are indeed impressive for sure,
But our stewardship of our planet is lacking, a true tragedy,
As the World Climate edges closer toward a vast cataclysm.

Our political leaders choose to bury their heads in the sand.
Now is the time we must face down all of these problems,
As Mother Nature herself cries out warnings to our deaf ears.

The classical scourges: Tyranny, Poverty, Disease, and War
Are still with us today as they have been from the very start.
They accentuate mankind's great shame for all of us to see!

Atrocities, Famine, Refugees, and Terrorism add their lot
To this growing list along with Nuclear Proliferation and
Political Mendacity for Personal Gain—with no end in sight!

Reasonable answers and solutions abound to these enigmata,
And people are in strife and rightfully want something better;
Yet the oft-noted solution is the "Head-in-the-Sand-Syndrome."

Despite any true faith in God, mankind must be self-reliant,
As a distant deity plays tough love with the bad decisions of
His "Divine Creation" as we all stumble along without a clue.

This creates fear, frustration, and anxiety that multiply readily,
Making potential solutions and decisions even harder to do.
There can never be easy answers under these circumstances!

The tasks facing mankind are many and Sisyphean for sure;
Yet, we must have the courage to face them down as we seek
Realistic accountability from our politicians and big business.

Meanwhile God is watching and Mother Nature is waiting...
For mankind to do the right thing and to step up to the plate;
For the "Collective We" hold the keys to make these changes.

Can we do it? Will we do it? Can we rectify our inhumanity?
Can our nation-states serve the people and not themselves?
Can we all realize that we are in this tragic mess together?

Tin-eared dictators and fools will gladly tell us all differently.
The temptation to take the easy way out is always there for us.
But are we prepared to inherit this wind and reap its vengeance?

Meanwhile we continue our present tortuous path oblivious now
To the realities facing us squarely down every minute of the day.
In a mythical sense—perhaps we wait for Jotunheim to save us?

Eventually all the sand in "Earth's Hourglass" will run out and
Our gig will be up, and all of us will be forced to Pay The Piper!
Are we not better than this? Let us hope we can find the courage!

October 29, 2015
(Tercet)

A Rainbow's Magic

A rainbow's magic reflects God's majestic and divine touch,
Giving us a panoply of colored images which mean so much.

The wonder of God's enchanted pictorial missives here on Earth,
Gives us an ethereal pause as we reflect on each rainbow's birth.

A rainbow is God's celestial medium of His images to treasure,
To help Man better understand Him and meet His deft measure.

The power of a rainbow is its picture-perfect aura of pulchritude,
Dazzling our visual senses and assuring us of Heaven's certitude.

A rainbow's very visage mesmerizes our human senses complete,
And embeds in us all, God's spirited message of His love replete.

A rainbow is a noble and supreme reflection of beauty at its best,
And of shades of heavenly images on Earth meeting God's behest.

A rainbow's magic is the power of God's message to us on Earth,
Subtly preparing Man for his heavenly ascent and his soul's rebirth.

August 13, 2015
(Couplet)

A Spider's View

Walking his web
At ceiling corner
Gazing downward
Watching and waiting
Patience absolute.

Growing hungry
Eyes focused
Two victims
Fly and Lady Bug
Trapped in web.

Sense of doom
Survival of fittest
Stronger species
Spider's appetite
Sustenance waiting.

Scheme of life—
With Darwin smiling
A winner, two losers
Strongest wins
And strongest eats.

A Spider's View
On a typical day
Each day similar
But different
Result—the same.

Fixed in place
Or hanging around—
Multi-legged
And multi-eyed—
An Acrobat Supreme!

February 18, 2015
(Accentual Meter)

A Spirit Leaves the Body Seeking Eternity

A Spirit leaves the body while crying aloud as
Cursing blind hate enters without conscience
A Hell for the wicked casting names as called
Tears of love weeping in sorrow and anguish
Dripping red from the heart beating so dear
Devouring feelings eating into emotions I laugh so
To stop the weeping stirring in deep rocks below
Echoing waves of turbulence and such gale force
Inside one soulful cry sounds in a whispered dream
Begging, desiring to move on from this mortal coil!

But pray tell—must wicked negation like this be
Ever so, if so, then why so?
Man-made negation, negativity should never be
Allowed and the soulful cry must be heard, answered
Divine intervention, angelic powers to the rescue!

A Spirit leaving the body—a solemn event it is, for
There is no place for such mortal wickedness in this
Instance as the Spirit begins it transformative ascent
Toward the Heavens and the power of the Almighty
Shall answer in kind those mortals who bring their
Perfidy to this most wondrous process that severs
The mortal bonds of the Earth dimension as the
Spirit moves on in its new-found state and presence
As Peace and Happiness envelop it soothingly and pure
Preparing it for God's most precious embrace into Eternity!

January 6, 2015
(Free Verse)

Author's Note: A Collaborated Poem with Liam McDaid.

A Teardrop Falls

A teardrop falls now deeply slicing and aching with
a sad hurt and twisting knots around our fingers as
I love you from my heart's warmest emotions, so that
in each kiss of your beauty I may feel all of you now,
and that's worth the suffering and pain that happens
as we both share such deep and profound emotions,
and an undiminished love and happiness that are such
precious gifts for us forever as the teardrop falls now
freely in your honor, and as it spills warmly and gently
in your name, my love, as grace is my honor to bear
this most noble sacrifice with a true joy, as I find you,
my sweetest sunshine with our happiness being that
one-way ticket to a real paradise that lies in your arms
forever.

June 9, 2015
(Verse)

Author's Note: A Collaborated Poem with Liam McDaid.

A Time of Bliss

Love's a mystery to everyone falling under its magical spell,
And it would be natural to think we all know it so very well.
But with emotions ripe and afire in this special time of bliss,
It's easy for those so smitten not to sense something amiss.

Love's a most potent alchemy enchanting at once one's soul,
And when it's returned in kind it makes one's life quite whole.
The pure passion that love excites is beyond all earthly compare,
Which makes it an emotive force not subject to any trifled dare.

Love's a time of bliss when a couple's love melds them as one,
And affairs of the heart shape their fate as two souls form as one.
This is the moment when lovers rejoice in such unbridled pleasure,
When each knows they've found a rare love for eternity to treasure.

February 1, 2015
(Rhyme)

A Tree

I'm a tree lining a country road
Along with hundreds of other
Trees in the direction of a verdant
Forest—full of scenic wonder and
Teaming with life.

All of us stand tall and firm with
Such majestic beauty and geometric
Symmetry and precision which is
Evident from the angles and curves
Of each tree and the fact we all
Practically line up in a straight line.

The simplicity and beauty we display
To the human eye disguises the actual
Complexity beneath the surface of our
Existence which could even be likened
To some form of a thought-provoking
Algebraic equation.

We all represent the wizardry of Mother
Nature and the divine thought of God and
Have been an integral part of this Earth
Far longer than Mankind—and do we have
Some stories that we could share with you!

As a tree I'm nurtured daily by our Earth,
But as I take, I also give back and help to
Bring balance to Earth's daily Carbon
Dioxide output in the greater scheme of
The worldwide environment.

And so, as a Tree, my life and function
As a living organism and an entity here
On Earth is a testament to the wonder of
Creation, and both the marvel and mystery
Of the Universe, and the omnipotence and
Divine power of God.

February 15, 2015
(Narrative)

Author's Note: A Collaborated Poem
with Ingrid Krukenberg-Bateman.

A Winter's Night

This winter's night is cold and bright;
frozen air brings fresh fallen snow.
It reflects now God's true starlight!
This winter's night is cold and bright;
a brilliant scene, this dark cold night!
Mother Nature smiles, now aglow!
This winter's night is cold and bright;
frozen air brings fresh fallen snow.

November 19, 2015
(Triolet)

A Withered Rose

Our love dear
is now but a
"Withered Rose."

And I really
don't know if
you care—I
must suppose.

We once had a
most radiant love
full of wonder,
joy, beauty, passion.

And now it's quite
hard to accept
the reality
that all is ruined
and all is gone.

I sleep now dear
with utter despair
in a soulless torment
that is unending
knowing our once
"Red-Rose Love"
is gone forever...

And in its place
I have nothing
but an image of a
"Withered Rose Memory."

February 4, 2015
(Accentual Meter)

Almighty Lord God

Heavenly Master—
Always omnipotent, yes!
Our Lord God is Love . . .
Always omnipresent, yes!
Eternity's Divine Force!

June 26, 2015
(Tanka)

An Autumn Portrait of Beauty

On this quite beautiful and most radiant Autumn day,
I marvel at Mother Nature's smile of silent pulchritude,
As I make a loving glance at such luscious scenery today,
In this country scene—a glorious gift of God's certitude!

The trees and their fallen amber leaves adorn this Earth,
As a shimmering reflection pervades from a green pond,
Of Nature's wonder with colors arrayed in a sacred rebirth,
Affirming God's heavenly promise true and His holy bond!

This view of trees, grass, leaves, and a shadow near the pond,
Captures the glory and grace from God's colored-palette true,
That affirms His desire of rendering this beauty from beyond,
And I thank Him with all my heart with joy and blessings true!

Yes, God doth paint this world with such love for all to see,
His Autumn portrait here is of unparalleled artistry and grace,
That I interpret as a heavenly-made moment for all of us to be,
As I reaffirm the beauty of Nature's gift in this wondrous place!

November 6, 2015
(Rhyme)

Author's Note: A special tribute to a former high school classmate that portrays the radiant beauty of the landscape behind her home on a beautiful and memorable Autumn day.

An Echo Through Time

An echo through time follows us all now in kind;
As it's the moment when poets find their rhyme!

Past-Present events give us a mirror to see from,
Of what Present-Perfect events have now become.

Poets must write the truth of what surely they mean,
With such wondrous verses that readers shall glean!

Writing with tone, tenor, and syncopation is grand;
Giving poets the mellifluous effect desired by plan.

The echo quality of a great poem bespeaks its passion,
Whilst its literary panache shall always be in fashion!

An echo reflects a poem's true resonance by its intention,
Ensuring one's mind shifts onto an intellectual dimension.

The poets' rendezvous with this echo through time is divine;
As it helps us enshrine our thoughts now in continuous time!

November 27, 2015
(Couplet)

Angel Eyes Loving You Forever

Always a dream as the stars wink and smile
Never ending beauty shines picture perfect
Gifted when the moon smiles silver waves
Endless pleasure in a breath of wind sweet
Love blowing goodnight wishes to Heaven

Everlasting happiness sings with such elation
You bring joy when echoes fall silent smiling
Eyes of emotions sparkle golden warm kisses
Sweetly the sun kisses a new day with you

Longing for your passionate caress every day
Oxygen needed to calm me down as we touch
Vivacious you are My Sweet always on my mind
In love always every day with you my Dearest One
Never ever wanting to leave your side in this life
Great things in abundance result from our true love

You are simply the most wonderful person to me
Our love is a mutual bond that binds us together
Unique signifies the nature of our love My Sweet

First always you are in my heart and soul My Love
Our love, desire, and passion are boundless always
Ready always to take you in my arms Dearest One
Ever precious you are as my true love and soulmate
Very intent and passionate always when thinking of us
Ever present we are now in each other's life My Love
Remembering the love we share forever as always one

January 24, 2015
(Acrostic)

Author's Note: A Collaborated Poem with Liam McDaid.

Animal of the Night

The animal of the night has an evil courage as its defense,
And with simple lies it now catches the filthy beast easily,
And now can stand and bask in God's purest of sunshine,
Whilst valor and glory speak all power to one's destiny!

Darkness doth now pervade and drinks slowly from that
"Chalice of the Faithless Heathen" who hides among the
Soulless Ones who are consumed by their hateful actions,
And spit thoughtlessly at your good will and human pride!

Hades' very own dark demons tilt their evil night shades
Whilst justifying the hurt and depravity of an "Ugly Brute,"
An utterly lost soul without any mercy, blind, as "He" throws
Freely a nasty spiteful spirit on your earthly fire of reality!

Hence, Hades' mark and mask of utter darkness and terror
Descend now into the very conscience of your Spirit World;
Burning hot with the force of "The Furies" seeking revenge:
Tisiphone, Megaera, and Alecto all appear *sans piete* now!

As their eternal gorgonesque spirits creep upon you furtively,
Your once handsome visage turns into a sad and horrid portrait
Of an old animal soul in the mirror never to see the Light again,
As clouds darkly shade your horizon and fate in Hades' name!

In this eternal land of darkness, the dead do not suffer this fate
So easily, and cast not without honor in their chains the notion
That fear itself, vice destiny, cries out now for your forgiveness,
As One-Eyed Beggars seek and see the basic good within you!

Each day now fades into its own doom, into a dark mist of evil,
And hides carefully inside a "Mountain of Consciousness" where
Your ethereal spirit knows who you really are—as black snakes
slither slowly and silently toward your spirit-mirrored reflection!

You—that "Animal of the Night," wear now your deceptive mask;
The reality of who and what you really are makes my skin crawl!
You can never return from this darkest "Pit of Hell" my old friend,
For thy animal-human spirit is doomed to all this darkness forever!

November 22, 2015
(Quatrain)

Author's Note: A Collaborated Poem with Liam McDaid.

Autumn's Promise

Autumn's promise of love compels us true,
As we walk in this magical moment.
This change of seasons reflects Nature's will,
As the trees shed their leaves freely and the
Afternoon wind's protean emotions—
Touch ever gently our bodies with their
Cool-warm breath as we hug 'n kiss deeply,
In this passionate moment of true love.
'Tis this very moment we cry out our
Pledge to love one another forever!

August 28, 2015
(Blank Verse)

Blood Red Moon

Deep devouring passions bleed now from this solar eclipse
As black-blood flows from an evil army of "undead" beings
Whose fangs hideously and cruelly pierce the veins of their
Mesmerized and unsuspecting victims who are held at bay.

In such a silence, burdens prowl inside deep sad heartbeats
As ghastly living shadows now creep eerily in and knot the
Tortured guts of a twisted and scarred bloodless life falling
Now under the dark macabre gaze of the Blood Red Moon.

At night, uncanny black magic spells are chanted from an
Old Latin scripture as large spider webs cast a sad, gloomy
Presence and enshroud now all those trapped by them as the
Misted breath of bleeding hearts howl now to Heaven's roar.

Standing at a lonely mountain crossroad on this darkest of all
Nights, there can be no release from the horrid, devilish glare
Of this "Blood Red Moon" whose evil presence engulfs each
And every breath you take and casts a derisive demonic stare.

My senses are now frozen in place as a deep and frigid chill
Shakes my soul to the very core of its primordial existence as
I react to the rimy cold of a dawning maleficent darkness that
Invades every corner and space of my psyche and existence.

The wicked jaws of a rabid beast seek now to bite and rip out
The last vestiges of beauty and thoughts I hold close and dear
As I gasp now for my life and painfully feel my tired heartbeat
Slow as my immortal soul numbs, crying out to Almighty God.

I'm cursed now to walk alone forever as my spilled remains are
Cut out, and my precious ties to all humanity have disappeared
Putting me on the ground, on all fours, as I ponder my ultimate
Fate in the hands of a dark supernatural force beyond any mercy.

As the shadow of Lucifer's Blood Red Moon passes over my sad
And tortured face, I spy a look at one demonic siren who prompts
Me to follow her as my body is now placed upon a sacrificial alter
And my life ebbs away as I'm kissed by the spirits of the damned!

October 11, 2015
(Quatrain)

Author's Note: A Collaborated Poem with Liam McDaid.

Bryant's Necropolis Conceit

Silent halls of death appear
William Cullen Bryant
Thanatopsis supremus now
A sepulchre awaits us all.

Dour darkness and shroud forever
Thanatopsis-Phantasma
The spirit world so beckons us
We all shall so wither and fall.

January 15, 2015
(Double Dactyl)

Celtic Dreams

The Celtic dreams come forth through auric visions of an all-seeing eye. An ancient calling where the mystic rivers flow down a rugged mountain whilst Angels bathe in the springs of an everlasting and radiant beauty. The Soul grasps at memories enfolding within fields of emerald green, where the sun kisses the golden barley as it dances softly to a warm and beautiful breeze.

I see my blessed star once more awaiting me upon the great golden plain, enchanting the beautiful songbirds' sweet melodies, and holding the air one breathes. I come on the breath of a sigh, as the haunting Celtic pipes are calling and resonating breathlessly to your adoring beauty, with a true angelic music playing wondrous tunes to you over the mountains forever more.

From the Kingdom of Arrach, I stand looking out over a magical mountain river from where mighty waters roar, and find now deep ethereal senses pure where the mind's eye sees through the murky depths, on the edge of a dark mysterious voyage toward the dreams of my past. Stars twinkle bright in an azure sky, and within these stars my "Diamond Queen" is shining, as a liquid gold melts, blending gently with the radiant colors of a misted celestial light.

I stand as the true power of an ancient time, and the past lives live on within my warrior heart. High above the mountain an eagle spreads its wings now, evoking the horizon and sounding soft echoes as an affectionate calling. My beloved, this Celtic heart beats only for you. Come to me from your star, and we shall join once more, uniting dreams under the sleeping eyelids, and later shall awaken the whispers in the seed and pollen that are freely floating in the enchanted night air.

The eagle circling ever so slowly in descending circles, with a halo vision, falling to the spirit of Celtic beauty. A flaming heart burns once more, you come as promised, eclipsing upon this earth. I kneel before you, my gracious one, to softly kiss your breathless petals. A thousand dreams take flight. The lonely wolf on the highest pinnacle of Arrach awaits his love as the eagle flies in search of a new Celtic dream to be reborn into this life.

Lighting moonbeams dance with the shadows of sparkling starlight glistening silver, born into an existence from a black void of nothingness. The wolf and the eagle shall now join as one in human shape and form. It's at this moment that new legends arise in the sunsets, holding your slender fingers to my heart with the deepest joy that skips inside a chain that kisses your every command.

And now behold the glory of the coming dream and reality, as light explodes in such colored hues. If I could blow onto your hair a gentle whisper where a Soul floats and breathes as a warm treasure sparkles with a very special gleam that would indeed be a most glorious event. Once more King Aird Righ and his Diamond Queen come forth to redeem again the mantle of Celtic glory and all of its storied greatness.

A gift gem of a thousand lifetimes, beyond dreams of sweet honey, awakening in the morning as I bask in your very light and mythical presence. On the breath of a sigh you come from your peaceful sleep, called by our Love speaking from our ancient time, and with each passing moon, I sense whilst gazing at the stars ineluctable feelings and emotions as the divine dewdrops of the morning speak.

You are the greatest jewel these blue eyes shall ever see—a diamond that shines bright in my darkest hours—you are my Supreme Love! This Soul calls over the the vast ocean waves to you, as each magical echo in your voice ripples like a tiny hummingbird, as its heart beats rapidly and its flowers kiss all over your soft and sweet dreams.

August 25, 2015
(Narrative)

Author's Note: A Collaborated Poem with Michael Clarke and Liam McDaid.

Christmas Love

December's that special month,
For heavenly thanks and grace;
Family renewal time,
And our special love!

We celebrate with great joy,
And think of others we love;
A time now for God's Blessing,
And His sincere love!

December 1, 2015
(Dodoitsu)

Chronicler of Events and Emotions

As a Poet and as a Writer...
I'm a Chronicler of Events and Emotions.
I watch, observe, and record all that I see.
It's truly enough to absorb and understand
Both the grandeur and depravity of mankind.

As I observe events—past, present, and future
And delve into any emotions that are at hand,
I make doubly sure to comment, at will, while
Showing no fear and sparing not the "sting" of
My words, as a poet, as any situation may require.

I can and I should do no less on every theme that
I approach as a poet and a writer, as I seek always
To pursue a thoughtful path of refined exposition.
We must realize that though we may fulfill a very
Notable function of recounting and relating events,
Situations and emotions—we should never fear
When we must provide, at times, a much-needed
"Conscience" to any theme, event or situation as it
unfolds.

And so, it's necessary for us poets, at times, to act
As a "conscience of mankind," and to be not afraid
To reflect this in our poems when the urgency of
A circumstance or situation pleads for it out of a
Compassionate need for human understanding and
A true sense of obvious decency.

And, who are we, as poets and writers, if we don't
Undertake a deeper and more exalted approach to
What we do and really attempt to become "one" with
The human event, emotion, situation or relationship
That we are writing about?

If we don't do it—who will?

February 7, 2015
(Didactic)

Count Dracula's Love

Count Dracula's love is blood—sweet and bright red,
And he wants to bite your neck while you're in bed!
Seeking his next eternal bride on this All Hallows' Eve,
His "undead" bite makes him happy and isn't a pet peeve!

October 25, 2015
(Clerihew)

Creative Process

Can I really write something profound, grand, and glorious as a poet?
Reality should be a part of all I consider when approaching a theme.
Events often drive and form the poetic fabric of what we write about.
Avenues of true passion and emotions pervade our conscious thoughts.
Taking our thoughts, fantasies, and metaphors to the readers are essential.
Initiating a positive aura of excitement makes all verses interesting to read.
Viewing themes from a detached perspective gives us variety in discourse.
Every idea or theme is considered fair game when we poets spill our ink!

Poetry is a superb medium for relating themes to all human circumstances.
Rigid ideas and concepts can be artistic with the right nuance and metaphor.
Onomatopoeia is an expressive sound imitation of words for a poetic effect.
Creativity forms the very warp and woof of what we do as poets and writers.
Exceptionalism is an attitude helpful to poets as we focus on what is unique.
Syntax is the structural medium for how poets write and express themselves.
Sensitivity is an attribute essential for how poets evaluate ideas and themes.

February 7, 2015
(Acrostic)

Dance through your life

Dance through your life always
And listen to your inner melody;
And dance through your life with
Much joy and lightness for God's
Love is always unconditional and
Special to each and every person
Who aspires to do good deeds and
To evolve toward greater spiritual
Awareness seeking God's blessing;
Dance through your life as you seek
To pursue God's plan and work to
Better yourself in all endeavors you
Undertake while being unafraid of
Challenges and never forgetting to
Always be kind and of a charitable
Heart and tenor to your fellow Man;
Dance through your life to the very
End understanding our mortal coil
Is indeed finite but is part of a much
Greater cosmic purpose whereby our
Souls will one day make that majestic
Journey with angels to God's heavenly
Home where all of us can dance on in
God's Grace and Light for an Eternity!

February 23, 2015
(Didactic)

A Collaborated Poem with
Ingrid Krukenberg-Bateman.

Despair

A life negative—
No person's immune from this.
Fight back hard always...
No fear—be courageous now...
And never ever give up!

February 16, 2015
(Tanka)

Destiny and Fate

Fate is that noble force in future time;
Destiny's look asks why and how in kind.

Destiny bespeaks the past as prologue,
As Fate shapes desire—leaving us agog!

Both give us a special import to reach,
And a rendezvous with what both can teach.

Destiny's past is now motion frozen,
As we await Fate's events as chosen.

Destiny and Fate walk with us in hand,
As our lives pass hourly like grains of sand.

Each differ by nuance of certain time;
Poets can muse past and future in rhyme.

Destiny and Fate form life's mosaic,
As we each seek life's joy and not heartache!

November 1, 2015
(Heroic Couplet)

Dream with Me Always My Love

I see you my Love every late night
In my most private of sweet dreams
As we share our most pure thoughts
Of our truest love, feelings, romance

Your passion sets my very blood afire
Your desire captivates my soul entire
Your love's more precious than all gold
Making my passion all the more so bold

Our song of romance, fun, and pure love
Serenades us as we dream always as one
Making our love so joyous and ever fun
As our souls meet as one in Heaven above

What more could we ever hope to ask for
My Love as we live our lives to the hilt
And never be afraid at God's very door
For we shall be there together My Love

June 1, 2015
(Lyric)

Enchantment

A type of magic—
Charming those involved always.
Enchantment it is . . .
A motive force for poets . . .
To captivate readers whole!

January 3, 2015
(Tanka)

Frankenstein's Monster

Frankenstein's Monster has that cosmic glow,
And only wants to be a common Joe.
Looking now for his oh-so-special-mate;
Beware ladies, HE could be your next date!

July 25, 2015
(Clerihew)

God's Christmas Angel

God's Christmas Angel is full of His love;
A Guardian to those lost to His light.
Restore them to God's path of divine right,
This Angel's charge be with His grace above!
This Angel's mission is replete with love,
And one prized in God's holy presence bright;
One passion perfect in His holy light;
And one blessed by heavenly Saints above!

This Angel cloaks those lost in love replete;
With true passion and holy spirit now,
To fulfill God's wish—His eternal vow!
Love is this Guardian's power complete;
Her spirit to redeem those lost on Earth,
Bringing them God's love and divine rebirth!

December 2, 2015
(Petrarchan Sonnet)

God's Return Ticket

Did you ever wonder about the Almighty's criteria or selection process for reincarnation of souls back on Earth? Just think—some famous politician, movie star, sports figure, criminal, dictator, and so on could use "God's Return Ticket" to appear once again on our earthly plane one day as another person in body and spirit. Yet, how would you react as a transient soul in God's Kingdom if you found out that your return options would be perhaps as an elephant, a gorilla, a lion, a toad, a snake, a bird, a dog, a cat, a fish, a whale, a snail, an octopus, a flower, a tree, an insect or even some type of inanimate object? The possibilities when one thinks about these options could be practically unlimited!

Now that I've perhaps captured or at least heightened your attention to this spiritual possibility—even if just for the sake of conversation—imagine for a moment in the reveries of your mind and inner psyche of what it might be like to return to Earth as one the following:

A Former Man as a Woman: This time around you might have a definite edge since you subconsciously know how men think!

A Former Dictator as a Peacemaker: Historical first-hand knowledge of having been a brutal leader may enhance your efforts in negotiating peace in the world. (One can only hope!)

A Former Hobo as a Wealthy Person: You've got a man now who may be respectful of those who are less fortunate. Such a wealthy person may become a budding philanthropist!

A Former Criminal as a Man of God (priest/rabbi/minister): Well this would be a turn-around, whereby a former criminal now has the advantage of being a Man of God and has a direct connection to what he perpetrated and experienced when he was on the other side of the law. This experience may make him a better priest, rabbi or minister in the end. Amen!

An Elephant: A quite stately and wonderful mammal indeed whose presence certainly enhances the Animal-Mammal Kingdom on Earth. Elephants are vegetarians and by their nature are not a threat to anyone. Returning as one today could be problematic given all of the mindless decimation of their herds worldwide by poachers and criminals who are sadistic, pathetic, and despicable by their merciless actions. Let us all hope that these individuals one day go straight to "Hell" when they die for what they're doing to our elephants!

A Gorilla: This could be viewed as a step backward from whence you came as a human being, that is, depending on your views and beliefs concerning evolution. I would think though it would be better to come back as a Gorilla in the wild than being one in a zoo. At least you would have your freedom, but then the challenge to this would be doing your best to survive the many poachers who want to capture or kill you and your Gorilla loved ones!

A Lion: This choice might not be so bad. Just think, you could return as the "King of the Jungle." A word of caution is in order though: stay in the wild and avoid being captured and put in a zoo or your "King of the Jungle" days will be past tense!

A Toad: Just think, you'd acquire the unusual ability to hop around on "all-fours," eating your favorite insects, and making croaking sounds all through the night! What more could you ask for?

A Snake: These reptiles are quite scary and are probably not the very first choice for reincarnation, although some humans might be tempted to make this changeover depending on the tenor of their personality and character. The real question might be what type of snake one would choose to come back as. Good Luck!

A Bird: Coming back as a bird would give you a chance to switch over to a diet of worms and help you to hone your skills in chirping and whistling all day long. Very Enchanting!

A Dog: This could be an interesting return to the mortal world. The question would be, what size and type of dog you would come back as, and would you be the "quite type" or a "barker." At least you'll be man's best friend!

A Cat: Being reincarnated as a cat could make you very popular with cat lovers, and just think, you may end up inheriting the gene set for the nine lives' gift of regeneration. Not bad at all!

A Fish: Returning as a fish may give you satisfaction in knowing that you are a vital part of the world's food consumption. If you should come back as a type of specialty fish, this might not be the case. Beware of returning as a Piranha, unless you plan revenge on someone who had wronged you in a previous life. But as a Piranha—you won't have many friends!

A Whale: Returning as one of these majestic mammals might indeed be a quite fabulous experience. Size matters in this instance and commands a definite respect, but beware of poachers—another courtesy of mankind at its very worst!

A Snail: This existence on Earth may not be the most pleasant for you since you may be subject to possibly being eaten or squashed by any inattentive passerby. Your very slow, self-mode of movement will be challenging too!

An Octopus: Imagine your ready mobility in the sea and the newfound extent of your manual dexterity as you move under the water. Just think, you would be quite popular and possibly an instant hit favorite of the underwater sea party!

A Flower: This could be a wonderful experience especially if you were to be a radiantly beautiful flower. You would be a welcome addition to the plant world, and could be the focus of people who seek out your beauty or perhaps want to pick you as a symbol of true love and emotions. If this is so, then . . . Think Red Rose!

A Tree: Well, a tree may give a reincarnated soul a chance at a much longer finite life on Earth before dying or being destroyed by man. At least one may have the satisfaction of knowing that one's long presence as a tree would help to improve the carbon dioxide imbalance on our planet. Go Green!

An Insect: A lot of insects are really nasty, but if you can make it back as a Honeybee or a Butterfly that would be just grand!

An Inanimate Object: Just think you could come back as a plain old rock or a stone or even a seashell!

Enjoy all of these possibilities!

February 7, 2015
(Narrative)

Goethe's Emissary

Mephisto-Diabolical
Johann Wolfgang von Goethe
Faust on the Brocken Summit
Go our own sweet way for show.

Walpurgis Nacht's spirit of perversity
Mephistophelian
Time now for your eternal soul
The Evil One's sitting in a fiery glow.

May 19, 2015
(Double Dactyl)

Halloween Eve's Double Tanka

Halloween Eve's here—
Departed souls cross over
The Veil is open...
The living are always scared...
Of things they understand not!

Halloween Eve's here—
A Jack O'Lantern smiles now
His grin's inviting...
Kids find him so exciting...
Question: Where's the candy at?

October 9, 2015
(Tanka)

Halloween Treat

This
Cold night
Of such fright—
This Halloween
Scares the Bejesus
Out of me for sure since
I fear being the fresh treat
For the Devil's big appetite,
And his desire to consume my soul!
Old Hob shall see my crucifix tonight!

September 22, 2015
(Etheree)

Halloween's Evil Visage Cometh

Halloween's Evil Visage Cometh alive now in this famous predestined time
Where dubious shadow-shades run a riot as the ghastly, ghosts of darkness
Begin calling to all goblins, ghosts, ghouls, and witches in the graveyards;
To come alive—as black cats call out their signals to all lost souls seeking,
Powerful black magic spells to aid the spirits of ancient alchemists as they
Brew their potions to dull the senses and conjure all the evil spirits on Earth.

A falling silver-layered mist appears as these uncanny evil spirits invade our
Mortal plane and lost ghosts appear as hungry human skeletons looking for
Sustenance and seem to be horrified at the stillness broken by a death cold.
They scream as bloodless fingers touch cold shivers without a warm heart;
And who knows for sure the sad and mournful song from an ancient grave,
As "The Undead" conjure ravenous demons seeking warm blood to feast on.

Blended into the dust are the crows whose shadows, as a "Dark Phantom,"
Form now and take his eerie shape—yet, fear not the potent occult light as
That special Halloween Eve super moon beams bright and brilliant, making
Its presence known as your destiny and destination are already decided by
An ancient alchemist who beckons us all to drink widely from his mystical
Chalice of Darkness as all malice is attuned and the birds and beasts speak.

Life as we know it, is offered upon the *Demonic Alter* as the Dark Phantom
Initiates all human sacrifices as a drool-dripping envy of all existence drops;
And the lustful and vengeance-seeking Vampires rub now along the walls as
Sharp, poisonous thorns begin tearing behind their secret inner-vision as the
Deep, dark, and dismally-damp curtains open and eclipse the radiant dawn as
An unpleasant and horrible pain visits and our heartbeats grow faint and stop.

An unending agony screams sonorously as a deafening silence falls over us.
In this "Land of the Dead," they make their own laws overwriting all limits,
As a vile, creeping, malevolent mist crawls down into the valley deep below;
The Devil's Advocate slithers on in a nasty, vicious way under your own skin,
As shivering timbers of truth of a living being watches outside our bodies on
This Halloween Eve as our individual dreams enter the Twilight Zone forever!

The Devil's clever wizards and witches concoct an ancient poisonous mixture,
As the boiling cauldron of demonically-enhanced soup is stewed with care and
Fresh toads, spiders, worms, beetles, ticks, and tiny black snakes are added in.
This unholy and potent poisoned soup from centuries past is now blessed by
The Dark One—to take life from the living and give nourishment to the dead,
As the veil between The Living and The Dead disappears on Halloween Eve!

October 1, 2015
(Narrative)

Author's Note: A Collaborated Poem with Anne-Lise Andresen
and Liam McDaid.

Heart of Eternal Beauty

A flame burns now in the heart of eternal beauty
As one doorway opens calling out to our future
And your wondrous love burns bright, white-hot
As our faith on this Earth is reflected for all to see
As hope knows no bounds and earthly limitations
Join with me my love on this mystical seventh wave
As you rise now to the highest peaks of true eternity
And kneel so graciously with all the knowledge of
Such a majestic and priceless cosmic jewel that's
Chained inside a bond kissing the heavens above
As golden links hold our emotions in a circle of light
And as our true-gifted feelings unite us always as one
As our hearts and souls bask in God's precious light

July 27, 2015
(Verse)

Author's Note: A Collaborated Poem with Liam McDaid.

How Shall I Say I Love You

My Darling Love, how shall I say I love you?
You know I do, but how can I portray this to you in words?

Let me try My Dear One—

With a Smile when I think often of the sheer radiance of your beauty.
With Thoughts which I have of you daily and the sweet things you do.
With Emotions ripe and afire when I think of the pure passion we have.

With my Inner Psyche when I get in touch deeply with my ethereal self.
With my Eyes as I gaze into your eyes with noble tears of joy and love.
With my Touch as I hold and caress you in my arms and share my love.

With my Heart which is the driving force of my love and emotion for you.
With my Laughter that helps to lighten even the most trying of situations.
With my Prayers which reflect my connection to God and belief in you.

With my Spoken Words which reflect my true heartfelt emotions for you.
When Holding your Hand at any time on any day for no particular reason.
When Walking with you day or night at anytime, anyplace, or anywhere.

When Writing Poetry since you are always my special inspiration and muse.
With my unbridled love and respect for you as a warm and loving person.
With my warm inner feeling for all of the special things we do together.

My Final Thought: As imperfect and inarticulate as I surely am, at times—
My Darling Love these are some special inner-felt notions and emotions
reflecting always my view of you and feelings for you as the most important
person in this world to me!

My true love always and forever!

June 5, 2015
(Free Verse)

Author's Note: This poem is a very special tribute to my wife and eternal soulmate.

"Words are all I have but they are what I use to paint my thoughts and feelings on the inner canvas of my true emotions and my heart and soul."

I Shall Feel Your Touch Always

Whenever I think of you my dearest one regardless of the time of the day,
I sometimes lose myself in moments of deepest introspection, but I know
and realize that I Shall Feel Your Touch Always!

Within the divine clouds of Heaven far above,
I shall feel your touch always!

When I dream of you so deeply during the night,
I shall feel your touch always!

With the gentle cool breeze of a fresh Spring morning,
I shall feel your touch always!

With the warm sweet wind of Summer kissing our faces,
I shall feel your touch always!

As the cool-warm wind of Autumn caresses our very souls,
I shall feel your touch always!

As we walk in the fresh-frozen wonder of a bright Winter morning,
I shall feel your touch always!

When we walk together closely now hand-in-hand,
I shall feel your touch always!

By the beauty of a most radiant starlit night,
I shall feel your touch always!

As we walk in the shadow and smile of a full moon,
I shall feel your touch always!

As I look passionately into your most loving eyes,
I shall feel your touch always!

When I think of your special smile and funny presence,
I shall feel your touch always!

After a soft rain as a magical color-arrayed rainbow appears,
I shall feel your touch always!

When I hear the mellifluous voices of angels in my dream world,
I shall feel your touch always!

When our earthly presence ends and we walk on eternity's footpath,
I shall feel your touch always!

As we one day stand before God in Heaven after our final ascent,
I shall feel your touch always!

And, as I declare my eternal love to you forever my dearest one,
I shall feel your touch always!

November 12, 2015
(Epiphora)

Ich weiss schon, was du meinst

I do know what you mean!
Trust me my dearest love—I do!

Whether I say this in German or in English,
my thought and intention with this are the same!

Since we first met years ago the love, fire, and
passion in my heart and soul for you have never
ceased or abated—and they shall never do so!

And the compelling force and the palpable feeling
created by the alchemic nature of our relationship,
shall be with us always in this world my dearest love.
I say this even until it's time for us to shake off this
mortal coil of ours!

Yet, I say even beyond this mortal plane, the love and the
feeling we share shall find their rightful place at the center
of our respective souls, as we gain our entrance into God's
Kingdom in all of His Divine light, love, glory, and eternal
harmony!

Worse it could be though, but I dare not ever think of this,
for I believe in the depth of our love, the strength of our
sacred convictions, and the power of our emotions—all
of which shall stand the ultimate test of time and the surety
of our commitment!

And so my love, I say be not ever afraid—for I shall be
with you in your moments of joy, happiness, sadness, fear,
rejection, illness, and celebration. That's the joyous bond
we both eternally share in God's very eyes!

Life can be great, it can be glorious, it can be challenging;
and it can be unfair, and it can be wicked for sure—given
the unfortunate ways and foibles of human nature!

Even with all of this said and done—this shall never, ever alter the love, fire, and passion I have for you in my heart and possess in my soul my dearest love!

And so my dearest love . . .

I do know what you mean!
Ich weiss schon, was du meinst!

November 8, 2015
(Free Verse)

In the Dark Night Sky

In the Dark Night Sky, a "Pale Moon" now arises suddenly,
With clouds of ice sparkling in a frozen-cold ring around it;
While your bright, rosy-cheeked face appears as a paste-like
Image of a grinning and laughing White Dwarf so happy!

A Million-Times-Brighter-Hell-Hot Supernova emerges now,
With a colossal colored-array of jewels firmly fixed upon the
Trajectory of a brilliant star trailing and exploding its waves,
As it shakes its cosmic dust on all of your light-filled dreams!

Divinity travels through my veins like warm blood free-flowing;
And as one radiant supercharged beauty kisses God's very face,
She finds His divine and infinite picture—His view of our Cosmos,
Where the souls of Mankind seek the final spirit of their being!

Wild Moon Dogs howl joyous echoes bouncing into an infinity,
As they choose to dance to an ancient song of peace and love.
This is the final message of the pale moon's image cresting now
Lonely across the Dark Night Sky as it reflects God's Starlight!

November 17, 2015
(Quatrain)

Author's Note: A Collaborated Poem with Liam McDaid.

Intelligence

A superb virtue—
Use for good, and not evil!
Smart is always good ...
Man's differentiation ...
To be nurtured at all times!

May 15, 2015
(Tanka)

Into Eternity's Arms

I dream of Heaven...
A deep dream beyond—no fear!
A happiness abounds, yes!
Hold me now tightly,
And give me your love always.
My soul has now come home Lord!
I see your kind face—
The Angels brought me to you.
Your presence is most divine!
I see Heaven's light,
Radiant and inviting.
My soul is so happy Lord!
Love and peace so pure,
Harmony abounds always.
Ethereal bliss sublime!
I wait for my love...
My Earth soulmate comes one day.
A heavenly bond to prize!
With her one day here—
Our love will be blessed on high,
As we walk Heaven's footpaths—
Into eternity's arms!

February 14, 2015
(Choka)

Je Suis Charlie – Afterthought

The shock of this most frightening tragedy is absolutely beyond the pale of any reasonable or adequate attempt or effort to explain it or to rationalize the horrible circumstances surrounding it.

Let me just say that all of us who are writers and poets ply our poetry, "our intellectual wares," if you will, in a common written medium that expects the same unrestricted level of freedom of speech and expression exercised by those extraordinarily brave artists at "Charlie Hebdo" who were recently murdered in cold blood by self-styled Islamic extremists in Paris.

It is also equally saddening and deplorable that some courageous police officers died in the line of duty defending these freedoms, as well as some other security people and hostages who were also caught up in the midst of these most terrifying circumstances.

The heinous actions perpetrated by these armed extremists destroyed innocent lives and affected the lives of a number of loved ones whose burden of sadness and tragedy is unimaginable. Their actions were also an attempt to strike at the very heart of those sacred freedoms that all of us who live in open societies and democracies cherish as part of our everyday lives. The armed extremists, by their actions, also personified and demonstrated an obvious affectation for barbarity, stupidity, ignorance, and cowardice which were all on ample display as a result of what they did.

Freedom of speech and expression are among those certain historic and inalienable rights given to all of us by the divine hand of God Himself, and not by the generosity of any government or particular religious group regardless of faith. The brave souls who died at Charlie Hebdo, died while exercising this most sacred franchise.

The point I am driving at, is this: Those extremists who committed these most reprehensible actions of hate against their fellow man, did not win, in spite of their collective efforts to destroy lives and to sully the honor of these precious freedoms that all of us as writers and artists hold so very dear.

The outpouring of real emotion and sadness in support of these slain heroes, in the face of this most despicable crime, is very compelling. It underlies the continuing determination of all of us who love and and cherish the freedoms of speech and expression, to continue our efforts in speaking out and in exercising these sacred rights without any reservation.

With all of this in mind, I humbly and proudly conclude my narrative to all of you here by saying and echoing as loudly as possible: "Je Suis Charlie!" . . . "I am Charlie!"

January 10, 2015
(Narrative)

Joy

Live life to the hilt—
Master your own destiny!
Determine your goals . . .
Seek happiness everywhere . . .
Live life with a proud purpose!

February 17, 2015
(Tanka)

Keats – Romantic Humanist

Romanticus-Extraordinaire
John Keats
La Belle Dame sans Merci
Circe-Enchantress to all.

Beautiful, deadly in her elfin grot
Supernatural-nous
She wept and sighed full sore
Hath thee in "Keatsian" thrall.

August 17, 2015
(Double Dactyl)

King Vlad the Greatest

Supremus-Dictatoris
Vladimir Vladimirovich Putin
Bamboozler-Provocateur
Arrogance absolute.

Master of Malarkey
Bolshoi-Apparatchik
Mask of a Monster
Hooliganism to boot.

August 20, 2015
(Double Dactyl)

Le Mot Juste

The right word indeed is what we poets always seek
As we use our imaginations in finding and identifying
A theme of interest and one that allows us to work and
To weave a tapestry of poetic virtue and enchantment.

The right word for the sake of poetic discussion can be
A singular word, two or three words, or even a group of
Words—yet, it is how a word or words are placed in
Verses which account for proper emphasis and nuance.

The right word gives us that certain image or metaphor
So necessary as we dexterously process artistic thoughts
Which meld into verses conveying a wondrous message
To our readers yearning for the magic that poetry brings.

The right word often sets the tone and tenor of each verse,
And it influences the desired effect of each verse as it flows
And follows, and interlocks with the other verses in a poem.
These attributes of tone and tenor are always very important.

Using the right word impacts what we say and how we say
It and how our poetic thoughts may or may not be correctly
Understood, which means "Words Count" always—and we
Poets should consider their effect in portraying our message.

Le Mot Juste in the French language very exquisitely means
"The Right Word" and seemed appropriate as the title for this
Poem to emphasize the critical nature of using the right word
As we poets seek to make our thoughts known to the public.

February 3, 2015
(Quatrain)

Looking So Deeply into Your Heavenly Eyes

It's such a beautiful cosmos I see in your eyes My Love,
When I'm looking so deeply into your Heavenly Eyes.

I sense love, harmony, and such a true passionate feeling,
As I ponder the warmest images I now see and feel, My Love.

And, as you look now so deeply into my eyes, My Love,
I hope you see and feel the desire and love I have for you.

What more could anyone ask for in this mortal life, My Love,
For without love, any celestial metaphor is truly meaningless.

During each and every night as I dream so deeply of you, My Love,
Our souls meld as one as I look so deeply into your Heavenly Eyes!

And I want you to know that I shall be with you always My Love,
And for the rest of my life and beyond—my heart is forever yours!

January 16, 2015
(Couplet)

Lord Byron – Genius Unchained

Primus-Supremus-Romanticus
George Gordon Noel Byron
Destiny in Missolonghi at 36
A soldier's death.

Legendary immortality
Mega-accomplishment
For him, the best
And now he's at rest.

May 6, 2015
(Double Dactyl)

Love is

Love is special
Romantic feelings
Sensual thoughts
Hope and expectations
Seize the moment!

Love is a real drug
Casting a spell
On one's inner psyche
Bringing pleasure
Leaving a message!

Love is with you
As one sees answers
In the eyes and heart
Emotions so special
Feel our love whole!

Love is alchemy pure
Paracelsian—yes
A dramatic power
Emotion + Passion + Joy
Equals Love so pure!

Love is the reddest rose
Supreme symbol of love
Flower of pulchritude
Sends a clear message
Love's signal affirmed!

Love is magical
Love is majestic
Love is divine
Love is God's Gift
Love is God's Love!

June 13, 2015
(Accentual Meter)

Love Star Night

We walk in love
hand in hand
under the stars
star night pure.

Our love's real
your touch warm
so inviting now
star night white.

We stop walking
embrace as one
kissing deeply
with passion
our souls now one.

We gaze skyward
see stars so bright
with radiance pure
this love star night.

February 13, 2015
(Accentual Meter)

love you can paint all colors of the sky azure

faraway as it opens your eyes chocolate melts now
wide with awe of a diamond wonder shining gleams
only if you were here embracing life magic majestic

love to spoil and cook for you something so delicious
putting your feet up softly watching a real-heart movie
sounds real my dream bride very beautiful and so real

as I looked into a candle as it flickers alone quietly
one light thinking dancing in thoughts all together
night shades color the luster of a silver star winking

a small shadow pervades ever so blotting starlight
slightly as I hear you calling me as shades whisper
in our crowded corner thoughts of passionate love

distant faraway wonders breathless whispers calling
me toward simple things catching my breathing sighs
just throwing a few more turf on that fire right now

starting to heat up my frozen breaths icy steaming
clouds misting as the sky clouds my breath true blue
sweet dreams princess sits regal crowning charming

with the angels filled within love flying without wings
catch you now in my dreams tonight 'til the sun kisses
your face and eyelids all golden warm beautiful bright

May 14, 2015
(Tercet)

Author's Note: A Collaborated Poem with Liam McDaid.

Love's Import

Love's import results when two lovers meet,
Merging their emotions as one—what a treat!

With an emotive force beyond all to compare,
Love blinds all of us, at times, even on a dare.

The longing and passion of two souls in love,
Comes with its heavenly destiny from above.

Cupid's influence is oft felt in an eye glance,
Which can bring two together in life's dance.

Love's message is always special as two kiss,
Seeking their moments of such romantic bliss.

Love's a special moment in eternity's parade,
As two souls dance to God's heavenly serenade.

Love's import says much when two say "yes"
And live their passion as God above has blessed.

July 1, 2015
(Heroic Couplet)

Love's in the Stars

A romantic moonlit or a soft-starry night . . .
Are both special times for a sublime love so right.
Freshness pervades the scent of the sweet night air,
As I hold you close now looking at your face so fair.
I'm hopeful we both have that rare love meant for two,
Which we shall always cherish and hold so dear too.
    Love's in the stars—and so is our destiny my love!

February 19, 2015
(Septet)

Love's that Magical Wonder

My passion for your love is beyond any measure,
And as I reflect on your angelic wonder my love,
I know that God blesses us always in Heaven above,
And that our life together is such a special pleasure!
I know my dearest that your love is my true treasure,
And as surely as I ponder my thoughts of you thereof,
I can always take such heartfelt solace in our love,
By feeling the warmth of your being with such pleasure!

We should always think of love as that magical wonder,
And its power in making us as One, not to be torn asunder!
Love, my dearest will help us find happiness in this life,
As we chart our mutual destiny as both husband and wife!
And one day when our souls ascend to Heaven high above,
Our spirits will be together as One feeling God's pure love!

January 17, 2015
(Petrarchan Sonnet)

Love's the Soul's Fire

Love's a mystical force, that's laden with nectar and emotion,
That many people sacrifice so much so often for in this life.
Love has the properties of an all-powerful alchemic potion,
Which is said can better help those in such a forlorn strife!

This famous four-letter word has such a unique persuasion,
And has made those lost in it so hopeless to understand it.
Love's been known to make people quite crazy on occasion,
Which makes it most alluring and for some—a proverbial hit!

Love does make one very crazy at times because of its sheer power,
And its ever-emotive force affects surely the body, mind, and soul.
Love's all-pervasiveness puts it in demand daily and by the hour,
And its deep influence is felt so special within one's mind and soul!

Love's that special emotion that many never really get enough of,
And as the language of Cupid, it sends signals not always clear to see.
This fuels a person's fury when he or she only desires to be loved,
And will sacrifice all so greatly while crying even on a bended knee!

Love's the soul's fire and it makes one's life whole and worth living,
And it's the balm which calms frayed emotions—a surcease of sorrow.
Love's an enchanted state of being, that when shared keeps on giving,
And with its angelic qualities helps all of us find that better tomorrow!

Love's the soul's fire, influenced by Cupid's most wonderful intent;
And Love, worth its weight in gold is most worth having in our life,
As one seeks its solace and divine rapture on that final angelic ascent,
When God calls one's soul to Heaven love abounding, free from strife!

God's message is simple—a special need of love in one's life and soul,
And that's why love's the soul's fire, which makes us human and whole!

January 4, 2015
(Rhyme)

Lucifer

Son of the Morning—
Symbol of false perfection.
Lucifer is thus...
A tempter and deceiver...
Praise only Almighty God!

June 5, 2015
(Tanka)

Medusa's Love

Medusa is a hideous and vile creature of Grecian yore.
Medusa, once a high priestess in the Temple of Athena,
Suffered Athena's unforgiving wrath for violating her
Sacred temple as she and Lord Poseidon made love there.

Medusa's love entices all of her naive human victims,
Up to that special mesmerizing moment of her icy shock,
As they end up unwittingly gazing into her evil, hellish
Eyes and their bodies harden and turn to stone forever.

You can never trust those Gods who relish in making
The plight of mortal man more challenging on Earth.
Once a perfect paragon of radiant female pulchritude,
Athena transformed Medusa into this mythic monster.

As if this life isn't frightening enough, with the advent
Of Halloween Eve and the cold, dark nights preceding it;
Medusa's restless spirit as this grotesque Gorgon can be
Conjured from her lair at the entrance to the Underworld.

From the hissing and viperous serpents adorning her head,
To the ever-present shaking death rattle of her reptilian tail;
Medusa's sneering and unholy visage paralyzes her victims
As her fiery and demonic eyes bring them a stone-cold death!

October 1, 2015
(Quatrain)

Moments in God's Cosmic Time

A fleeting, finite time space one now may define;
A flash of seconds for poets to see and find rhyme.

Fashioning a human understanding of God's Time,
Gives us a hint continuant, complex too—yet Divine!

Einstein's $E = mc^2$ gives us all a most gifted treasure,
With "c" as light's constant nature for us to measure.

These moments can concatenate continuously as one,
Or may be revealed in time by mere eye-blinks for fun.

By teasing our thoughts, God infuses our spirits now bold,
With life's knowledge over time, worth more than all gold!

Being of God's self-image defines who we each are in life;
It's for each of us to master our destiny before earthly strife.

Teasing our thoughts with heavenly images of eidetic clarity,
God speaks to us all subliminally over time—never as a rarity!

God's the only true divine mystic when it comes to Cosmic Time,
And the master for setting the Universe in perfect Cosmic Rhyme!

December 12, 2015
(Couplet)

Mother Nature Cries

Mother Nature cries now her deep tears of true sadness,
For all the years of Man's sad shame and utter madness.

Man has brought this lovely lady quite often to tears,
By his poor and pathetic care of our Earth over the years.

Mother Nature's been with Man now it seems forever,
And he does nothing at all and always tells her never!

Man's climate sins are so tragic and always most telling,
And all he does is bitch and moan and keeps on yelling!

Man's span of existence is short in our Earth's long life,
And all he has done is to corrupt, pollute, and cause her strife!

Mother Nature cries at this sad tragedy Man has thus wrought;
She knows his life on Earth may be short and he will learn Not!

Mother Nature will adapt and evolve over time with no problem,
And she knows Man's adaptability to change may be a problem.

Perhaps Man will learn this sad lesson here before all is too late,
And seek climate harmony in all he does and make positive his Fate!

Mother Nature cries—yet this can change with Man's redemption,
If Man becomes Earth's Good Steward and lives by God's direction!

February 12, 2015
(Couplet)

Mother Nature's Little Prince

A most beautiful little green frog swims quietly and so gracefully
While his eyes gaze gently on a mountain looming in the distance.
He's at ease as he swims in a deep forest pond warmed by the sun.
Lost catching flies inside the shadows as an echo holds on to a
Certain gentle stillness within him humming with burning sighs.

This little green frog was called "Froggy" by Mother Nature,
And he was her little precious star-light promise of pretty colors.
Froggy was the Gem of Her Eyes: handsome, funny and intelligent,
With a kindness so overwhelming and a soft-touching tenderness.
He was talkative, and quiet princely by his apparent noble mien.

Froggy had a divine hope and destiny to wish for a dream princess.
Mother Nature knew that "Her Froggy" was indeed so magical as
His golden fingers of light painted a rainbow array of newborn life.
"Her Froggy" was much more than a mere amphibian in this life,
Although he was dark green and sprinkled with light black spots.

Froggy lay on a lily leaf faraway as his thoughts sailed freely into
Another world, where his most infectious and funny smile made him
Quite popular and noticeable to a beautiful young fairy princess who
Was smitten instantly with his looks and his princely correct behavior.
For the young fairy princess it was love at first sight—and so precious!

Froggy was slowly changing, and love became his desire and passion.
With a purity shone silver in streaming beauties of light pure gold,
At the rainbow's end was a bridge of his loving tears as he sang a
Melodious song of love with a supreme confidence for the princess.
Upon meeting his princess their mutual fate was woven now as one.

Mother Nature's enchanted wish for "Her Froggy" and "His Princess"
Was now at hand for their love and emotion were now blended as one.
All that remained was that magical kiss to make them both human.
When these two beings of wondrous beauty kissed—the very stars and
The comets in Heaven above shone so brightly that night became day!

With love and the omnipotent and majestic whisk of God's divine hand,
Froggy and his princess metamorphosed now into complete human form!
This was a sight in Heaven itself to behold and cherish for all of eternity!
Now they were a royal pair: A prince and his princess in love—reflected
In the radiant colored light of a mystical rainbow from heavenly direction.

Mother Nature cried joyous tears of hope and happiness at this splendid
Occurrence, making the very rivers on Earth flow in a great abundance
With the sweetest and purest mountain spring water one could imagine!
Now as "Her Froggy"—a real prince now—kissed his princess again,
God's angels anointed them with heavenly star dust shining so brightly!

The new prince now known as "Frederic," and his princess took their
Royal places in human society with no one ever suspecting or knowing
From whence or where they came from, and their divine relationship to
Mother Nature herself, which was her secret and their secret shared now
Together and forever to the very end of time!

July 5, 2015
(Narrative)

Author's Note: A Collaborated Poem with Liam McDaid.

My Heart is Yours My Love

My heart is yours my love now forever,
As your fiery passion enchants my soul.
I shall with such love desert you never.

Our life is now filled with joy and pleasure,
As we share life with so much to extol.
My heart is yours my love now forever.

The desire we share is Earth's great treasure,
Making our souls one—a heavenly goal.
I shall with such love desert you never.

Our love knows no bounds of passion ever,
As we follow God's plan and pledge so bold.
My heart is yours my love now forever.

Your beauty my love brings me such pleasure,
Knowing its worth exceeds all Heaven's gold.
I shall with such love desert you never.

Our love as one is a grand endeavor,
In God's light as two spirits with one soul.
My heart is yours my love now forever.
I shall with such love desert you never.

July 16, 2015
(Villanelle)

On Valentine's Day My Love

Our love is quite wondrous and divinely enchanting all the yearlong,
And on Valentine's Day, its sparkles radiantly in Heaven's very light.

As I look into your eyes My Love I marvel so at your very beauty,
And all the little things we do as One while renewing our love daily.

We seek our fortune and destiny together in all we do in this life,
Making every second, minute, hour, and day count for an eternity.

We are so blessed My Love that God helped us to find one another,
And to make our union of love, respect, and happiness so special.

As we walk now through this life in love as a couple together as One,
So too our eternal souls shall walk on Heaven's footpath always as One.

Valentine's Day gives us that time to reflect on our love so cherished,
And on all the things that matter the most to us beyond any human strife.

And so, My Love, as we renew our special commitment of love on this day,
We should rejoice in God's true blessing that our love shall be One forever!

February 7, 2015
(Couplet)

Our Cosmic Existence

We think what we know but the key confusion is always there,
When we ponder situations or events that have such high import,
And what we're used to dealing with daily, at times, on a mere dare.

In this cosmic realm what we don't know we sometimes try to purport;
Significant because of the infinite nature of the deep, dark outer space,
Which points toward an existential dichotomy of a most intriguing sort.

Our knowledge of what we don't know is of such an infinite pace,
Confounding whole the mortal complexity of a cosmic coldness,
And defying our very consciousness in the monotony of dark space.

We must confront our cosmic existence with such a confident boldness,
Whilst calculating what we know and don't, without any scintilla of fear,
And seek a God-given azimuth beyond this aura of such a fearful coldness.

Our cosmic existence lies in God's light beyond this darkness and fear;
Meaning we must reach out beyond our mortal state into an aura of grace,
With our thoughts, our hearts, and our feelings so God can make all clear.

We can pursue this divine challenge now as we live in the human race,
And when we realize and reach out with God's help to find His light,
And prepare one day for our mortal transition beyond to God's place.

Our cosmic existence is that spiritual effort that we must try to get right,
As we seek out and find our way ultimately to God beyond our mortal life;
Confident in our quest through a pathless land toward eternity into His light.

May 1, 2015
(Terza Rima)

Author's Note: A Collaborated Poem with Ingrid Krukenberg-Bateman.

Our Destiny

Life's choices come to us by divine plan or fate,
With these options each shaping destiny's date.

How we each now proceed defines who we are,
As we seek a life beyond living in this Bell Jar.

To find this rare azimuth requires so much care,
And make not your choice on a whim or a dare.

One's destiny is such a complicated proposition,
Which sometimes calls for a divine supplication.

If the Almighty wanted to make easy our life's path,
Then he would have laid out a way in our life's past.

For it is within His divine power in Heaven above,
That we all may fly beyond the sky so blue above!

God inspires us to master our true destiny every day,
So we can ascend to Him in Heaven on our final day!

April 29, 2015
(Couplet)

Our Earthly Appetites

In our earthly appetites our love is now one
To hear your heartbeat next to mine always
Oh yes—a sweet beautiful rose of paradise
You came to me by the river my bonnie lass
Whilst branches of birds whistled tunes of love
Drifting on a summer breeze warmly whispering
Moaning as gentle thoughts murmur your name
Carried on a majestic breath of warm luscious air
With echoing babbles from a most precious maiden
Memories with one dream holding a forget-me-not
Unveiling so fair your impression left on my heart
Dancing on every pulse beat sweetly sings a siren
I watch the sun as it fades into the deep blue sea
We both sail upon one warm beauty breeze of sighs
Whilst behind these eyes the truth forever is dawning
One flower nods in a rainbow array far beyond compare
Whilst you who drink from love's very chalice so true
A magical and enchanting blessing holding no disguise
You're the precious breath of my life and existence . . .
My true love! My bonnie lass!

July 21, 2015
(Verse)

Author's Note: A Collaborated Poem with Liam McDaid.

Our Excursion is a Pathway

Our excursion is a pathway we must follow
in our life journey beyond this universe as we
seek that precious eternal emotion called "Love."

Poetry is that true sweet music—light or dark,
that's bound from the mystic union of our hearts.
Without poetry, our minds are only a whirlpool.

Disoriented and lost without song and sense
there is a unique understanding with delight
that moves us toward the direction of words.

Believing in mortal life as it exists on Earth
is a true proclamation of faith holding strong
with a heavenly promise beyond our grasp.

Eternity embraces our eternal existence in each
and every daily aspect of our lives and our souls
as light holds the final godly power over darkness.

May 25, 2015
(Tercet)

Author's Note: A Collaborated Poem with Liam McDaid.

Our Two Stars Sparkle as One Soul

They whisper their sonnets and surrender their thrones gracefully,
Consuming tunes sweetly echoing and crowning a heart with love.
Your gentle words, your tender touch, so much divine beauty as
Our two stars sparkle as one soul with one golden smile of eternity.

When the sun rises in the east and the sun sets in the west, we know
Whilst looking upon a dream holding the deepest vision awestruck,
The new sun across the sky passes so the soul can reach its destiny,
And you vanquished all doubts of me burning as one flame on fire.

Knowing the winds in Heaven mix forever in a powerful divine glory,
With one angel standing before our eyes as destiny sparks its promise
That in God's way it must be the message of love we feel so strongly,
Embracing forever the alchemy of two stars blazing hot with emotion.

Dreams and fantasies merge with this wonderful bliss ever so gently
As faraway rising is your sunshine holding hands warmly as a regal gift,
And a truth filled with blessing, deeply peaceful and complete as we pray
Under a bridge of hope with colors kissing the heart and soul of a dream.

Love and devotion pervade our eternal desire of oneness with the Lord God
As His heavenly guard ushers our souls together with purpose before Him,
And as a choir of angels sing their majestic paeans honoring this moment,
We see now our dreams melding as one, as our two stars sparkle as one soul.

June 11, 2015
(Quatrain)

Author's Note: A Collaborated Poem with Anne-Lise Andresen and Liam McDaid.

Our Winter Love

We walk sweetly on the fresh snow,
this sunlit morn all bright and white;
making snowballs as we now go.
We walk sweetly on the fresh snow.
Nature's snow makes our love now grow!
Our love's alchemic and so right!
We walk sweetly on the fresh snow,
this sunlit morn all bright and white!

November 19, 2015
(Triolet)

Paracelsus

Supremus-Alchemist-Occultist
Philippus von Hohenheim
Alchemist, Astrologer, and Physician
Arrogant to a fault.

Medical genius
Paracelsianism
Iconoclastic for sure
Ignorance he couldn't halt.

June 15, 2015
(Double Dactyl)

Paradise Lost

Today I could feel only burning salty tears of sadness
Alone as I walked slowly along the beach pondering
Sweet memories pervading my inner psyche deeply
With coiling inside gasps of heavy breathless moans

Sweetest honey holding precious memories so real
Faraway looking into the sun setting warm—a utopia
As a special friendship was born under a sweet kiss
Whilst conjuring true a most incredible dream shone

Visions flashback into far-distant everlasting thoughts
Full of smiles adoringly walking along the golden sands
Feelings with joy as magical tunes are so divinely sung
As large waves crash over and over in the mind's eye

True emotions burning with love stays forever so pure
As tears fall upon the sand symbolizing a rapid change
In realizing your very touch means and meant so much
As a salted-heart of burning flames stir unquenchable fires

You who burns inside this candle lost in your very space
Darling the happiest day of my life came on our meeting
As I found you fortified in a castle of one mystic dream
As whispers cast over the warm sea finding a true love

Carnations lovely crowning petals of a most regal life with
Beauty whose golden visage lights faraway sunsets so real
Whilst smiling gently and graciously before her—Our Queen
Who seeks with her tears and toil to restore our Paradise Lost

June 6, 2015
(Quatrain)

Author's Note: A Collaborated Poem with Liam McDaid.

Paris November 13th Makes Me Weep – Afterthought

The shock and tragedy of this most horrendous event of slaughter, murder, and unmitigated evil are indeed a very sad commentary on the state mankind finds itself in today as the dark specter of terrorism and chaos attempts to engulf our entire world.

We can never forgive, nor should we ever forget the evil that these minions of darkness—in their acts of barbarity, cruelty and cowardice—perpetrated upon the innocent, unsuspecting people in the magnificent city of Paris during the evening of November 13, 2015.

The death and destruction wrought by these armed terrorists, although similar to that which occurred to "Charlie Hebdo" earlier in the year on January 7, 2015, was unfortunately executed on a much larger scope and scale resulting in the deaths of 129 people presently and injuries to over 350. All of this transpired in the later evening hours with a cold and quick military precision among terrifying shouts of *"Allahu Akbar"* by ISIS-associated terrorists.

All of this was done by these terrorists in the name of God! Huh? Really? All of this was to satiate a dark thirst and to justify an evil philosophy of murder, rape, pillage, and destruction *en masse* in the Middle East—and now brought to the evening-hour streets of the great city of Paris.

This makes me weep the deepest tears possible for sure, as I am also sure it does Almighty God in Heaven! This horrific event is beyond the pale of any semblance of human decency and dignity, let alone morality! These self-styled Islamic terrorists and extremists filled with hate and anger committed the cold-blooded murder of innocent people to fulfill their warped vision of Islamic sanctity—and in God's name! This was an abhorrent act of absolute sacrilegious depravity on the part of these terrorists!

These individuals may perpetrate this evil and stain the streets with the blood of innocent people presently, but they shall never be allowed to win in this ultimate struggle. The motto *"Liberté, Égalité, Fraternité"* (or "Liberty, Equality, Fraternity") for France stands at the vanguard of freedom and justice as a timeless symbol and legacy from the Age of Enlightenment that is now inextricably bound as part of the French national heritage. I pay my humble tears and respect for what this historical motto stands for and means today.

The freedom-loving countries of the world and their people must stand together now with France in this hour of maximum danger and help support its government and people in combating and destroying this dark specter of terrorism that has entered its borders and murdered innocent people without any iota of conscience or remorse whatsoever.

With all of this said, I offer my sincere respect to all of the dead and injured victims who had to endure this nightmare tragedy in Paris on the evening of November 13, 2015. May God protect the eternal souls of those who perished in these coordinated acts of senseless violence, and give solace and peace to their families and loved ones who remain behind.

I know that I shall never forget this evening of terrible violence inflicted upon Paris and its innocent people, just like the violence and death during 9/11 in the United States.

May God Bless the victims' eternal souls forever and let us pray that the murderous violence of ISIS and other radical movements analogous to them are one day stamped out from the face of this Earth!

Amen.

November 15, 2015
(Narrative)

Past Ghosts

One's thoughts occasionally wander into the past
conjuring deep memories of what was and was not,
what might have been, and what should have been.
This type of "past is prologue" gives one perspective
for the present, and a requisite azimuth for the future.

Some may say to forget about Past Ghosts and move on.
This is sound advice when such ghosts harken one back
to a time and place of unhappiness or emotional despair.
Yet, one must, at times, be not afraid to confront The Devil
who lurks in the deep and dark regions of one's memories.

Finding one's self means knowing one's self, and always being
willing to change and adapt to new challenges and thoughts as
one, and as all of us move forward now with our respective lives.
Past Ghosts, in the form of people or experiences, shall always
be with us no matter how hard we try to shut them out and forget.

And so, our Past Ghosts become part of our selective memories.
Embrace and bring those to light that are pleasing and positive,
and deal with the less pleasant ones more restrictively for sure.
Our Past Ghosts are an indelible aspect of our life progression
as human beings, and so—live, go forward, and always fear not!

July 3, 2015
(Quintain)

Peace, Love, and God's Greatest Gift

The mellifluous musical tones of the village bells
Echoing chimes over the cold snowcapped mountains
Both finding their way to people in the valley below

Christmas songs—let your spirit sing freely and loudly
Welcoming the Birth of Our Savior and Baby King
Who so charms the Angels on High and God Himself

On this night, The Star was so beautiful, clear, and shiny
Crisp and so crystal-bright, centered above and beyond
Reflecting now the Lord God's most divine and holy light

There is a real magic in the night air as Heaven rejoices aloud
The child and the infant's divine soul breathe life now intently
Fulfilling truly God's very promise and His hope to Mankind

Keep this Christmas spirit—share it with others near and far
Grace filled with good tidings as we dance on wings of joy
We all now celebrate in great happiness, love, and kindness

Christmas is forever—and you must never ever close this door
Faith always enters, carrying His guiding torch high and proud
And encouraging Man every step of the way on his long journey

Even in a simple cradle where the Baby Jesus so innocently lay
Heaven doth bathe His cradle with the warmest rays of divine light
Bespeaking the heavenly beauty, joy, and wonder of Our Savior

Amazing peace makes a lovely gift, I wish for all of us to have
As new life blossoms, wrapped in petals of an immaculate heart
God's holy blessing, love, and intention are clear for all to see

That Holy Night the Angels entire sang mirthfully on Christmas Eve
Praising Almighty Lord God in Heaven on the birth of His only son
The Angels' paeans echoed in their divine beauty across the Universe

To bring peace now, glowing with your love, is His divine intention
Rejoicing in God's Greatest Gift to Mankind who was born in a manger
Destined to become Our Most Holy and Divine Savior—Amen! Amen!

December 1, 2015
(Tercet)

Author's Note: A Collaborated Poem with Anne-Lise Andresen and Liam McDaid.

Prufrock's Symbolic World

Metaphors-Extraordinaire
Thomas Stearns Eliot
Metaphysical consciousness
Aura of aging and decay.

Streams of consciousness forever
Proto-disillusionment
The mermaids singing each to each
The mermaids will not sing today.

January 14, 2015
(Double Dactyl)

Rapture

A wondrous delight—
Spiritual movement pure!
Rapture is that joy...
A magic force for poets...
Arrival now in God's arms!

January 3, 2015
(Tanka)

Santa Claus

The Children's Hero—
Promotes the Christmas Spirit!
A Big Kid himself...
Omnipresent, forever!
A divine mythic image!

December 3, 2015
(Tanka)

Sentiments of Love

Our passion defines two loves now as one,
And what we share now is life's great treasure!
Our emotions My Love burn hotter than any sun,
Ensuring that our rapture as two is such a pleasure,
And that a love so grand is truly beyond any measure!
When we stroll together—and talk, embrace, and kiss;
It's like being in Heaven—something never to miss!

February 19, 2015
(Rhyme Royal)

Shelley – Romantic Visionary

Maestro-Romanticus-Supremus
Percy Bysshe Shelley
One Heaven, One Hell
Promise of a later birth.

About a little soul
Epipsychidion
One immortality, one annihilation
Wilderness of this Elysian earth.

August 5, 2015
(Double Dactyl)

Smiling Spitting Deadly Sins

Son of the Devil—evil and twisted as his mask falls away
Through the curtains of death he turns truth into dark lies
With horrible shadows haunting over Love's light so pure
As jealousy reveals shades of a Soul's envy at this moment.

Cunningly you crawl behind colors pride with selfish hurting
Innocence casting stones—the fruits of a hideous lurking evil
Filling you with stupid, silly emotions crying crocodile tears.
Hate is your playground game as the Dark One takes his souls!

Weeping from the deep wounds inflicted on others at your wish
While fighting one lost battle as your words burn from the ugly
Fork of your tongue while spitting venom, they become a vile
Poison in which every last drop makes one's very skin crawl!

When I see the light of truth awakening in your Soul's eyes,
I really see a Hell-Fire scorching red-hot who is the real you.
Your pretty tongue of thy father speaks the evil words of the
"King of Lies" to my heart as it's touched by the serpent's rasp!

Yet ever, you can never always hide behind this perfidious mask,
And such words of beauty will not always hide what lies within
Those darkest outreaches of your Soul's descent into damnation.
For Love itself is a journey of the gentle, divine, and the innocent.

But those who breathe the Hell-Fire can only fool us all so long—
And when their mask falls away, they speak with a serpent's tongue
So vile and gruesome that they know not of Love as they strike and
Bring eternal pain and the Devil's sword with their blackened hand!

Causing pain with greatest relish as they laugh heartily at the pain
Inflicted on others, not really knowing what they hold in their hand
In hate and anger, whilst they strike out at all innocent souls as their
Double-edged sword waits for those from the depths of Hell itself.

August 9, 2015
(Quatrain)

Author's Note: A Collaborated Poem with Michael Clarke and Liam McDaid.

Solitude

Walking alone
Often outside
In deep thought
About things of
Great importance.

I wonder aloud
Thoughts amassed
Priorities now
Solutions not clear
Seeking inspiration.

Time's fleeting
Which is always
Tied to many
Dynamic actions
Begging resolution.

I stop now—
And look heavenward
Solutions abound
Choices are difficult
I'm staying focused.

Using my intuition
Request divine help
Do Nothing
Take your pick
Nothing's easy.

My soul's focus
Trust yourself—
First and foremost
God speaks silently
Do it now!

January 27, 2015
(Accentual Meter)

Starlight

Heaven's light source pure
Radiated light-years beyond
Man's conscious knowledge
And cosmic understanding

Various brilliant streetlights
Of the universe charting
Courses through stretches
Of eternal darkness deep

God keeps this Starlight
True to his every word
For when darkness wins
The keys of enlightenment

Fall prisoner to Lucifer
Who controls them for
His advantage over Man
At odds always with God

Starlight reflects the way
For mankind's quest in
Seeking ethereal guidance
And spiritual illumination

This heavenly pure light
Keeps mankind on track
Despite Lucifer's intrigues
To do just the opposite

Man's Earth time is short
And his date with destiny
Finds his fate held in the
Balance of God's Hands

But there is always the
Chance to ask God for
His advice and help—then
Waiting for the answer

And God's answer is
Coming in different ways
And—at the end, Salvation
Is granted by the act of God

Being in God's arms and
Looking back the way Man
Came reflects that everything
Was part of God's divine purpose

God's grace and protection
On each and every one of the
Stones on the way and back
Was part of God's divine plan

At the end it turns out that
Everything was planned
From the very beginning
By you and God together

The godly part created in
Man is the divine guidance
Which brings everybody
Back into the arms of God

Being in conscious awareness of
God's plans and creation
Man can now enjoy with inner peace
Starlight—Heaven's light source!

January 30, 2015
(Quatrain)

Author's Note: A Collaborated Poem
with Ingrid Krukenberg-Bateman.

Striking Deeply a Painful Reminder

Striking deeply a painful reminder comes of you now.
Salt falls inside my open wound bringing untold pain.
My soul has one choice to make amidst all this pain,
Telling me the considered direction I must take now.

Washed through a dirty ocean lining all foamed up,
We are frustrated with ourselves to no end today,
As we stand at the crossroads of our broken lives
Asking sad, difficult questions and feeling all alone.

Begging the wrong side for forgiveness is no fun at all.
We must answer whilst looking at two sides of a story;
As a wounding confession now exacts promises only,
As a flash of darkness blinds out a tragic haunted mist.

Warm dawning radiant colors say love to both of us now,
As they elicit a soothing and gentle compassion of hope;
Yet, real tenderness is nothing but an illusion as deep pain
Lives now in the shadows without any remorse or apology.

Invading poison of a snake bite brings such sweet love,
As your alter ego robs me of all my dignity and grace.
I listen now to the stark tonal sounds of the seagulls,
As they mix their cries over the ocean dark and deep.

Kissing salted waves filled with the care of true angels,
I cast now cruelly all bitter stones in the Garden of Eden,
Whilst touching an apple once bitten, never to shy away.
It's funny how one can see such a tragedy in the daylight.

Sacrifice a dove dancing within the light now turning dark;
Behind the curtains a grotesque, ghastly face appears now
As the double side of your coin is exposed for all to see—
And when flipped, the truth opens its book quite readily.

Dropping down, a snake crawls upon its soft underbelly,

And behind the scenes people find this image repulsive,
Since it portrays how a poisonous viper strikes fatally as
His very mask falls away for all to see his diabolical grin.

Forbidden is the soul of who you are and want now to be;
A sweet-talking deceiver I know too well for my own taste;
One who hides behind a false face but revels in his own true
Deception as the dark demons mask their fear and cowardice.

Dusk blends into the night now as death comes to life;
With this I realize the hellish intent of Lucifer's demon
Who stares intently at me with his blackest of eyes as
I see my mortal soul consumed in the flames of Hellfire!

With all my final strength and emotion, I drop to my knees
And cry out fervently with every ounce of my conviction—
Almighty God in Heaven! . . . Almighty God in Heaven!
Please save me now! Please save me now! Amen! Amen!

October 25, 2015
(Quatrain)

Author's Note: A Collaborated Poem with Liam McDaid.

Stupidity

A tragic foible—
For those so blinded in life.
Stupidity's sad . . .
Negation's ugly face . . .
To be challenged at all times!

May 15, 2015
(Tanka)

Sunshine Radiance

Your love is my true sunshine radiance,
That greets me every day with such passion.
It sets my heart and emotions afire!
Words often fail me at times dearest one,
As I seek to share the depth of my love
For you and how it makes me feel daily.
The brightest of moons and stars in Heaven
Can't match the splendor you bring to my life.
My heart is joyful when we touch and kiss!
Our love basks in your sunshine radiance!

July 7, 2015
(Blank Verse)

That Spring Love in Your Eyes

Spring Love's in your eyes for me now to see,
And it reaffirms thoughts of our special love;
And there is no other place I would rather be,
As we kiss deeply under the moon light above!

Darling with you in my arms this spring season,
My feelings are of such passion with true bliss;
We are "two" together by His Heavenly reason,
And for this our time together is never amiss!

With spring in bloom and God's blessing above,
My heart's yours forever my love please know;
For I know our emotions are of the deepest love,
And for this Darling to the Earth's end I would go!

With that special spring love dear one in your eyes,
Nothing on Earth compares with this Heavenly prize!

May 10, 2015
(Shakespearean Sonnet)

That Sweetest Starlight and Heavenly Embrace

You are that sweetest starlight shining now across all the oceans pure,
enchanting my dreams and thoughts aglow as I bask in your true love,
whilst you touch my heart and soul now with your beauty and wonder.
If we were together, I would hold you so gently and warmly in my arms,
and, I would kiss your adoring lips forever with a passionate goodnight.

Love is that faraway feeling rising in the morning sunshine's warm rays,
and the light of your presence glows brilliantly as you enter my dreams,
of a pure, sweet surrender and a kiss that touches now my immortal soul.
You are the light of Heaven's own dream of a rainbow's flight of angels,
arriving at Heaven's gate to greet me on that mythic beam of silver light.

Mesmerized I am, as I embrace you now as the heart, soul, passion, and
desire of my life, as I see you as my truest dream and my heart's delight.
Feeling the wonder of your palpable caress as you ask me now to kiss you,
I know for sure you are the one I have dreamt of in my deepest of dreams,
and I know you are the one, my love, with that sweetest heavenly embrace!

September 15, 2015
(Quintain)

The Evil Enchantress with the Greenest of Eyes

This lady is most lovely, luscious, and fascinating with her greenest of eyes,
And she'll easily captivate and bewitch all men she meets with no surprise.
This lady has the reddest of hair, long and full, with such a lustrous sheen,
And with her soft skin and a nubile appearance she looks just like a queen.
This lady's grace of movement and her mellifluous voice are most charming,
Which makes her all the more enthralling to men and at once most disarming!

Now one can see why this Enchantress with her comely visage of pulchritude,
Can make easy work of the men she meets and mesmerizes with such certitude.
This reflects that some people in this life are not always who they appear to be,
And this Enchantress wears such a mask hiding her true self for no one to see.
Since this is the reality for men who fall for this lady whilst making their pitch;
It shall be obvious to many of them over time that this Enchantress is a Witch!

For men who succumb to the spell of this Enchantress, it's time to pay the Piper,
And so they'll now meet the real person behind her mask who is Satan's Viper!
With powers of evil sorcery supreme this Enchantress sets her nefarious goals,
To sow real fear in her victims whilst bringing eternal damnation to their souls!
For men who may meet this Enchantress, don't look deeply into her green eyes;
This shall lock your soul under her evil power and bring on your timely demise!

January 20, 2015
(Rhyme)

The Evil Hands of Tyranny

"*The Evil Hands of Tyranny*" grip the coils and springs,
As they crush the throats and lives of all innocent people
Who cry out for fairness and justice, only to get a deaf ear.

Dealing cards falsely makes a laughingstock of us all now,
Whilst we gaze at that *"Dark Spirit"* with his ghastly grin,
And his evil intentions to steal our very souls like Mephisto.

From power hungry fools, a greed envelopes all who pay
Attention not to the real evil that some men do to others,
But to those who appear to be fooling themselves true.

This brings pain, suffering, bitterness—and not peace,
And disturbs mankind's harmony and hope for a better
Existence as the rapacious *"Dogs of War"* are unleashed.

Twisting wars to suit underlying issues is that all-too
Occurrence in our world as the young, old, and weak
Face *"The Grim Reaper"* who snickers at this chance.

The rich get richer with a poisonous ill-regard for those
Others not so blessed who live in this precarious moment,
As the innocent endure such a monstrous and virulent evil.

This manifests itself in a hideous mask of hateful deceit
And true lies toward any poor person who objects to this
Horrid reality and challenges *"The Evil Hands of Tyranny."*

September 22, 2015
(Tercet)

Author's Note: A Collaborated Poem with Liam McDaid.

The Final Dance

Death is that final dance we face in life,
He comes for us whether one's young or old,
Courage is the answer to this sad strife,
Which means fear not this specter—be ye bold!
And prepare now your soul as God has told;
Death appears dark as Heaven's light shines bright;
Angels bear ye now so true in God's light!

October 18, 2015
(Rhyme Royal)

The Fire in My Soul is Real

The fire in my soul is real,
and you left me now in such strife,
and no magic nor miracles
may now restore my troubled life.
Nothing's left for me now my love,
the fire in my soul is real.
My spirit cries and I so wince
in pain with a love now so lost.
We must try to find now our love
again, if we ever can since
the fire in my soul is real,
and I can't go on as before.
I shall pray to God in Heaven
on how we can love and be one,
and restore what we once had as
the fire in my soul is real.

August 30, 2015
(Quatern)

The Frozen Ghost

All Hallows' Eve conjureth yearly a foul evil of such a mythic yore,
As a ghastly icy spectre walketh silently now through our very door!

This frozen ghost of yore giveth we the living his curses on this night,
With his blackest of eyes and icy hands delivereth he his horrid fright.

The frozen ghost's unholy eyes mirror crystal-clear Old Hob's real plan,
To spread his evil, fear, hate, and Hellspawn in God's own divine land!

Mankind hath a sacred duty so true to fight Old Hob's vile temptation,
And to resist the frozen ghost's message whilst praying for redemption.

We pray now to Almighty God to send this frozen ghost on his way,
Back to Old Hob, never to walk on this Earth another night and day!

We honour now All Hallows' Eve and think about departed souls' wit,
Knowing the frozen ghost hath gone now, buried so deep in Hell's pit!

October 7, 2015
(Couplet)

The Might Have Been

Illusion so bespeaks the might have been,
Which passes not for real, done, and when.

A grammar notion meant for a moment;
Descriptive too of a heartfelt lament.

Imagination swims in might have been;
A world of fantasy until time when.

Emotions so thought and not yet expressed—
Now cannot cancel such moments depressed.

Stating what you thought—but it happened not;
Meaning might have been is all you have got.

The might-have-been pervades such actions past,
And no forgiveness for mistakes made fast.

An event that never was scares one true,
When the real event makes one so blue!

July 6, 2015
(Heroic Couplet)

The Moon, The Swan, The Rose

I see an enchanted image that you've never dreamed of
With reflections twinkling while dancing on wave drops
Of a dreamy blue lake that is a mirror of one white swan

A dancing beauty with a pureness that blesses this water
She floats like a princess with such an elegance and grace
As splendor ripples through a lens of her divine existence

A canvas painting as one masterpiece beyond compare
As the moonlight manifests a sweet rose in my dreams
Beautiful to desire now that nothing shall be disturbed

Within a frozen memory a brilliant diamond illuminates
As the full moon's image enters the depths of her soul
And a sad, certain loneliness leaves her spirit exhausted

Arising before my eyes on the wings of angels, I see all
Clearly now with an excited, fluttering magical heartbeat
Believe me—that this eternal blue sky is incredibly real

With a golden orb of light colors reflecting so exquisitely
Now as majestic images of God's Heaven appear above,
I see His very image of the Moon, the Swan, and the Rose

September 2, 2015
(Tercet)

Author's Note: A Collaborated Poem with Anne-Lise Andresen and Liam McDaid.

The Never Will

The "never will" is sometimes...
left alone;
and the never said... never happened;
and so who shall ever question?

The "never will" can be:
the never did,
the never can,
the never could,
the never have,
the never had,
the never would,
the never would have had,
the never shall,
the never shall have,
and the never shall have had...
(with all of its grammatical bliss).

The "never will" emotes
a determination—
and a pulse and a force of
masterful and demonstrative negation;
sometimes never to be really and fully understood.

Our lifetime is spent with the "never will"
as part of our inner psyche
and as...
a daily aspect of one's Cosmic DNA.

It lurks as our constant companion,
...*im Gegenteil*...
to the "always will" which means it always will.

It will follow us too on our eventual Soul Path
to that Great Beyond . . .

But only God can make that decision.

May 8, 2015
(Lyric)

The Power of Love

God's eternal message is "The Power of Love."
The power of love is magical and enchanting,
The power of love is exciting and compelling,
The power of love is in truth and honesty always,
The power of love is reflected in one's good works,
The power of love is reflected in one's true humility,
The power of love is integral to always doing the right thing,
The power of love is a catalyst for humor and fun,
The power of love is what makes our world go round,
The power of love is reflected in your lovely eyes,
The power of love is in your smile and laughter,
The power of love is with us all in times of sadness and loss,
The power of love is with us all in times of happiness and joy,
The power of love is the glue that binds two people in love,
The power of love is a potent alchemic mix of radiance and wonder,
The power of love is in the romantic aura of God's starlight,
The power of love is magnified by the glow of God's moonlight,
The power of love is in every rainbow that appears on Earth,
The power of love is manifested in our mortal being and spirit,
The power of love is at the very center of one's eternal soul,
The power of love is in the fantasy and magic of the Unicorn,
The power of love is Mother Nature's majestic and magical touch,
The power of love is at the very center of hope and prayer,
The power of love is in the DNA of our cosmic dust,
The power of love is in the destiny and hope of mankind,
The power of love is in the glory and hope of all Guardian Angels,
The power of love is Almighty God and all of His Angels in Heaven,
The power of love is in God's eternal message of hope and freedom,
The power of love is the positive impetus to influence people and ideas,
The power of love is in the absolute divinity of God's heavenly kingdom,
The power of love is one with mankind and all of the creatures on Earth,
The power of love is in the wind, the rain, the soil, the leaves, and the trees,

The power of love is in the glorious nature and beauty of the Earth's clouds,
The power of love is in one's civility, manners, politeness, and good nature,
The power of love is in the utter simplicity and wonder of all children,
The power of love is God's undeniable divine force in the Universe.

November 2, 2015
(Anaphora)

The Reaper's Return

The cockroach crawling inside a satin evil darkness
as one clown weeps into silken-soft sensual feelings,
as a blinking starlight beacon awaits a tense message
of doubts from all living dreams becoming nightmares.

Bleeding trapped within a shadow's eerie smile whilst
grinning through the hurt smiling at the joy cheering,
at twisted laughs with needles of pain, lust, passion
and gasping of a victim choking in deep-labored breaths.

Choking one heart now taken tragically away from us
with a nightshade vision as we blindly walk into the
dark night in the realm of the dead, forever gone now,
with sad, ice-cold whispers playing aloud and so deeply.

A taste of Hell and a fool's game of serious malediction
whilst cold whispers compel us ever so against the wind,
as a restless soul is cutting ice frozen in a time dreaming
of things past with hypnotic jewels of a deepest beauty.

When little gestures that meant so much to us all, whilst lost
in a space-dark matter invading and pervading our lives now,
a mysteriously hot sulfuric fire burns down the mountainside,
as an ice-cold stream in the ocean now becomes a mystic dream.

May 15, 2015
(Quatrain)

Author's Note: A Collaborated Poem with Liam McDaid.

The Stars at Night

Gazing at the stars at night I marvel at their divine beauty,
Knowing that God created them as reflections of His Light.

The stars, in a sense, serve as light markers to mankind's
Very existence on Earth and in other celestial dimensions.

The stars have served as romantic backdrops for people,
As they seek love, find love, and desire a life together.

The stars with their infinite beauty and God-like presence,
Shall always have import in the lives of men and women.

The darkness of night itself creates a motif that contrasts with
The very wonder and hope for mankind that starlight brings.

Love itself serves as that quite special emotion which brings
Two star-crossed lovers together in love as one in God's eyes.

The secret of the stars is the magic and majesty of love that they
Engender as two people find each other and fall in love forever.

The stars at night mirror God's eternal presence in the cosmos,
And represent His love and desire to be with mankind always.

The stars reflect an infinite beauty and God's grace and love,
Which shall always be part of mankind's existence on Earth.

June 23, 2015
(Couplet)

The Sweetest Starlight and Heavenly Embrace

You are the sweetest starlight shining now across the ocean so pure,
Enchanting my dreams n' thoughts aglow as I bask in your true love,
Whilst you touch now my heart and soul with your beauty and wonder.
If we were together, I would hold you so gently and warmly in my arms,
And, I would forever kiss your adoring lips with a passionate goodnight.

Love is that faraway feeling rising in the morning sunshine's warm rays,
And the light of your presence glows brilliantly as you enter my dreams
Of a pure, sweet surrender and a kiss that touches now my immortal soul.
You are the light of Heaven's own dream of a rainbow's flight of angels,
Arriving at Heaven's gate to greet me on that mythic beam of silver light.

Mesmerized I am, as I embrace you now as the heart, soul, passion, and
Desire of my life—I see you as my truest dream and my heart's delight.
Palpably feeling your wonderful caress as you ask me now to kiss you,
I know for sure that you're the one I dreamt of in my deepest of dreams,
And I know you're the one my love with the sweetest heavenly embrace!

August 2, 2015
(Quintain)

The Tides of Our Passion

The tides of our passion cry out my love,
As we seek to define who we are now.
To live this special life gives us that how,
And when and why we must seek God above!
Our souls blend one perfect constant of love,
As we prize God's cosmic eternal vow.
Our passion defines our life and us now;
Our love basks in Heaven's own light above!

Our passion's rapture is love replete,
With brilliant emotions forever bright,
As we kiss softly under God's moonlight!
Love's magical force makes our life complete,
As we seek happiness here on God's Earth,
Knowing love shall transcend our mortal birth!

July 28, 2015
(Petrarchan Sonnet)

The Walk of Love

With you now entering this heart enchanting with rose petals
You are the sweetest flower dancing tunes inside one's mind
Once upon a fairy tale dream adoring you my loving princess

You begin rising in the east amazing light crowning sunshine
Ultraviolet radiance glowing warm with rays of deep breaths
Inner sighs as you walk softly on the deepest of sands My Love

Your footprints are so soft and deeply touching Sweet Honey
As your loving gentleness sweeps me away into a paradise pure
Where we walk hand-in-hand smiling with such feeling and joy

In a thousand dreams floats one treasure of Golden Happiness
Your joy sparks liquid honey melting gold into our heartbeats
Fluttering on wings of a butterfly silently flying in the cool air

With the sweetest scent of the purest jasmine now pervading all
Breathless beauty as an angel of the heart sings a paean of delight
Whilst the warm air dances on a flower kissing a breeze so softly

Flocks of beautiful birds sing you praises of glory that be forever
As they fly with such grace and their hearts beat softly in rhythm
Landing on paradise as your words touch with whispers my soul

Resonating into the deepest crevices of my ethereal psyche true
Whilst echoing inside the chambers of your lucent pretty presence
Holding hands as the sunlight beams your every foot step now

As shadows silver dancing waves call out one name within each
Echo crashing salted sure your spices kiss our magic moments
As a gentle but sensual wind kisses the lips of a lovely Sweet Siren

As she holds us in her dreams of a wonderful love so rich and pure
We share the Dream of a thousand lifetimes beyond all compare
As twelve rich-red roses blush in the heavens where one diamond

Gary Bateman

Shines so brightly with a rainbow array of heavenly colors pure
Reflecting God's own divine design and wish for us to keep our
Eternal promise now My Love with a ring symbolizing us as One

July 12, 2015
(Tercet)

Author's Note: A Collaborated Poem with Liam McDaid.

The Warmth of Our True Love

The warmth of our true love is forever,
As we walk hand-in-hand in God's bright light.
Our love is God's gift and shall leave us never.

We know dear one our love always feels right,
As we savor all of this emotion;
As we walk hand-in-hand in God's bright light.

Our desire is a magical potion
Of heavenly force and cosmic power,
As we savor all of this emotion.

This is our love's ecstasy and the hour,
We find our destiny and feel God's hand
Of heavenly force and cosmic power.

Love is God's music in His angelic band;
Its divine nature touches our souls true.
We find our destiny and feel God's hand.

God's love for us binds us like cosmic glue;
Its divine nature touches our souls true.
The warmth of our true love is forever;
Our love is God's gift and shall leave us never.

July 23, 2015
(Terzanelle)

Gary Bateman

Theatrum Mundi

T*heatrum Mundi*, derived from the Latin, means: "Great Theater of the World," was famously incorporated by William Shakespeare for his certain well-known metaphorical world-view often referred to under the rubric of "All the World's a Stage," as it applied to many genre specifically, I take *Theatrum Mundi* a step further at a macro level and consider it under its more precise definition as "the world thought of as a theatrical presentation of all aspects of human life," while considering all of us who live in this world who are, in a sense, on a stage as our very own actors in different roles.

I believe that many modern-day poets tend to follow a multifaceted approach to many compelling and captivating themes and problems that form the verbal and written mosaic of what we call human life or the human experience. This is not so different from poets of a bygone age; yet, we tend now to be more influenced by the technological age we all live in, but this should not at all detract from our poetry and how we frame and stage human events on paper with our pens.

Despite our technological prowess nowadays in the twenty-first century, the certain true genesis and exposition of what we poetically write and how we write it, should continue to follow the traditional formats and the structural methodologies passed on to us from the poets of past centuries. The true art of poetry will always be in the same tradition; yet, it's worth noting that the increased proliferation in the use of "free verse" is indeed more telling today in this modern literary age. Regardless, traditional poetic formats will always remain too, and play an ever-evolving and significant role in the warp and woof of what we do as both poets and as writers in general.

That's what makes writing poetry indeed so special today in comparison to strict prose and journalistic writing. For me, really good poetry invites readers to think, and to use their imaginations while venturing into the inner sanctum of allegory, assonance, imagery, metaphor, metonymy, onomatopoeia, and so on. And so, we poets tend to have a virtual, unending group of ideas, themes, and subjects to consider for developing and writing when we look at the vastness of the human experience in society today in this century and in centuries past.

Theatrum Mundi is very much applicable to an all-inclusive view of themes and works across all genres when one considers the veritable magnitude of the human condition in today's world. And, in this sense, poets are also actors on the global stage—and we will always have much to observe, discuss, and write about—no doubt whatsoever!

February 11, 2015
(Narrative Essay)

Author's Note: This specific definition of *Theatrum Mundi* was cited from *The Oxford Dictionary of Foreign Words & Phrases* (New York: Oxford University Press Inc., 1998), 431.

Tilting at Simplicity

William of Occam
Harbinger of today's
"Occam's razor"—
His simplest solutions
Bespeak not always
Accurate conclusions.

A Simple Simon
Binary approach
Style vice logic
Solutions not always
Truest to measure
Requires real
Human variety.

Heuristic methods
Abound—of course
Tied to many
Scientific efforts
But how about
The Messy?
The Complex?

Simple rationale
On each conclusion
May be suspect
With only barest of
Variables considered.

Take your pick—but
Use your intuition
The easiest are not
Always most correct
Use common sense too!

When in doubt
Trust yourself
Keep objectivity
Fail not to ponder
The complex too!

September 14, 2015
(Accentual Meter)

To Be, To Feel, To Love, To Live, To Die

TO BE is that existential moment that defines each of us on our respective life paths as we each individually acknowledge the reality of our human existence on this Earth. To be able to laugh and cry, to think and wonder, to create and perpetuate, to read and write—among many other human actions—all help to define our human experience as we individually and collectively pursue a philosophical and ethereal realization of our cosmic existence.

TO FEEL is a special characteristic that reflects the nature of human compassion as it is often associated in consonance with a genuine understanding of relationships and all-important human interaction. To be able to feel something positive for someone is a grand and marvelous thing. It is definitely inherent in our human psyche as we each reach out to one another in those times of certain joy and sadness, crisis and affirmation, and friendship and love.

TO LOVE is that most special emotion which has a tremendous effect in covering the vast expanse of our daily human experience. Love excites us and makes life worth living. Love warms our hearts with a true passion and purpose. Love makes us happy as it touches our hearts. Love is that special alchemic catalyst that transforms us as we each seek our respective destinies in search of that other one person who loves us and opens our hearts and souls to a heavenly redemption.

TO LIVE is what we humans do on this precious planet that we now inhabit—this Earth. Although we all live here in this everyday world, there is for many people, little or no real understanding of the special relationship to their Soul Body beyond the limitations of this certain mortal coil. To live and to live well, one should have a capacity for both empathy and compassion toward one's fellow human beings. Our days living here on this Earth do mark our mortal time which will eventually run out for each one of us like grains of sand in the fabled Hourglass. Beyond our challenge to define ourselves on this mortal plane, lies that divine and ethereal world of God as our souls seek their place and destiny as they journey toward eternity.

TO DIE is that special final moment that describes the action ending of our mortal existence on Earth as our individual souls seek to find and fulfill their destiny with God Himself in the very outreaches of His infinite kingdom of wonder, beauty, and divine glory. This whole process gives each and every one of us the closure we need to sever the earthly bounds that have defined and circumscribed our existence in this finite, mortal world. This process is inevitable and is something not to be feared, but to be understood and embraced as God helps each of us on our eventual spiritual journey along His footpaths to eternity and into the everlasting light beyond.

August 29, 2015
(Didactic)

Valentine's Magic

Love is eternal—
Expression of love so pure!
Valentine's Day is . . .
That magic moment of love . . .
Renewal of love always!

February 8, 2015
(Tanka)

Valentine's Unicorn

A magical and most wonderful creature of times old,
With a holy soul filled with love and a heart of gold.

Harmony, peace, and love pervade her very essence,
And they define all that is good and grand in her presence.

She loves poets, musicians, and all of us who so often dream,
And visits us all in ethereal visions on a radiant light beam.

This Valentine's Unicorn is a precious bearer of purest love,
Who possesses angelic power from the very heavens above.

She lives in our hearts and souls as an enchanted dream,
And shares her love and trust with us all as we dream.

She shares our dreams past, present, and future—
And shall always be a spirit of majestic love in our future.

On Valentine's Day her love is felt on Earth and in Heaven above,
As she sends us harmony, peace, and love on the wings of a dove!

February 9, 2015
(Couplet)

What Kind of People Are We?

In a Shakespearean sense of true tragedy and doubt the famous "To Be or Not To Be" from *Hamlet* is not the question I shall discuss in this narrative. Rather, I shall consider a few things concerning the current Middle Eastern and European migrant situations that have riveted the attention of the countries in those regions as well as the rest of the world. And, it is my opportunity to reflect on some of the things that have occurred (and are still occurring right now), that I find quite troubling and morally offensive, and totally reprehensible to me as both a concerned person and a world citizen.

As a writer and poet, and as a moral human being, I must say that I was truly shocked at the sight of an innocent, young Syrian refugee boy named "Aylan Kurdi," who had drowned and was lying face down on a Turkish beach near a resort with his head turned slightly on its right side, as the ebb and flow of the salted waves pushed and pulled on his little body. A real tragedy for sure that might have been prevented, if humane, thoughtful, responsible, and responsive migrant immigration policies had been in place so his father would not have been compelled to put his wife and both of his sons—who all drowned together—on that fateful boat at the very mercy of ruthless and evil human traffic smugglers.

These horrendous scenes played over and over on the twenty-four hour news cycle of the migrants and their innocent children from Syria, Iraq, Turkey, Afghanistan, and other countries being treated like cattle (or even less than cattle), and indiscriminately pushed around and tear-gassed by unfriendly and unwelcoming jack-booted *Magyar Rendőrség* (Hungarian Police), and were certainly terribly shocking and disgustingly revulsive by both their malicious tenor and and insidious intent. The actions also of some right-wing Hungarian demonstrators hurling loud and abusive comments at the refugees was quite tragic and disturbing. In particular, I found that the actions of the Hungarian Police under the direction of Prime Minister Viktor Orban to be similarly reminiscent of the actions of Adolf Hitler's Gestapo and his *Sturmabteilung* or the SA Troops after 1933 in Nazi Germany. I say, Shame on them! Shame on them! This is the same old tired bigotry and rank stupidity that is on ample display in today's world. Hence, stupid is as stupid does for sure!

Despite these despicable actions of the Hungarian Police and many of Mr. Orban's governmental officials, a number of Hungarian citizens still showed their kindness and humanity in helping the migrants at various junctures on the autobahn as they trekked toward the Austrian border in route ultimately to Germany. This caught my obvious attention as well.

For me, the "so-what?" of this situation turns upon the demonstrative human question: "What Kind of People Are We?" The migrant problem as we know is largely the result of the massive displacement of people that has occurred (and is still occurring) in the war-torn countries in the Middle East and in certain areas of Southeastern Asia. This tragedy is one of many of our world's current and future challenges we are facing now in the twenty-first century. In reality, how each of us choose to react as "concerned citizens" in this instance, in consonance with the policies and actions of the various governments in the countries we each live in, will play an obvious role in reflecting, in the end, the kind of people that we really are.

For me, the nationalistic actions of the right-wing parties and extremists, in many countries (including the United States), and particularly now, in Europe, provide no real solution at all, and the despicable nature of them have become a convenient excuse for many people today to forsake their conscience and basic humanity—and to stick their heads in the sand like a bunch of frightened ostriches who are lost in the reveries of their hate and prejudice, and disgraceful cowardice! There can never be any apology nor justification for this type of behavior ever! This behavior manifests itself, in fact, as a type of deep-seated cancer ever-lurking in the genes of our human society and in mankind's soul, awaiting its chance to awaken, as it metastasizes and reeks its horrible destruction upon innocent victims.

The point I wish to emphasize here, is this: The responsible actions of a number of world leaders, particularly those of the European Union, appear to be taking several of the right steps in helping these refugee migrants and their families to deal with the terrible strife forced upon them by the tyranny of war and the resultant poverty and dislocation that has upended their lives. It is also worth pointing out that being stupid, hateful, and clearly prejudiced as some people are, as well as certain governmental leaders in our global community today, is not the answer and it never will be!

To people who really do care about this ongoing migrant tragedy, it is time to rally and act in support of local, regional, and worldwide efforts to help these migrant people and their families so afflicted by poverty, disease, war, injury, death, and territorial displacement.

For me, on this matter, I desire to make my voice heard in my own way, both loud and clear as a writer, poet, and a concerned world citizen who passionately believes that all of us as human beings and citizens of this world can and must do better than this!

It is certainly worth keeping in mind that many of us are descendants of families from various countries in this world of ours, who at one time or another, were migrants from other countries escaping the whip and lash of cruel dictators and their terrible regimes that masqueraded as so-called legitimate governments of the people.

With all of this said, in my final estimation, the kind of people we should hope to be or aspire to be are those who relish the winds of freedom, the certainty of justice, the spirit of friendship, the values of fairness and fair play, the magnificence of humanity, the desire for cultural diversity and inclusion, and the love of our fellow man under the aegis and true glory of Almighty God Himself.

What kind of people are we?

This is a question worthy of profound contemplation that lies at the very heart, soul, and consciousness of all mankind. We should always dare to do the right thing! Why not?

With this, I rest my case.

September 11, 2015
(Narrative)

What Our Angels on High Meant

One whose heart and soul are pure
And are full of love and content,
Is one whose life and deeds have
Been gloriously fulfilled and knew
What our angels on high meant.

Is it to be part of our fate and destiny?
To wonder why things are as they are,
Or is it to seek a spiritual approach and
A metaphysical concept of much greater
Import than we can possibly imagine?

This indeed gives us all a noble purpose true,
Whereby we can all aspire to the course that
We take on life's road in fulfilling our sacred
Fate and destiny in our Lord God's name—
For this is what our angels on high meant.

February 11, 2015
(Quintain)

What the Heavenly Angels Above Speak Of

Mankind's love, passion, and truth on this Earth
Are what the heavenly angels above speak of
As part of our continuing mortal experience.
No power on this Earth can ever diminish our
Love nor tear asunder the aura of this uniqueness.

Our heavenly dreams and ongoing desire for
Cosmic Awareness are ingrained into our souls
And our very DNA—forming that rare divine
Wanderlust characterizing humanity's efforts
To synchronize its spirituality with God Himself.

This gives us all cause to reflect on and think of
The higher path that brings our hearts and souls
Together as one as we seek our cosmic destiny,
As part of Almighty God's plan for us in Heaven.
This is what the heavenly angels above speak of.

August 9, 2015
(Quintain)

You Told Me Never Again My Love

Love's a most sacred trust between two people meant forever,
And yet you treat it, at times, as a sham and forever is never.

The bond of love is considered sacred in God's very eyes,
And you should know dear one—that God tells us no lies.

My thoughts and feelings for you are beyond earthly measure,
And the love we share is quite special and always to treasure.

You once told me you would never again ever doubt me,
And yet I've found your doubt is back now to haunt me.

Love's that infinitely complex and most perplexing emotion;
Its mysterious power is the very alchemic force of its motion.

And so my love, it's time now for us to seize once again our life,
And to renew all that's special between us, and not just the strife.

You told me never again my love, and say I the same to you my dear,
For life with a true-found love is one we must nurture year by year.

October 25, 2015
(Couplet)

Your Beautiful Heart Doth Beat

Your beautiful heart doth beat with rapture,
And the sweet of your kiss doth now swoon me.
We caress now and my soul you capture;
My love no place other I wish to be!

When we embrace my love in joy and fun,
Our hot passions spark an alchemic fire.
Our spirits soar high now becoming one,
Affirming love only God can inspire!

Your heart beats a brilliant tempo of love,
That enchants our eternal souls replete.
It's God's gift to us from Heaven above,
And His divine love is true and complete!

To God now I pray your love forever;
I declare my love leaving you never!

November 14, 2015
(Shakespearean Sonnet)

Your Touch Means So Much

Your touch means so much to me my love,
As we hold each other with intense passion.
We know our love has God's blessing above;
Our bond for eternity shall always be in fashion.

As we hold each other with intense passion,
We dazzle with emotion pure on this Earth.
Our bond for eternity shall always be in fashion,
As we approach our souls' nexus of rebirth.

We dazzle with emotion pure on this Earth.
We know our love has God's blessing above,
As we approach our souls' nexus of rebirth.
Your touch means so much to me my love.

July 31, 2015
(Pantoum)

Your Warmest Embrace My Love

I treasure ever,
Your warmest embrace my love.
It captivates my soul pure!
I see your dear look—
Mesmerized by your presence.
Your touch is so rapturous!
I taste your warm lips,
Luscious and most inviting.
They excite my passion so!
I love so your smile,
So pure, cheerful, radiant.
It fascinates me always!
Your touch is magic;
Your presence stirs my passion;
Our emotions now on fire!
Our bodies meet pure;
They unite one locked in love;
Sublime ecstasy complete!
Our love is now one,
And our shared passion is true.
Our destiny is now one!
So as I write this
My Sweet—I think of you now,
And our love so wonderful—
Your warmest embrace My Love!

January 9, 2015
(Choka)

Zephyr's Magic

I feel the true delight of Zephyr's Magic,
As I walk in the nighttime mist majestic.

This West wind caresses now my very soul,
As I walk earful of an ancient faint bell toll.

This West wind is so warm and compelling;
It envelopes me whole now—quite so telling.

Zephyr enchants my slumber on the beach,
Charming me to dream of a love past my reach.

With Zephyr's spell I dreamt so deep and well,
Of that lost love I missed—I shall not ever tell!

Zephyr's wind touches and warms well my face,
As I sigh now and look on in endless space.

Walking home Zephyr's Magic follows me more,
Enchanting me until I walked through the door!

February 15, 2015
(Couplet)

CHAPTER THREE

Selected Poetry
(2016)

**Alchemic Notions
Beyond the Veil
Moments of Love
Life's Realities
and
Spiritual Epiphanies**

A Love So True

A love so true is what I found in you my dearest one!
The depth of our shared emotions defy all description,
As they excite and enchant every aspect of our lives.

A love so true is a quest I started long ago to find you!
One so special with that undeniable smile and laugh;
One possessed with that rare angelic heart of gold.

A love so true binds us together even in strife and tribulation!
We find our shared thoughts and love do sustain us each day.
We renew our passion and commitment without reservation.

A love so true blessed by our Lord God in Heaven above!
He watches over us now and gives us His true love always.
We walk in His divine path now, two souls forever as one.

January 13, 2016
(Tercet)

Ancient Shadows Awaken into God's Light

Underneath the deep seabed the stirring sands of time have passed on.
Ancient shadows continue to haunt all of us from the oceans' depths,
And insidious and violent nightmares portray bloody and evil visions,
As an old treasure chest is opened and a gull's cry foretells tragic stories.

Untold riches awaken Neptune's deepest waves as the tides turn inward,
And a star-gazing dust trail turns into a golden circle of subtle measure.
The dark moon's horrid howl sounds in its crimson cradle over the ocean
As the cruelest beast from evil Hellspawn creeps and invades all energies.

The moon's beam feasts on poor and lonely souls under the cover of night,
Whilst savagely touching the sad forlorn places between Heaven and Earth.
These unholy places of dark origin beckon the spirit of a vile Vampire who
Cometh from a deep-darkness creeping around under the Devil's own aura.

This Prince of Darkness bringeth enchanting soft-sweet kisses of solitude,
Tempting now the innocent silhouette of a ravishingly beautiful young lady
Whose true desire and passion for love leaps over an ice-ruby magical fire,
As her robust heartbeats incite the Vampire's ravenous thirst for her blood.

The sensual fire stoked by this lady's heartbeats and lifeblood burn sold
Down a macabre river of true darkness, all perfect up, as she gasps aloud
For air, wincing and moaning audibly, as she expires with a most ghastly
Death rattle as the Prince of Darkness gleefully smiles at her godless soul.

This gruesome image invokes a blending of human bread eating into the
Suffering eyes of salted fish bait trapped and gasping for air, for mercy,
Just like a trapped drunken sailor now swallowed inside hungry ghouls
Who haunt over dark sea whispers that chill to the bone mankind's future.

Those souls lost within the land of this living dream bask now positive as
The darkness turns into sunlight in God's own yard of supreme radiance,
Metamorphosing into a lovely butterfly emerging from its silken cocoon,
Now so cotton-soft and swallowed by the bright light of the human soul.

The soul's lucent energy of heavenly radiance comes forth for all to see
As the Devil's dark beast now sings its paeans of utter joy as this terror
Transforms itself, yet ever so slowly into a calm sea of true change.
With this miracle change cometh a peace sanctuary of God's angels!

That is a thousand of God's angels now chanting with a pleasured delight
As a heaven-sought change comes to nurture the plight of all lost souls.
With this aura of change, love's sacred light shineth now so ultrabright,
For even the darkened heart of the beast can find peace in Heaven's light!

We await to see where this beast shall go and what shall follow in kind.
Shall this former beast of the Devil himself experience a final epiphany
To be like the blessed butterfly or to return to the black heart of the crow?
Almighty God does indeed move in the most mysterious of ways!

The Prince of Darkness laughs no longer as his long-lost soul burns hot
And blue-bile-black-red in Hell's own deepest, darkest inescapable pit!
No redemption for him and for his master, the Devil, confined below.
By God's holy command, all ancient shadows shall awaken whole into
Heaven's eternal and radiant light! All by God's divine grace and mercy!

Amen! Amen! Amen!

November 16, 2016
(Narrative)

Author's Note: A Collaborated Poem with Anne-Lise Andresen, Michael Clarke, and Liam McDaid.

As Liquid Fire Melts

As liquid fire melts with twinkling sunshine in your eyes,
Opening wings now embrace deeply all of my true emotions.

Feeling the warmth of your beating heart now fluttering so,
I see a radiant chain of daisies growing in the deep green grass.

Every choice I have ever made throughout my long life,
Has led me now to you at this very special moment in time.

Beholding ivory silk starlight whispers of heavenly angels true,
I have now a clear vision of my life, my destiny, and my fate.

Becoming the richest person in this giant, lonely world—
Means finding you and sharing our love unconditionally.

All real emotions we have beholding in this life of ours,
Are part of that God-given sensitivity from the Almighty.

Truly, as liquid fire melts beyond in the great stars of the cosmos,
I think of you, our love, and the starlight whispers of angels true!

April 21, 2016
(Couplet)

Author's Note: A Collaborated Poem with Liam McDaid.

Autumn's Kiss

The colors of autumn abound for all to see,
while the layers of fog spread gently over the fields,
and the fine wet teardrops weigh heavily on a spider's web,
making the spider's web dance with great joy.

Autumn comes around the corner by God's eternal plan,
as Mother Nature brings her wondrous bundle of bright colors,
and as the Sun's warm rays touch the leaves ever so gently,
making everything most radiant and brilliant.

The Sun's warm rays begin to dissolve the layers of fog,
covering the fields for miles on end which are now spreading
out before the open eyes for all to see.

The last days of summer are now kissing gently and softly
the cheeks of the arriving autumn with a great expectation.

Enjoy this treasured time in between,
for every moment is such a precious God-given gift;
this must be done before the winter arrives,
with its long-dark nights and its cold-frozen days.

All of these marvelous seasonal aspects of Mother Nature,
Reflect a divine certitude and the ultimate power of Almighty
God's cosmic plan and His omnipotent touch!

October 22, 2016
(Free Verse)

Author's Note: A Collaborated Poem with Ingrid Krukenberg-Bateman.

Believe in Angels

Believe in angels with all of your heart and spirit,
and they shall always believe in you holy in kind.

And when it comes time for your heavenly ascent,
the angels shall be with you by God's own assent.

What more could any mortal surely hope for with
the assurity that the angels shall always be with us.

July 4, 2016
(Couplet)

Fickle

The ebb and flow of life;
Fickle is, fickle does, fickle so
Yet struggle we all to know,
Can we really do this?
Love—yeah, Friendship—yeah,
Character, Smart, Dumb, Fun;
Do we know what we want?
Forever fickle can be that
Forever pickle that we laugh at
With Mankind locked in that
Forever maze ever mercurial.
Frazzle, frizzle, razzle are the now;
Dazzle is the How and When?
One who is portentous in thought,
Whose mind is open but adrift,
May know this How and When.
Shall it be him or her or both?
Just maybe—it is no one at all!

March 28, 2016
(Verse)

God's Holy Whisper of Love

I long to hear now God's holy whisper of love,
For its sacrosanct sound abounds most high above.
This subtle-soft tone mirrors forever God's grace;
It maketh our souls one in His heavenly place.
God's whisper reflects his love and passion in kind;
It is His wish for poets to set them in true rhyme.
God's whisper is our music on this mortal Earth;
It sustains our love's spirit for a holy rebirth.
Warm tears always symbolize our human passion,
As now we seek God's plan for His divine action.
God's whisper sustains us true in all times of need;
He teaches that love conquers all, and we must heed.
God's love shall be with us all until the end of time;
And He knows that poets shall set His words to rhyme!

July 15, 2016
(Canzone)

Hobbyhorse

Hobbyhorses live—
Some bosses like to ride them!
Yes, repetition...
Over, over and over...
Until all their points are made!

November 10, 2016
(Tanka)

Love's Alchemy is Eternal

Your look, touch, and scent now so perfect pure,
Enchants my true emotions and soaring passion.
I know now darling our love shall always endure,
As God unites our souls as one by divine action!

Our sensual passion defines love's spirit entire,
As we caress and kiss for this moment's bliss.
Love's alchemy maketh our spirits soar afire,
As we embrace, our lips find that deepest kiss!

Our hearts beat now in a sacred tempo of love,
That reflects our real destiny, two souls as one.
This is God's gift to us from Heaven high above,
As we wish these magic moments of eternal fun!

By Heaven, I pray our love's alchemy is forever,
And I declare my love, I shall not leave you ever!

June 27, 2016
(Shakespearean Sonnet)

Meretricious Spirit

This spirit is modern society's cancer
Replete with rank, flashy vulgarities
Pervading our social fabric and soul
Unbridled, unbowed, unapologetic;
It can be a curse to mankind itself,
Engulfing some people in moments
Of childish deception and insincerity
Which challenge our human civility;
Petulance, at times, can be seen to
"Rule the Roost" in certain personal
Interactions to make each of us seem
To be less than who we truly are in life;
Always follow your life's passion and
The spiritual heart and tenor of your soul,
For they shall be your true moral compass
As you face the daily slings and arrows of
This life as mankind's fabulistic tendencies
Seek to tarnish one's very spirit and worth
In this thing we all call—our mortal coil!

October 11, 2016
(Didactic)

Our Human Nature

A real aspect always part of a person's life;
One that can bear fangs and pangs of strife.

A living barometer replete with its choices;
Leaving each of us puzzled, full of voices.

It prays on our very emotions and naivete,
Leaving us at times in moments of disarray.

Man by his nature is fickle and imperfect.
God by His nature is divine and perfect.

A person's decency is so wonderful to tell;
Another's depravity is so worthy of Hell!

A person's good deeds mark now his true measure,
Bringing him God's divine love always to treasure!

Never trust what you can't feel deep in your heart;
This makes us divine in God's eyes and sets us apart!

January 5, 2016
(Couplet)

Phantom Slippers of Thoughts

Without soul nourishment our spirits shall wither and die.
Words are a mere instrument, but can reflect truth to power.
With our faith in love and understanding—truth begs mercy,
Whilst melting honey-sweet crystals kiss thy soft warm cheeks.
We dream and bathe inside the sun's most radiant gift of desire.
Cool waters of divine creation lovingly quench this desert fire,
And the haunting spectre of death shall never be an end to us!

Winds of such deep-thoughts softly and sweetly sting at once,
When I show you a mirror-image of what our destiny can be.
Adrift in storms of fervid emotions I give in now to your love.
I see a temple of beauty I once bowed down to under your gaze,
As your red-hot daggers strike deepest cords in this coldest breeze.
Now holding hands sunlight-sparkled with you inside this dream,
This heartfelt satisfaction's worth more than all the world's gold!

Riches fall from Heaven now in shining jewels of misted pearls,
Whilst I walk alone in deepest thoughts in my blue suede shoes.
Living-loving inside a sole-soul of dreams—true and unbounded,
I hear songbirds whistle and whisper in such joy by God's grace.
Our souls may nourish themselves on the eternal power of our love.
With God as our witness—we fear not what death shall bring to us,
For our love and true destiny exist far beyond this mortal world!

May 15, 2016
(Free Verse)

Author's Note: A Collaborated Poem with Liam McDaid.

Poetic Encryption Like Ancient Egyptian

This terror and threat to poetic clarity,
Becomes a pet rock for some poets.

Words do count for sure, but so does
Clarity unless poets put a mask on.

Encryption can be used to mask certain
Vaticinal pretensions that many poets do
Harbor, at times, when waxing eloquently
About some trendy theme or some idea
Or notion deemed as avant-garde.

If hieroglyphics were to be readily used
In our now advanced world of modernity,
Would they be viewed as:
A rifacimento? A renaissance? A code?
It all could be plain nonsense too!
Or maybe not . . .

In T. S. Eliot's, "The Love Song of J. Alfred Prufrock,"
He enchants and captivates his readers to a rare and
Flavorful taste of *vers libre*, if one might be so bold,
That is selectively sparing, and yet, well-calibrated,
With intermittent sprinklings of superbly crafted
Visual imagery and eloquent tonal alliteration—
And varied meter, rhythm, and rhyme.

"Prufrock" is palpable with emotion and metaphor, yet—
Detached from a ready explanation of the delicious
Power of the words with which Eliot mesmerizes his
Readers with the devout cleverness of a Pied Piper.

One could see the eternal **Footman**
And hear his snicker—and be afraid;
One could roll one's trousers;
One could dare to eat a peach;

One could walk upon the beach;
One could hear the mermaids sing;
But will the mermaids sing to him?
Only Eliot really truly knows . . .
The real Prufrockian mien here.

Are not such metaphors there . . .
To make us think?
To enchant our senses?
To play on our fears?
To be emotive?

And, yes . . .
To tantalize our passions?
And, yes . . .
To excite our psychic yearnings?

Yes . . . Contemplation is always vital!

Some poets speak in a self-tribal code.
Sometimes artful obfuscation is the real goal,
And sometimes—maybe not.

A cacophonic scramble of
Demonstrative and passionate
Words, thoughts, emotions.
All so pure and all so real,
And all in the poet's mind!
All so exact and all so real!

Some, like the legendary Sylvia Plath,
Bring the reader to a forlorn world of
Lost faith, utter despair, and loneliness
In the midst of such a sad dream world.
Plath's lyric poem — "Edge"
Summons readers to the brink;
Occurring one week before her
Untimely suicide.

The power and symbolism
Resident in this, her final poem,
Point toward . . .
A perfection, A completion,
A tragic tribalism.

Plath's symbology is both
Intense and compelling;
Forming its own sense of
Encryption while embellishing
A supernatural aura of immortality.

The redoubtable Ezra Pound in his
"Hugh Selwyn Mauberley," and in
Many other of his complex poems,
Personifies a certain form of encryption
With his use of symbols and metaphors,
A mix of foreign languages, and a definite
Convulsion of syntax which makes for an
Intellectual "Rite of Passage" defying, at times,
A clear analysis and ready understanding.

Pound in "Mauberley," writes on various
Levels begging much pre-knowledge from
Each reader while amply teasing us with:
His gnomic predilection for novel themes;
His thirst for the unexpected and unusual;
His formidable knowledge and language forte;
His array of uniquely woven-word tapestries;
And his referential flair for striking aphorisms.

Pound does all of this so magnificently . . .
All the while forming imagery challenging
A reader's sense of understanding . . .
Leaving a sense of syntactical encryption Writ Large!
Always challenging and never ever dull!
That is, if one's cup of tea is reveling in the complex!

There is a profound literary sense to what some may say,
Is Pound's Janus-faced proclivity for genius and madness.
Pound will not disappoint you regardless of which bipolar
Face you ascribe to him.
Although, contrast and comparison are very important...

Yet, I proffer that deep thinking and sometimes actually
Being confused at times...
May result ultimately in a true epiphany,
Leading each of us to a spirit of greater understanding!

I end with John Keats, who has left all of us, as poets,
With his immeasurable sense of naturalistic Humanism.
Keats' pursuit of metaphor, nuance, descriptive imagery,
And sagacious symbology reflect the highest degree of
Poetic mastery and a strong sense of perspicacity obvious
In all of his works!

Keats also uses a type of poetic encryption—
With his diction, imagery, thoughts, and verse syncopation;
He is quite elegant with his varied and fluent thematic reveries.
They are always a joy to decipher, whilst leaving us to bask in
Their powerful sense of clarity and persuasive meaning!

Many of Keats' works reflect this form of encryption...
"La Belle Dame Sans Merci"
Particularly comes to mind in this instance,
As well as his famous "Ode" narratives;
And his superb Grecian epic fragment: "The Fall of Hyperion,"
Presents the reader with a veritable smorgasbord of contrasts
And imagery, and an imaginative view of the classic conflict
Between the Olympians and the Titans!

Divining the complex, chaotic, and unpredictable
In our world of arcane symbolism and imagery,
Reflect the modern world we live in today.
Poetic Encryption is indeed...
So like Ancient Egyptian!

Hieroglyphics, after all, form their own
Sense of imagery and word pictures . . .
Analogous to what we do today with the
Words, images, metaphors, emotions, and
Other symbols in our poetry!

Poetic Encryption is so like Ancient Egyptian!
Amen! Amen!

April 25, 2016
(Narrative)

Sailing Beyond My Dreams

Sailing deeply into my dreams—
All night long, I could sense it,
The ocean in its pure magnificence and majestic wonder.
I smelled Nature's soft salt from the sea in the air,
Savoring complete its true sensorial magic and delight.
I heard the rhythmic melody of the waves breaking at the beach.
I heard the wind's sonorous echo loud and clear,
And felt the force of its glorious power and pitch,
Whilst nurturing its earthly promise for a most exciting day!

And now I was finally on the ship—
With its big white sails,
Along with all other people
Who share the same goal.
Despite of any differences, different jobs, and families,
We all are joined together on this unique sailing trip.
Everyone is excited,
And full of hope for a wonderful day!

And now the ocean itself seemed to be very
Excited, full of enchanted hopes and dreams,
Whilst looking forward to everything,
And to what each new day may bring!

And more and more and more—
With every movement of the ship,
I could sense, see, and palpably feel a mystical
Dancing with the waves and the wind
In the midst of this great ocean entire,
And then, I could feel it again:
Freedom, total precious freedom!

And now, at the very same time—
Everybody on this magical ship,
Is so familiar and close together
In this marvelous joint venture!

At this special moment of divine
Wonder and purity,
The idea of God's own creation
Presents itself with an absolute clarity:
A sense and realization of total freedom,
With all earthly elements arrayed in their
Purest and most radiant nature!

I'm part of this fabulous and fantastic adventure,
In each and every moment—
Yet, at the same time,
I'm never ever alone!
I'm part of the people—
I'm part of everything—
And each and every element and aspect of what
God in His most holy and divine grace meant
When He created this miraculous Earth!

I am at peace. Here I am. Right now.

November 11, 2016
(Free Verse)

Author's Note: A Collaborated Poem
with Ingrid Krukenberg-Bateman.

The Bewitching Call of the Siren

She ululates a forlorn desire for a human love;
She's pure evil, not from God's Heaven above.
This siren's seductive melody is heard on all seas,
And even on the largest lakes and flowing rivers;
Bringing even seafarers near *Die Lorelei* to shivers!
Beguiling young sailors to such a ghastly death;
This vile creature's venom is felt with each breath!
Her visage is one of true love and a blessed pulchritude,
Yet Lucifer's mask is dark with a great evil certitude!
Her perfumed scent enlivens her victims' senses,
Whilst her dark green eyes and deep wet kisses;
Mesmerize her prey, oblivious now to all consequences;
Now feeling her fatal bites and hearing her hideous hisses!
She taketh all pleasure in her world of this evil measure,
Enthralling all her sad victims to a most horrible death;
Now Lucifer counts with joy the lost souls' treasure!
Always *sans merci* this siren be to those in her grot,
As her victims find their souls lost to Hell's dark rot!
Beware say I to all good seafarers, do heed this tale well;
Be deaf to this siren's call or your life shall end in Hell!

July 4, 2016
(Canzone)

The Christmas Spirit

All year long a lot of excitement,
surprising developments . . .
up's and down's
fear, anxiety, conflicts, sadness
all over the world—
and given this . . .
where now shall the
Christmas Spirit come from?

Remember also . . .
the year of your friends and family—
situations when you met your friends
with laughter and joy,
while living and always treasuring family values
at home with true love, feelings, and caresses.

That soft and caring embrace
in the morning . . .
before going to school or work;
that kiss and hug in the evening
when you're finally coming home.

And, this is where the "Spirit of Christmas"
comes from . . .
it comes from deep within your heart,
where it meets every heart around you,
where it touches the depth of your humanity,
and a soft whisper comes from there too . . .
Merry Christmas!

December 18, 2016
(Free Verse)

Author's Note: A Collaborated Poem with Ingrid Krukenberg-Bateman.

The Demon's Shrill Cry of Dread and Horror

This tale of "The Demon's Shrill Cry of Dread and Horror" lives on in the mountain village of *Gpeth Tor* in the outlying region of the "Dark Forbidden Forest" known for evil, death, and lost souls. This tale passeth from generation to generation, to the present, and still frightens all people who hear its grim message as it sends an icy-cold chill that stabs at the heart of one's holy eternal soul!

A young boy who just turned six years heard this tale so told by both of his parents who shivered with a great foreboding fear. Their story of the Devil's Demon of the Dark Forbidden Forest mesmerized this young lad, giving him gruesome nightmares, whereby the Devil's Demon whispers cruelly to him in the darkest corners of his mind and in his deepest moments of sleep!

The young boy's recurring nightmares show him running each night deep into the darkness of the Forbidden Forest while both shouting and screaming his desire to see and to serve this foul "Demon of the Wild," while forsaking Almighty God in his inner thoughts! This ghastly dream world each night is like morphine to his brain, as this young boy suffers, feeling the chains of its cruel and merciless torment!

But this story of the boy is now twenty-two years ago as he's now progressed on to manhood—driven to the very depths of depravity and insanity as he witnesses nightly in his heavy-padded cell, the evil actions of both Ghouls and Ghosts who'd open up the graves of past rotting souls. This insane young man now sings paeans with a fulsome alacrity as he celebrates the shrill and haughty cry of the Devil's Demon!

Does anyone really believe in happy fairy tales when Hell itself corrupts the mind and spirit of the young and unsuspecting?

Does anyone believe a young fairy princess who kisses a frog and says that the frog is now a dashing, noble prince?

Does anyone really understand and believe there are real monsters who roam the maze of one's mind crying now into a dark abyss, while Goblins and Ghosts float freely robbing the living of breath?

The Dark Forbidden Forest of this evil lore does indeed exist, and it lives freely in the dreams of young village children so frightened and terrified by the dark-demonic visage of a bile-black-blooded Bogeyman who resurrects himself nightly in their true dreams of a sweet innocence in the place where scars are born every waking day, as the lid of terror is lifted open, spewing legends and tales of the macabre stealing the very life-force of heartbeats leading to Death!

The local people of this legend in the village of *Gpeth Tor* do speak freely of shrunken heads in large glass jars deep in the bowels of the Forbidden Forest, where the threshold of pain and absolute madness knows no bounds of moderation, and tortured beings and lost souls cry out loudly as the Dark One takes his due while the broken bones of those who remain are crossed—weighted so heavy like an anchor!

Invisible and evil forces at the Devil's command have taken control of the Forbidden Forest, where nasty beasts with a rabid blood thirst for torture live in the very cells of the chained and forgotten souls who have lost their way to Almighty God and His Angels in Heaven above.

Grotesque stories still abound to the present time in this century of the perverse and maledictory nature of this dark forest that borders so close to the ancient village of *Gpeth Tor*—of what can happen to those who dare to speak of the unspeakable, as "Specters of the Undead" feast upon the heartbeats of innocent victims until they are fully consumed, and their souls are condemned to an unending damnation, torment, and agony!

It's been so many years since I graced my presence again in this ancient "Village of the Damned." Mea Culpa! Forgive me! A difficult journey! I've now lost my way into the light and to the holy path to God Himself.

Gpeth Tor and its people live on into this twenty-first century as it is, a place where the *Fire of Gehenna* means something for real and is not at all to be considered as illusory or deceptive regardless of how any events, situations, or human interactions may seem or appear at first blush. The frightful memories and presence of the Forbidden Forest are real, and are still devouring the very living thoughts and ideals of the young. Many moons later the sacrilege of this reality still lurks and crawls beneath one's own human flesh as the divine answers to "God's Truth" lay, locked far away in the depths of Lucifer's Kingdom here on Earth!

August 20, 2016
(Narrative)

Author's Note: A Collaborated Poem with Anne-Lise Andresen and Liam McDaid.

The End

Seeing through these cold dead eyes now,
This world looks much different.

The scars of one's life entire,
Appear now for all to see.

What once meant everything,
Really means nothing now.

I still see and sense things mortal,
But the earthly world can't hear my words.

Lying on an ice-cold white slab this darkest night,
I see the pale-yellow moon's sad face in the sky.

With visions of people who've crossed over before,
I wonder when Charon shall finally appear?

Shall it be him who appears on this new horizon?
Or shall it be someone or something else?

The everyday mortal world moves on as before:
Regardless of one's wealth, poverty, fame, shame, infamy.

I guess now all the ancient mysteries of the universe,
Shall become obvious and answered in kind.

I wonder what shall be said to me and the reception?
Thumbs up or Thumbs down—I guess I shall find out.

The pale-yellow moon now appears brighter . . .
As if a special message cometh soon from a winged angel.

Hope this helps to answer my lingering questions . . .
As the dark void from the mortal world grows greater now.

I feel a gentle tug pulling me upward now from Earth's grasp,
Into the majestic arms of infinity and into God's eternal light!

June 12, 2016
(Lyric)

The Magic of Christmas Divine

Christmas cometh only once in each year,
Infusing us with moments so divine,
Giving us God's love in His cosmic rhyme,
As mankind basks now true in hope and cheer!
God brings us His Son's love precious and near,
In a mystic rhythm of iambic rhyme,
Whilst we seek Christ's holy embrace in kind,
Praising Him with our love true and sincere!

Christ's passion gives us His true love replete,
As we bathe in Heaven's light ever bright,
Sharing His endless love on Christmas night!
Christmas magic touches our souls complete,
As we celebrate Christ's love here on Earth,
Praising His transcendence from mortal birth!

December 16, 2016
(Petrarchan Sonnet)

The Master of Nuances

Supreme literary intensity
Rainer Maria Rilke—
Inspired as Orpheus sings
Predilection for Die Dinge
A mastery of true nuances
A thirst for poetic symbols
He sings now with Orpheus
And with angels in Heaven.

December 5, 2016
(Verse)

The Old Dark House

This tale of "The Old Dark House" is one that's replete with a devilish horrid sense of evil and macabre, and is worth being retold each year during the deep-dark hours of All Hallows' Eve before the chime of midnight when the thin veil separating the land of the living and the dead momentarily dissolves, bringing both worlds together until the break of dawn.

Beware of this house's mythical and ethereal presence in the shadow dreams of the innocent, and be forewarned to never conjure its image in your unconscious mind. If so conjured, The Old Dark House shall become an unending reality to the innocent and uninformed, and on All Hallows' Eve, the "Evil "Demons of Hell" shall come for your very soul! So Beware!

The Old Dark House is one that is bathed and cursed in absolute hellfire and damnation by Lucifer himself. It's one that creeps a chill and frozen reminder into the very frame of its nasty, putrid structure. It shall guarantee you the worst possible nightmares as your very soul cries out in agony and pleads in a resolute and an unrelenting fashion for mercy!

Your nightmares are, in turn, amplified and born into the very structure of this house with ivy creeping as you palpably sense the wretched ice-cold fingers of Hell opening the doors to the cavernous basement where shadows of goblins, ghosts, ghouls, vampires, and werewolves parade openly from their past lives.

Everyone who suffered the curse of the damned was captured here when they visited, and became prisoners to the darkness of a true evil, that was far away from the sacred light of Heaven and the divine spirit of mercy and the love of Almighty God.

Six generations of my family dwelled beneath the ghastly rafters of The Old Dark House where these demonic forces proliferated in a state of constant play, as their hot sparks burned the tongues of lost souls there who cried out in vain as their world was pulled into an unforgiving vortex of darkness, whilst their blood-curdling screams could be distinctly heard during the night on All Hallows' Eve. Ghostly images would appear out of nowhere supported by the frightening ferocity of Lucifer who is the true Dark Prince and the Ultimate Tempter of Mankind!

The horror I felt as a young boy trapped in this existence is truly unimaginable. The image of The Old Dark House still haunts my adult consciousness, even today, as I would shudder in the cold night-sweat of sleep to purge its eternal presence from my mind! Cruel pictures adorn this hell-hole hall of the imagination as a grim and unbelievable power underneath wields its vice-grip of hideous words, whispering in the coldest of ice without the living being able to breathe in any cloud of mercy and forgiveness, within an ancient language of evil and evil-doings that twist the shape of words to suit one's human fears and cold shivers!

I still don't understand the full measure of things being lost in this dark pit of Hell in The Old Dark House. It's a place that's devoid of human meaning and worth as shrunken heads are disembodied! I hold on to what remains of a past shame, hovering high in the air as unclean spirits of a crooked vision-circle wander aimlessly as a Blind Sheppard leads our lost souls to the depressing Dark Land of Nowhere and Nothingness!

Every October as the full moon rises high in the dark-sky evening, a local coven of witches sets a ritual fire to celebrate the advent of All Hallows' Eve. These witches know well the power and evil of The Old Dark House. Their burnt offerings and black magic spells echo hauntingly as Hell's own fury is unearthed, challenging all the things virtuous in mankind's existence and in God's world of hope, beauty, kindness, light, and love.

These evil images of black magic and witchcraft haunted my sleep entire. I couldn't sleep at all before dawn. I constantly sense now an awakening madness in my soul, as if it comes from the hidden graves yet to be uncovered. Images and horrible memories of The Old Dark

House push me now toward the opening of unknown tombs, where I can actually now smell Death's own Sulphur-burnt flesh!

Doors begin to rustle behind me as I hear loud footsteps of a pin echoing deep in my mind. The echo shatters any illusions I have of human sanity and forgiveness. I feel now the sheer horror and begin suffocating as the stale air is trapped in each breath I take!

I sit up now—immediately confused, looking directly at a lonely and empty Black Void that goes on and on and on—to infinity!

Cell doors in the house basement were always closed tight with rusted iron links bound by heavy chains. As a poor child alone in this house with other condemned children, there were nice rooms upstairs that were always barred and shut to us as we suffered in the filthy basement below—in Lucifer's Hell!

I recall now too, from my memory, a gallery of special portraits in The Old Dark House, which formed a ghastly mosaic of pure evil.

These portraits were of human disciples of Lucifer who had served him well through the ages. All of these images were grotesque and supremely evil when taken as a whole.

What did I learn? Evil is what Evil is! And Evil does what Evil does!

I'm free now from the eternal curse of The Old Dark House. I finally escaped this mansion of the macabre as a young man and eventually found my soul path back to Almighty God with the faith and help of of a priest who found me, and helped me to step into the divine holy light of God's unending love, forgiveness, and redemption!

Now, as a very old man, I tend to sleep and dream a lot, and at certain times, I dream rather deeply. Usually my dreams, thank goodness, are pleasant as I draw toward the end of my mortal existence here on this Earth.

Yet, despite all of the good things in my life now, during the build up to October 31st of each year, All Hallows' Eve always prays close to me, whilst it infests the deepest and darkest recesses of my mind. It's during this very peculiar time of each year, that I recall very clearly that the ground floor of "The Old Dark House" had these frigid-cold wind gusts that spoke so chillingly to one's very own soul. And, being young kids, as we were, we would all sneak upstairs in this evil house just to hear all of the voices of the "Ancient Demons of the Night," as they wailed and moaned at a fever pitch, crying out with their loudest shrieks into Old Hob's dark web with its infinite vortex of perfidy and unmitigated evil.

I must say—Old Hob always had a way to speak to all of us as kids in His House!

September 7, 2016
(Narrative)

Author's Note: A Collaborated Poem with Anne-Lise Andresen and Liam McDaid.

The Soul's Path

The soul's path is one . . .
whose way
is oft
clouded and confounded
by a
myriad of challenges
and
rank superficiality
which
pervade the
very nature
of mankind's
mortal coil.

This means . . .
each of us
should seek a
higher ethereal
understanding of life,
and
be not afraid
to meet and embrace
our fate and destiny
head-on
with
courage and faith
in
God's holy guidance
and
His most divine grace.

The soul's path . . .
is an
individual endeavor,
but one
worth taking
so each of us
can find
our final way back to God.

July 17, 2016
(Short-Lined Free Verse)

The Unknown

While standing on a razor-edge end of my mortal time,
I'm not sure of what lies beyond and what I shall find.

Death's dead, cold eyes stare directly at me, as I wait;
My spirit sweats and shakes as my blood turns frigid.

His skeleton face is scary, horrid, pallid, and macabre.
His apparition floats freely full of fear this frozen night.

A little girl, long dead, steps toward me from this oblivion,
Her face sad, streaming tears as she hands me a wilted rose.

This strange netherworld has that dull, cold pallor of death,
Just like the smell, sensation, and sadness of a charnel house.

The moon on this eve is one blood-red, insidious in intent;
Fixed high in the cold-night sky, it gives one no hope at all

The little girl, long dead, returns and holds my left hand gently:
She says, "It's not yet your time . . . this is still only a dream."
She adds, "The River Styx lies ahead—cold, dark, and deep."
She says, "There is yet time to change your life for the better."

As I started to awaken from this intense and revealing dream,
I could hear a faint voice whispering deep inside my psyche.
It related to me a certain message that I shall never ever forget.

Follow your heart and conscience, find the goodness in your life.
Listen to God and what the better angels of your nature tell you.

This shall keep you on that path of the devout in the eyes of God.
The image of God is reflected in Man himself as he seeks to fulfill
Always his divine destiny!

January 1, 2016
(Lyric)

This Fury-Fiery Moment of Hot Sensual Love

This fury-fiery moment of hot sensual love nourishes us now,
As we move from a caress to razor-close, then to lover-close,
Intertwined as one in a true tempestuous storm sparkling afire!

We share such a white-hot passion with a boundless fiery desire,
Blending us deeply in a fury-fiery emotion of love's true inspire;
Bringing us to this apex with lust as love and love in lust's hour!

This magic moment melds our passion into a true alchemy of love.
This prized-perfect passion purrs us now into satiated contentment,
As our hearts bask-bright in a fury-fiery moment of sensual desire!

May 19, 2016
(Rhyme)

Trickster Extraordinaire

Eulen und Meerkatzen
Till Eulenspiegel
Medieval Clown
Fooled them all.

Mirrored people's vanity
Physiognomonic
Judge of humanity
Wasn't hard at all.

June 8, 2016
(Double Dactyl)

Turbidity

Turbidity is
An artifice of
Being Human
One who is
So confused
So disordered
Or even one
With a Turbid
Imagination!

Being Turbid
Allows its Owner
To be or seem to be
In turmoil or
In degrees of
Real or Fake
Confusion
Making situations
Quite interesting!

This ascribes
A most likely
Pejorative symbol
When intentionally
Used to obfuscate
Human interactions
Or to be just
Plain difficult or
Uncooperative!

Possessing bouts of
Seeming Turbidity
For the Poet
Can also be
That perfect
Literary Conceit

To challenge
To mystify
All readers true!

Such notions of
Verisimilitude
Or better yet
Literary Truth
Methinks this would
Maketh the likes of
Keats, Eliot, Pound
Among other greats
Jumpeth all for joy!

January 14, 2016
(Accentual Meter)

Winds of a Frozen Wasteland

Winds blowing down the mountain silver-capped so cold,
Howling fiercely with a herculean ferocity rarely ever seen.

A cold snap cuts straight and deep now to one's very bones,
As one's body trembles tremulously teetering toward a fall.

Beloved baby-black crows roost inside their snug warm nest,
As a hail-driven breath spits its hardened bullets piercing now.

On this frozen wasteland of one's soul—a lone rooster crows,
Seeing, feeling soft sunlight rays stroking his proud chest pure.

He's puffed up now breathing boldly the brisk cold morning air;
Singing with wondrous conviction true of daylight's awakening.

This lone rooster knows the gifts of nature's frozen wasteland,
As the warm sun's ebullient eyes flash bright inside dark jewels.

A crystal fountain baptized with Heaven's own purest light,
Appears as the sun warms a land frozen nightly by the winds.

Dewdrops now form as those teardrops of a life growing anew,
With brightest beginnings for God's hallowed frozen wasteland!

May 1, 2016
(Couplet)

Author's Note: A Collaborated Poem with Liam McDaid.

Your Satin Silk Touch

My darling love—you are the true angel of my existence!
Your satin silk touch mirrors your beauty in the moonlight!

Your satin silk touch always sets my true emotions afire,
With your scent of perfume and luscious red lips blushing.

Your warm tears are precious dewdrops kissing softly true,
As heavenly-honey crystals shine bright signifying our love.

I look deeply into your eyes and realize our life is so special,
And that the magic of your divine beauty is beyond reproach.

Touching becomes my every precious breath now gasping hard,
For fresh air as I lay my eyes on you and feel your angelic aura.

As the very salt is awash in my ocean of dreams my dearest one,
My heart and soul are always one with you—as my true love rare.

What we share in this wondrous life are Heaven and Earth as one!
Your satin silk touch is the enchanted alchemy of our forever love!

June 1, 2016
(Couplet)

Author's Note: A Collaborated Poem with Liam McDaid.

CHAPTER FOUR

Selected Poetry
(2017)

Soulful Thoughts
Human Realism
Rays of Light
and
Shades of Darkness

A Bohemian Maze of True Evil

Once so loyal and always true the gargoyles watch everything now
During their stony slumbers with their careful one-eyed open view,
As evil red-eyed demons rain down upon us in their dark-sprit forms,
Whilst our unsuspecting mortal Earth is flush in an aura of confusion,
And a cloudy haze of unrepenting sin that symbolizes Lucifer's work.

Malefic shapes of Hellspawn emerge now from an unholy alliance
Where venom and hate merge in a dark chamber of "The Damned,"
All the while their scowling and fiendish stares pierce us deeply,
And unrelentingly as they beckon our inner spirits backwards with
Their tinge and terror of true malediction and feverish desire for all
Things uncanny and unclean that bespeak of macabre pure.

Reasons dance upon slivered tunes and silvern tongues of the demons,
As they grotesquely mount the battlements with their smiles of true evil.
The hideous grimace on their faces is a devilish upside-down nasty smile,
That can only be possessed by the cruelest of creatures who are charged
By Lucifer himself, as a perverse group of miscreants who welcome all
Misguided visitors who arrive at this unholy and forlorn earthly cavern,
To cross the River Lethe into a state of oblivion from whence they shall
Never return to see nor to bask again in the glory of God's eternal light!

A radiantly beautiful mermaid entices her unsuspecting victims into a
Menagerie she maintains as one of Lucifer's most favorite disciples.
After entertaining each victim, she turns her deadly Medusa-like gaze
On them whilst sending icy-cold shivers through their dying heartbeats,
As red-eyed demons anxiously await each victim's painful demise.
There can never be any mercy shown to a visitor who unexpectedly
Enters Lucifer's Kingdom of Eternal Darkness and Damnation!

In this continuous unending maze of debauchery there are also other
demons who are specifically assigned to entertain the deceptive and
Spawning lies of those unusual aliens who co-exist on mortal Earth
With human beings and are hidden in plain, open-sight among them all.
These aliens, devoid of all human emotion, who show up unexpectedly
Are there to capture a view of Hell's eternity under an occult dais circle.

Endlessly as death comes—there is an aura to the emotional immorality
As Centaurs, Sphinxes, and Harpies transform themselves into a kind of
Ghastly, ghoulish, and deliciously evil group of dancing shadow-shifters
In the realm of half-lived lives whose mendacity is the main dish now,
Served where the only menu choice is a one-line trick possessed by the
Spectre of Death, the mythic eternal Footman himself—who doubles as
A most trusted prophet of imprecation and fear for Lucifer!

Self-appointed Demon Guardians of this lost world seeking fulfillment
Of Lucifer's masochistic imperatives rule the roost where those shells
Of former human beings who were once viewed as members of mankind
Are, indeed, viewed in contempt now as depraved hosts of the once great
Human Race deprived of any hope, shorn of dignity—now soulless figures
At the beck and call of everything that's truly evil in Almighty God's Eyes.

Entering this final gruesome portrait of undying hellfire and unmitigated
Evil in this Bohemian Maze are monstrous apparitions from bygone times,
Who come alive and take real form as Minotaurs, Echidnas, and Chimaeras.
All are profoundly frightening creatures who are ready and willing to do the
Horrible bidding of Lucifer at the very flick of his finger—as such creatures,
With this unbridled power and force of nature find their true home in this
Evil mephitic maze!

This ancient covenant of evil and moral deception is symbolically cast
As a vicious coiled snake—who bespeaks an aura of poisonous venom,
And an odious degree of moral depravity that's beyond any type of a
Normal description where Black Phantoms reign and freely haunt the
Consciousness of all mankind, as it hopelessly trembles ignorantly fretful,
Whilst all the while being truly unaware of the undeniable and unlimited
power of Almighty God in this instance!

To those who harbor their fears of the darkness, the unknown, and the
Evil intentions and machinations of Lucifer and his minions, they should
Understand that Almighty God's authority and power are omniscient, and
That His divine and radiant heavenly light shall forever crush the horrid
Impulse of darkness to fight and resist, and shall conquer creatures and all
Things presenting themselves as truly evil, uncanny, and unclean! Amen!

Deus miseratur! Deus tecum!

December 23, 2017
(Narrative)

Author's Note: A Collaborated Poem with Donna Loughman and Liam McDaid.

A Parable of Love's Spell

We danced and kissed passionately whilst feeling that frenzied,
flushed-rush of two people together now as one under love's spell.

Love's that mystical, magical emotion captivating every aspect
of our senses as we succumb to its aura of delicious enchantment!

Love's power is a divine omnipotence which touches us tender
now as we walk this night watching the Moon smile back at us.

Love's that moment when two people's eyes search and discover
each other and their hearts know it's much more than mere chance.

Try fate, try destiny, but know too that this special emotion is oft
beyond the pale of any ready explanation of the mere commonplace.

Love can be palpable, spiritual, promising, hopeful, bashful, and
even disappointing—but full of surprise and true wonderment too!

We savor our embrace now as two lovers mesmerized in this moment,
whilst we fall deeply under love's spell as the Moon smiles back at us!

March 28, 2017
(Couplet)

A Psychedelic Whistle Plays a Rhythm into the Darkness

Entering the dark side of a moonbeam on this evil lens of life,
A gruesome old man recreates a murder time and time again,
As the cold and lonely howling bitterness of the night escapes.
The psychic contrasts go on in a surreal smoke-filled eternity.
This is not lost to the all-seeing consciousness of the cosmos.

Moaning a malefic agony of selfish needs devours all that is good,
Whilst in black-leather gloves are the bleached deadly-white bones,
Filling a heart expelled with a legion of grieving spirits, sad and lost.
A maze doth open now as Dark Demons appear with their foul flesh,
And scraps of empty emotions that make them all so deliciously evil.

Inside ashes intoxicated with the Hallowed Eve's evil kiss bring now,
To all, a Gorgon-like gift cursed and raised in Lucifer's own Hellfire.
It leaves them to their executioners who wash their own hands clean!
Cain, within life's garden dwells as a zombie—a grief-stricken figure,
As a psychedelic whistle plays a rhythm into the darkness of the cosmos.

A deep darkness seduces as a fire burns black-ebony removing the flesh.
Ice-cold tears of anxiety fall, shouting loudly that nobody sees nor hears,
The jealous whimpering of jackals needing love with no way to find it.
There remains emotionless beings who kill passion with a crocodile's bite.
Fear not the tempting by Lucifer as long as the silver crucifix adorns thee!

Fireflies born in a hellish fury cast in anger the past sins of those doomed,
Yet they can be "Bearers of an Ancient Light" for things good and noble,
If they can pass through the ugly veil of evil and darkness into God's light.
When the smoke blows away pride, there's no remorse, only danger ahead!
The silence is deafening to those who possess such holy-pure mortal blood!

Understanding of reality loses its meaning in this evil realm of darkness,
As an agonizing pain is cleared in an eclipse found under "Hate's Trigger."
Under a deep crater, twilight ghosts rise as "Shadow Beggars of Despair,"
Whilst feeling an unholy torment in nerve fibers of a past-life enchantment.
Only Lucifer knows this truth as he collects new souls for eternal damnation!

Uncanny conversations are secret and bloody-confused in Hell's own pit.
Rising from the ashes unhappy beasts mark the ground with sharp claws,
As disoriented tongues of envy are struck down by lightning bolts blinded.
Lucifer knows the omnipotence of the psychedelic whistle as it plays its
Rhythm bewitching all lost souls as they enter the darkness of the cosmos!

May 5, 2017
(Narrative)

Author's Note: A Collaborated Poem with Anne-Lise Andresen and Liam McDaid.

A tiny little star lights the way

A long time ago it was told
That an angel appeared and
Spoke about a future time,
Where darkness shall come
No light can ever be seen,
And pain, tears, fears, sorrow
Shall befall all of mankind,
As the world descends into agony.

At the darkest time of that darkest year
A tiny little star shall appear in the sky,
And can only be seen by some people
Who are awake and full of awareness,
That this tiny little star is the one,
The "Chosen One" everyone should follow
Because it shall light up the way, the path
To the radiant heavenly light on this night
That shall save our world forever,
And this darkness shall disappear on Earth!

This is the time when Christ is coming,
At Christmas Time—and all shall be blessed!

Merry Christmas to all of you and remember
To look out for this tiny little star!

December 16, 2017
(Free Verse)

Author's Note: A Collaborated Poem with Ingrid Krukenberg-Bateman.

Angel in the Clouds

Sometimes you look up to the sky
And maybe you can find
In a large bank of clouds
The face and figure of an angel with wings
Who's looking down on you.

It may be someone
You knew from the past
Who went to Heaven a long time ago.

And maybe that angel appears here now for you
Just to say "Hello"
And to make this moment very special.

You feel an enchantment in your heart
And sense a soft-tingling on your cheek...

As if, this angel placed a kiss there
With an encouraging touch on your shoulder
Giving you a wondrously warm feeling inside.

With this magical moment as you're touched
By this angel...

You realize this angel loves you very much
And just came by to look after you
And to send you a joyous blessing
Right from Heaven—personally to you!

Amen.

May 17, 2017
(Free Verse)

Author's Note: A Collaborated Poem
with Ingrid Krukenberg-Bateman.

Death and Forlorn Time in the Shadows of True Evil

Death and Time hold onto the eerie and most frightening shadows,
Whilst pervading deeply within that infernal region where the dark,
Evil and uncanny mists occlude the terrifying presence of a great,
Dark Doomsday cult of vicious and horrifying beasts that are now
Perpetuated from a putrid hellspawn by Lucifer's own command!

Corrupted with the presence of sacrilegious beasts of true violence
Who hate all aspects of mankind with their real spirit of maleficence,
And wince not whilst decapitating the heads of those who disagree
With them, and creating a mindless havoc of unparalleled tragedy
That's become an expected, sad occurrence of mankind writ large!

Brandishing a razor-sharp, coal-black blade is their evil incarnation,
Of a time, that's totally indicative of their chaotic rampage of bloody
Burning attacks as battlegrounds are drawn into an eternal darkness,
From whence there may be no return since there's a dark, blood-red
Poison from the dark afterlife in which every drop of blood is toxic!

Every drop of this spilt, blood-red poison has a deadly-demonic aroma,
That produces nasty swarms of ravenous locusts to torment all innocent
Victims caught between the machinations of Almighty God and Lucifer.
In this reality, these evil spirits cast their malevolent spells without any
Scruple as they wish for mankind's swift destruction by Lucifer himself!

November 24, 2017
(Quintain)

Author's Note: A Collaborated Poem with Liam McDaid.

Death Comes

All arguments and denials were fruitless;
The deceased fell prey to the Master Thief.

The "One" whose icy-cold touch is . . .
Just Too Cold to Resist! . . . They Say!

No worries though . . . They Say:
"He looks so life-like!"
"He looks like he's sleeping!"
"They do wonders with embalming fluid, don't they!"
"Who wants to live forever anyway?"

The deceased's body epitomizes all four.
I'm sure the deceased appreciated them all . . .
As if the dead could talk and nod in agreement.

Alas! The body's texture is . . . Cold-Rock-Hard.
No surprises here!

The thoughts of what might've been,
Are now . . .
What could've been and what should've been!

"I guess we'll never really know." . . . They Say.
"I wonder what he would say?" . . . They Say.
"But the dead don't talk." . . . I Say.

That icy-cold touch of this Master Thief . . .
It was just too cold to resist!

The sweet 'n stale odors now so deep in the air,
Overwhelm everyone packed in the funeral parlor.

The loved ones, friends, and visitors all walk
Outside into the very frigidly-cold night air.

An anxious pale-yellow full moon now awaits us all . . .
It looms now larger-than-life across the cold-night sky.
It looks down at all of us . . . so sad and so forlorn.

All of us seemed to be momentarily spellbound by this
Mournful visage of the full moon on this very sad night.

Perhaps, this was an omen of some sort—I thought.
But what to do? What can anyone do?
A life is over . . . A person is dead and gone now.

I walked away now from the others in our group as I was
Preparing to leave very soon.

I needed to take some time, some moments, to collect my
Thoughts and memories of my dear, deceased friend who
Was lying now all alone only steps away inside of the
Confines of the dimly-lit chamber of the mortuary nearby.

As I slowly walked away, very deep in thought, it was only
A few minutes later, and then . . . I suddenly stopped . . .

Just when, I started to hear the faint echo of a deep-raspy voice
That sounded out some very strange words in the cold-night air.

These faint words had a definite imperative resonance,
Sounding almost like inexplicable, ethereous vibrations.

"You know the Myth, they say, is true my sad friend."
"Yes, my icy-cold touch is just too cold to resist!"
"But don't worry though . . . you won't feel a thing!"

The faint echo of this deep-raspy voice sounded once more . . .
"No worries though . . . it's not yet your time!"

The very last sound I heard before quickly leaving the area was
An eerie rattle of frozen-ice droplets colliding intensely in the air,
Whilst making a high-pitched crystalline-like type of sound.
It was all very spooky for sure, I thought to myself . . .

These frozen-ice droplets reflected the macabre image of a faint,
Blackish-grey frozen hand, arrayed with jaggedly-long fingernails!

I then, momentarily gasped and paused—then gasped again,
Whilst transfixed in a moment of true fear and mesmerization!

It was like my mind, my very being was in a catatonic state,
A mental stupor of sorts . . . and then, I snapped out of it!

Yes, ah . . . I thought, ah . . . Oh No! . . . Oh God! . . . It's Him!
It's Death Himself!

He's the "One" whose icy-cold touch is . . . Just Too Cold to Resist!

Death Comes!
May God Help Us All!

Requiescat In Pace.

August 3, 2017
(Lyric)

Deep in Our Hearts

Deep in our hearts there's a never-ending desire,
That seeks to fill our souls now so precious pure.

This desire brings our fiery passions to conspire,
As our emotions and heartbeats merge now as one.

Our love shines always ever-bright in Heaven's light,
As God's angels sing paeans to our passions' delight.

The true love we mortals find is by God's very design,
As we seek its meaning in the deep pool of our souls.

The enchanted beauty of this true love we have as two,
Brings our hearts to the moment when they beat as one.

This true love transcends the mortal limits of this Earth,
Whilst gently coaxing our souls to their heavenly destiny.

Deep in our hearts, our souls make this final sacred journey,
As angels accompany us into Almighty God's eternal light.

August 1, 2017
(Couplet)

Demagoguery

Scourge of weakest minds—
Always seeking more of them!
Infectious venom...
Pervasive and destructive...
Resist this stupidity!

August 29, 2017
(Tanka)

Dreams Divine

Dreams are deepest images formed in one's mind,
 Showing us events past, present, and future in kind.
Subtle faces be they that reflect in the soul's mirror,
Whilst pleading in hints the reason why—not clearer.
God gives us dreams of the divine to spark a fire,
And sustains us in our imperfect trials to so inspire.
God speaks to us in His spirit-dream code of passion,
Whilst Angels on high sing paeans to His divine action.
Dreams show us a mystic way to His love and light,
On trails of cosmic dust bathed, bold-bright at night!
God wants us poets to set these dreams now to rhyme,
So we can all dream deeply of His true love in kind!
Dreams harken enchantment beyond our every day,
As we mortals seek God's holy spirit in every way!

January 1, 2017
(Canzone)

Erkenntnis

Stillness
A thought
Knowledge
Peace

June 22, 2017
(Quatrain)

Author's Note: This special Quatrain poem was authored by Ingrid Krukenberg-Bateman.

Fall of Man

Adam and Eve
John Milton
Don't eat that fruit
Thought they could.

Tree of Knowledge
Insubordination
Downfall occurs...
"Evil, be thou my good."

August 13, 2017
(Double Dactyl)

Fires of Noise

These fearful fires rage inside and across
your soul when the twilight comes for you.

They begin by cleverly enticing your imagination set
deeply in your mind as you sleep soundly at night,

and all the while that big elephant in your room
sees everything that's going on as you sleep, and

being wise, he knows these fires greet everyone
they run into as they seek Death himself at night.

And now, as sleep comes amid all this noise
your eyelids are very heavy and start to close,

and you feel as though you just can't stay awake
anymore as sleep's soothing presence fills your body.

Beware, this is when the dead appear out of nowhere
and seek, by surprise, to take you with them at once,

and when the dead do appear and start to parade about,
give them a Loud Hoot and your best ever stone-cold look,

but never let them kiss your face and lips with their cold,
puffy-purple lips and their straight, glued-down hair—

for the dead and their ethereal spirits always love playing
little games in tricking and spoofing the living, why not?

And besides, the dead already know that "We the Living"
shall one day face the "Fires of Noise" when we die.

And so, Be Courageous! It looks like we all have something to look forward to when our earthly presence ends.

And, Don't Ever Forget! Give Death that Loud Hoot! He just might have a real sense of humor after all!

October 14, 2017
(Lyric)

For Our Love So True

For our love so true lasts now forever
For I know now I shall leave you never,
Here on Earth 'n later in Heaven's light,
Whilst God is with us on this cosmic night,
Angels sing to us with all due pleasure.

Our passions are beyond mortal measure,
As we walk tonight, hands held together,
We know our emotions feel now so right
For our love so true.

God's divine love is our special treasure,
Our souls, are bound now together ever,
We ascend now with the angels in flight,
We bask in God's holy blessings tonight.
With our souls now one, no one can sever
For our love so true.

November 18, 2017
(Rondeau)

Irish Nectar of the Sun Goddess

This mystical aura of golden radiant sunbeams so sublime,
With a warm mead laying lovely below its enchanted neck,
Is breathless releasing gasps of white-hot fire breaths now,
All spiritual within one and a thousand sighs, it whistles too.

Brightly your radiance shines through the deep blue oceans,
Where rainbows are misted with shades inside a desire born,
With curtains falling—revealing a beauty spot held precious,
Whilst in your heart glows warmly a true love pure precious.

A royal crown bestows upon thine mantel of soft and purest silk,
Now spangled as dewdrops glisten brightest on mirrored slippers,
As a divine swan upon one wave began dancing on joyous ripples,
An old Irish jig played on in this moment dancing you and I, as two.

The Merry Old Leprechaun looked on with his wee-soft eye twinkle
As the Sun Goddess giveth her divine breath to this sacred harvest;
Now to bear the sweetest of fruit with the warmest rays of gentleness,
So all may share in this grandest garden moment of holy eternal glory.

We shall all now, forever and ever, prosper in this heavenly abundance,
Whilst we shed our mortal, wee-curious light into this eternal paradise,
As you and me, and the Merry Old Leprechaun share a passion so true,
We drink so gladly the sweet and stout Irish Nectar of the Sun Goddess!

January 17, 2017
(Quatrain)

Author's Note: A Collaborated Poem with Liam McDaid.

It's Your Time

A mysterious voice in my deep sleep said . . .
"It's your time."

This was repeated several times,
Yet, as more of a faint whisper.

What an unusual way to be greeted—I thought.
I just hoped to have a night of sound sleep.

What appears now deep within my psyche
Are catacumbal visions, illusions, and truths.

Is someone telling me something?
Are these images part of my life-run?

I realize now much more:
They are a mystic kaleidoscope of human experiences.

The mysterious voice returns again declaring . . .
"It's your time now!"

A thick mist appears, blinding me.
A solar eclipse occurs, captivating me.

The brightest light of all appears out of nowhere.
My senses run wild, no mortal proportion exists.

This infinity of the deep-black-dark cosmos
Gives way now to His divine, majestic light.

The solar-eclipsed moon is now long gone . . .
An ethereal fragrance and happiness pervade.

A lovely and radiant angel appears before me,
Ah . . . she's the source of this mysterious voice!

Elysian perfection complete.
A beautiful, mystical Unicorn smiles at me.

There's no more anger, fear, sadness, and suffering . . .
Only the divine love, hope, and peace of Almighty God.

March 4, 2017
(Lyric)

Just a tree

He is standing there
Beside the road like all others in one line
It looks all the same
When people pass by
Just a tree—like all others?
 Or not?

This tree leans, and is not straight up
It looks like he leans away from the road
To make room for everybody passing by
At the same time protecting everybody
From wind, rain, snow
Whilst
Spending its shadow and shade on hot summer days.

The tree is there and doing the job
Like all others
But only here is the place
To do it in perfect harmony
With everything around him.

So, it is "just a tree" like all others
Doing the perfect job at the right place
Like it is meant to be
In God's divine creation.

But maybe this tree is the one
Who is very much connected
With Mother Nature and God's Plan of Creation.

And so, he knows on a very deep level
That only in alliance with God's Plan
Everything here is in its place
At the right time
For the right purpose
In God's Plan for Mother Nature.

So this tree may not be at all
"just a tree" standing beside the road
In the countryside.

But there are a lot of "just trees"
In God's Plan for Mother Nature
On this, our planet Earth
Fulfilling their sacred part
In God's Holy and Divine Plan of Creation.
They "just" do it!
March 19, 2017
(Didactic)

Author's Note: A Collaborated Poem
with Ingrid Krukenberg-Bateman.

My Supreme Goddess Thou Art

I can see Heaven clearly whilst gazing deeply into your eyes now,
Where the sweet caramel melts deliciously into heartbeats so pure.

The radiant light of our eternal love dwells deep within our hearts,
As our souls are captivated by God's aura of divine enchantment.

A nirvana fills our destiny as passionate lovers kissing softly so,
Mesmerized by the enraptured emotions we forever share as one.

A wild wondrous wallflower you are shining now ever-brightly,
As that angelic spirit in mortal presence on Earth by God's hand.

Dearest one, I say truly now my supreme goddess thou art,
As we hold one another in an ardent embrace by God's grace.

The fiery passion of our forever love is a pure beam of silken starlight,
Which bathes the darkest depths of the cosmos in a heavenly radiance.

What more can two people hope for in this world of finite limitations?
Our shared love and rich emotions form the destiny we seek with God.

April 29, 2017
(Couplet)

Author's Note: A Collaborated Poem with Liam McDaid.

My wish for you

Whenever I see you in the midst
of the struggle of life
dealing everyday
with issues, problems, and affairs;
I wish you could see yourself
the way God would see you:
The bright light in the middle
of Earth's life struggle—
bright, shining, and brave.

My wish for you would be
you could feel one time
the love that God has for you:
His love for you as a bright and brave soul,
that God sparkle he created
in the best of all moments of creation;
the perfect time to bring a soul into life
to fulfill its mission here on Earth;
to bring love and light into brightness there.

April 22, 2017
(Free Verse)

Author's Note: A Collaborated Poem
with Ingrid Krukenberg-Bateman.

Narcissism

It's all about Me!
This shall always be my wish—
A fool's vanity . . .
Thinking of only me . . . me!
I'm so wondrously perfect!

September 16, 2017
(Tanka)

Now is Our Moment of Forever Love

Now is our moment of forever love,
Whilst we embrace with deepest emotion.
God's blessed our love high in Heaven above.

Forever love is God's cosmic potion;
We bask as one in His heavenly light,
Whilst we embrace with deepest emotion.

Our passion and desire feel now so right,
As we kiss in the most tender of bliss.
We bask as one in His heavenly light.

Enchantment comes from our deepest kiss,
Whilst we bathe in the light by God's desire,
As we kiss in the most tender of bliss.

Our passions are one by divine inspire.
God's holy blessings caress our souls true,
Whilst we bathe in the light by God's desire.

Love is eternal in God's cosmic view;
God's holy blessings caress our souls true.
Now is our moment of forever love;
God's blessed our love high in Heaven above.

April 20, 2017
(Terzanelle)

Poetry and the Soul

The soul hungers now for all true metaphors replete,
With real nuances and a spirit of true love complete.

Poetry seeks always that higher human intent,
As the soul cries out that it shall never repent!

The soul thrives always for a cosmic reflection,
Beyond human thoughts by a divine direction.

Soulful poetic images seek angelic attention,
 As man's problems exceed earthly redemption.

Poetry is a medium for true ethereal reflection,
That mirrors the mortal coil for divine attention.

The past, present, and future sleep deep within the soul,
And poetry's a catalyst to awaken us to our divine role!

November 25, 2017
(Couplet)

Racism

Mankind's ugly shame—
False superiority!
Ignorance supreme . . .
Evil, wrong, and destructive . . .
We must stop this prejudice!

December 3, 2017
(Tanka)

Radio Music

I sense this music has a soulful touch;
A special purpose that only lyrics
Possess to enchant my inner being.
I oft pass up soft, soothing sleep late night
To marvel at the magic of some songs;
Tunes that draw me into deep moments of
Raw emotions that tease and test the kind
Of person—I am or wish I could be!
What else could one expect from the Cosmos
Laden with such lyrics, music, and God?

October 2, 2017
(Blank Verse)

The Butterfly and the Caterpillar

"This is the end," said the caterpillar. "
This is the beginning," said the butterfly.

The butterfly is fulfilling its goal by leading
the life of a butterfly.

Why should he live like a caterpillar, only so
the caterpillars can be less afraid?

Since the butterfly knows the life of a caterpillar,
he can help the caterpillars to be less afraid when
 they live the life of a butterfly.

Who knows the sweetness of nectar,
 shall never want to eat leaves again.

And how about you?
The rare moments you feel like a butterfly.
And there are days you feel like a caterpillar.
But isn't it you who is exactly that butterfly,
who is helping the caterpillar to be less afraid?

July 10, 2017
(Free Verse)

Author's Note: A Collaborated Poem with
Ingrid Krukenberg-Bateman.

The Curve of Time

This curve is the truest magic of space and time,
With one finite, the other infinite but not in kind.

Einstein's vision gave us this new fourth dimension,
Inspiring mankind's depth of a true infinite intention.

The infinite extension of this mystical curve of time,
Gives our poets much to ponder and to set in rhyme.

Piercing the veil of time travel exceeds finite space,
Whilst allowing man his place in this noblest grace.

Man's primitive view of our Earth as being only flat,
Gave way now to an infinite future view to arrive at.

This infinite future view bespeaks a constancy of motion,
Descriptive of time, people, events, passion, and emotion.

Let us all dream of the enchantment of this curve of time;
For this shall give our poets the chance to set all in rhyme!

July 22, 2017
(Couplet)

The dark blue night of sorrow

The dark blue night of sorrow
well-known to everybody on the path.
Only one little light seen
in the midst of darkness
until a newborn soul
will awaken into the rays
of the rising sun
on the new day still to come.

August 30, 2017
(Verse)

Author's Note: A Collaborated Poem
with Ingrid Krukenberg-Bateman.

The Demon's Poet

Wander the Earth
Mikhail Lermontov
Immortality his burden
Abandoned and alone.

The Demon's embrace
Excommunication
His fatal kiss
Tortured to the bone.

April 21, 2017
(Double Dactyl)

The Devil's Black Eyes

The Devil's black eyes burn red-hot on this night,
Their piercing stare cuts our souls now dark and deep;
His demons spread evil lies, fury and fright,
On innocents who lie-down now in sound sleep;
The Devil worships now his Unholy might,
As souls lost to God multiply in his keep!
We pray to God for his Holy redemption,
As Angels escort our souls on Ascension!

December 2, 2017
(Ottava Rima)

The Full Moon Makes Faces Tonight

Gazing out my picture window on this darkest of night,
The full moon shone true now with its brightest of light.

I spied its eldritch contours and its dark areas whole,
As this lucent orb made faces at me from pole to pole.

Methinks these faces were for this special moment now,
A teasing fantasy-illusion for me to wonder why and how?

This full moon had two eyes stone-set from East to West,
Giving me a very comical-look whilst winking all the best!

This lunar illusion silently sang a sly aria full of devilry,
As it mesmerized my senses replete with all due revelry.

As I studied this comedic-faced orb far from our Earth,
I felt its true spiritual intent was one for a cosmic rebirth.

The full moon made its curious faces on this darkest night,
Whilst I smiled big as I basked and bathed in its lunar light!

June 14, 2017
(Couplet)

The Hole Deep in One's Own Heart

In moments of greatest loss, sadness and sorrow,
A hole forms so deep within one's own heart;
There it shall remain so for each 'n every morrow,
Until life's end when comes our heavenly depart!

My dearest, such times of tribulation define us pure,
For we know not all the twists and turns of this life;
We must keep our faith ever true, never it to abjure,
Whilst seeking angelic guidance from this human strife!

As we recommit our true faith in God's blessings above,
We seek solace in His love that only our souls may find;
With this our passions 'n emotions form the deepest love,
Giving us His blessing as our souls return His love in kind!

God's love brings our eternal souls into His heavenly space,
And makes our injured hearts whole in His divine embrace!

November 11, 2017
(Shakespearean Sonnet)

The Holy Dust of Creation's Seed Sown

Born from this ancient dust of creation's seed sown now so true,
Whilst sparkling inside a mystical divine light on this dark night,
I'm nourished from the living waters—the oceans deep and blue.

Majestic wings rise high in the waves basking in Heaven's light,
Crowning the blest halo golden ring around this angel very dear,
Whilst I kiss warmly the salt of the deep oceans stirring at night.

Spiced now in a seabed, a rainbow's gem shines pure so clear,
That a traveler in this radiant world of delight knows real love
Is what we all seek as sparkling diamonds now appear so near.

Where the rivers flow down a mountain's verdant slope because
There, in the highs and lows of these rivers, tears soak the Earth,
Falling and rising from the dust, ashes are memories of what was.

I have abounding faith in this life's bond as Nature begins her rebirth,
Eclipsed by a peerless beauty inside, wild passions grown now strong.
A liquid sphere appears in our mortal lives reaching its point of girth.

In the cerulean oceans mystic gulls cry deep echoes bringing us along.
We find peace kneeling as a psychic mantel covers our thoughts pure,
As that special circle of brilliance radiates within life's treat so strong.

By God's hand the ancient dust of creation's seed is with us to assure,
Mankind's perpetuity on Earth as part of His most holy divine vision.
Only God knows mankind's destiny rests in His divine hands for sure.

The ancient dust of creation's seed is part of God's omnipotent precision,
For He's the one who shall guide us all heavenward by His final decision.

June 10, 2017
(Terza Rima)

Author's Note: A Collaborated Poem with Michael Clarke and Liam McDaid.

The light of a candle

The light of a candle
Can light up
The dark corners of a room
The darkness of a heart
The dark night of a soul.
The simple light of a small candle
Reminds us
In its pureness
Of the Flame of Eternity
As the savior from all darkness on Earth.

August 29, 2017
(Verse)

Author's Note: A Collaborated Poem
with Ingrid Krukenberg-Bateman.

The Oneness of All

Depths of wisdom
Hermann Hesse
Spirituality's quest
Soul's transformation.

Enlightenment assured
Corporealization
The oneness of all
Siddhartha's realization.

June 18, 2017
(Double Dactyl)

The Pied Piper from New York City

Dare his name be said?
I say, of course, Yes!

The Pied Piper, himself, is the man, the myth, the legend.
And they, the so-called incurious lot of the *hoi polloi* in
American society, are the ones who accept the:
bluster,
ignorance,
lies,
rudeness,
and rank buffoonery of this Pied Piper.

They are the ones who blindly choose to follow around this
Abject Charlatan and Bunco Artist without any question or
Thought or any civilized degree of true human concern, whilst
HE "pipes" loudly and rudely with an endless supply of hot air,
And with all due trickery and ferocity, his bombastic true-lies,
And his merry tunes of deceit, stupidity, and just pure-plain
"Baloney" for those seeking the simplest of answers to the
Significant questions and real problems of the day in our
Society and in the greater world, that cry out for and demand
Intelligent thought, discussion, and consideration of realistic
Solutions that directly affect people's lives and their well-being,
And the essential stability of our country and of our allies in
This very complicated world of the twenty-first century.

Ah . . . yes, I wish this were only a dream in the deep-dark center
Of the subjunctive mood of my grammar, but not of my heart, and
My psyche—for it's truly and unfortunately much more than this,
And it's much more than one could ever imagine or ever venture
To say that this "Alternative Universe of the Pied Piper" is one
That's a genuine "Nightmare," a panoply, replete with:
a few truths,
so many more half-truths,
untruths,
insults,

and endless deceptions!
And even incompetence to boot!

But look at this way, it's just more of the old fantasies just like
The people in the past who received a fake degree from his sham,
Real Estate program at good old "TU" in the Big Apple!

Ah . . . yes, The Pied Piper is one who always takes great pride in the
Barnum-Fields' popular *bon mot*: "Never give suckers an even break!"
He takes this zinger to heart as part of his dubious *modus operandi*,
Whilst joyously snickering, and laughing behind the backs of those
Who are gullible enough and have the proclivity to believe anything
They hear him say— just as long as, "it sounds simple and good!"
When I unfortunately hear things like this, I roll my eyes and think . . .
"Simple is as simple does, and stupid is as stupid does!"

Ah . . . yes, these children of misfortune and those full of anger and
Prejudice—including assorted Hatemongers and merry groups of
White Supremacists, Neo-Nazis, Ku Klux Klan, and those so-called
Righteous Apostles of the Alt-Right who now arrogantly march and
Strut their ridiculous stuff in a true lock-step fashion to the beguiling
And mesmerizing shrill voice of this supposed modern-day hero!
This well-known, thin-skinned man with his pair of clay-feet and an
Overblown Reality TV persona is Our New York Flim-Flam Man!

All this, is clearly on display when the Pied Piper reprises his most
Famous on-the-air gig in the Reality TV World as—The POTUS!
Horribile Dictu! Horribile Dictu! Oh yes, horrible to be told! And
Horrible it is to be told for sure! This is all I can say in response to
This troubling reality for America and for the greater world.
Let us all now pray! Let us all now pray!

These poor people have no idea at all that they are being played
As fools, suckers, and willing and unwilling victims, duped by
The Pied Piper's "Big Lie" mantra in the storied tradition of the
Twentieth Century by the clever propaganda machinations, that
Are truly reminiscent of past evil luminaries such as: Hitler, Hess,
Goebbels, Goering, Mussolini; and don't forget the likes also of

Lenin, Stalin, Molotov, Beria, Brezhnev, Andropov, and so on,
All the way today to the likes of Putin, Assad, Duterte, and Maduro.
Just to name a few!

Say it ain't true ... Say it's not possible ... But it sadly is!
What a motley gallery of rogues and apostles of deception,
And out and out liars and frauds to be associated with!

All the while the Pied Piper decries and bemoans the supposed
"Fake News," and the cherished, historical role of the Free Press in
America, as protected, along with the rights of Freedom of Speech,
Religious Worship, and Peaceful Assembly as all are enshrined in the
First Amendment of the Constitution of the United States of America.

All the Pied Piper's crying and bemoaning are quite telling and nasty
For someone who sang his paeans and voiced his fulsome panegyric
In support of "WikiLeaks," which took great pride in their role as a
Conduit for Russian propaganda and fake news, with the obvious goals
Of spreading lies and fomenting trouble in the hope of disrupting the
U.S. Presidential Election and the general electoral process in 2016.

The Pied Piper's despicable actions in this regard tear at the most sacred
Institutional fabric and foundation of our nation's grand Union, whilst
Threatening the very heart and soul of our precious democracy, and the

Accepted tenets of:
Good governance,
Tolerance,
Fairness,
Good judgment,
Moral leadership, and
Expected professional conduct.

In this instance,
His actions and those of his henchmen
Have been and truly are shameful!

The Pied Piper also chooses, at times, to defame and shame those who
Would dare to disagree with him in both the public forum and in private.
In exacting his revenge, one of the Pied Piper's favorite ploys is to wrap
Himself in the patriotic aura of the great American Flag, the famous
"Stars and Stripes," which is most sacred to our American history.
This is quite rich for a man who has never served in the military, and
For one who is certainly not a veteran! He lambasts his opponents in
This fashion by calling them both "Unpatriotic" and "Un-American."

This is quite despicable and very inappropriate for someone holding the
"Highest Office in Our Land." The Pied Piper hides his treachery by
Wrapping himself in the glory of the "Stars and Stripes." Talk about
True shame! He should look in the mirror!

The "Forgotten Man" who represents those who fell prey to the inflated
Promises and mindless propaganda of The Pied Piper, should not at all
Be surprised later when they suddenly discover—they've been "had,"
That is,
Sadly, forgotten by their Pied Piper,
Replete with his famous Trademark Attributes:
Thin-skinned,
Clay-feet,
Big-mouth,
Nasty-disposition,
Twitter-thumbs, and
A shrill-accusatory voice.

The Pied Piper, as a new-style politician, is also mired in some other
key controversies with his family that are worth mentioning.

Since coming to Washington, DC and ascending to the White House
on January 20, 2017:

The Pied Piper and his family have viewed the nation's capital and
the people's house as,

"Luscious Juicy Plums—Ripe for the Picking!"

And, the Pied Piper's various plans and actions since his ascension to the presidency are certainly not done necessarily in favor of the American people—if at all!

Characteristically, he enjoys playing to people's "Fears," rather than taking the higher road that any good leader would do, by appealing to the "Better Angels of Their Nature." For sure, an Abraham Lincoln, he's not, nor shall he ever be!

Indeed, the Pied Piper has done some very naughty things, among others, already to his credit and ignominy:

His poorly conceived and implemented Muslim travel ban.

Playing "Chicken" with the U.S. Congress on the state and quality of American healthcare.

Using the White House as his own personal ATM machine.

Becoming the "Patron Saint of Nepotism" with the inclusion of select family members on his staff. (What's wrong with a little nepotism, eh?)

Engulfed in multiple business conflicts of interest, both foreign and domestic.

Revelations of potential collusion with Russia and Russian surrogates to interfere with the 2016 presidential election.

Blatant violations of the Emoluments Clause of the U.S. Constitution.

And he's just now quashed executive branch protection of the DACA Dreamer Immigrant Program.

All these very naughty things are tragic, thoughtless, sad, stupid, and grossly reprehensible!

With all this, I now rest my case!

Yet, I would like to encourage everyone to reflect for a critical moment on "The Fragile Nature of Democracy."

"Democracy," itself, has been viewed and likened to: "That Most Precious Fabergé Egg."

We all must devoutly cherish this most precious *Fabergé Egg* called "Democracy."

And protect it always from the unscrupulous actions of the Pied Pipers of the World!

For us to do otherwise would be absolutely unforgivable!
Need I say more?
Yes, I must.

Our vaunted "Pied Piper" is historically most deserving of, at least, one more appropriate title that fits him to the tee, and is another perfect moniker for him:

"The Fabricator Extraordinaire." By acronym, simply: "TFE"....

God Bless Always and Save the United States of America!

In God We Trust!

But with "Our Pied Piper," "Our TFE," trust is not, and never will be an option! And, what about being honest and telling the truth for a change?

Johann Wolfgang von Goethe once noted: *Die Weisheit ist nur in der Wahrheit.* That is, "Wisdom lies only in truth."

And, "Our Pied Piper" is woefully deficient and inadequate in being able to tell the truth. And, honesty? Forget about it! It's not in his vocabulary nor is it in his DNA! A *non sequitur* at best!

May God Bless the USA!

May democracy continue to reign supreme always!

In God We Trust, and in the Pied Piper . . . Never!

Amen. Amen.

September 7, 2017
(Political Verse)

The Strange Parable of Umpti

Good Old Umpti lies now slowly moldering in his grave
whilst coffin flies and maggots feast merrily on his flesh!

With such a morbid occurrence—the rats now join in too!
Mirabile Dictu! Umpti's skeleton and teeth remain intact!

An ethereal jig is merrily danced daily in Umpti's very name.
It's ever-quite so marvelous to speak of his of "pearly whites."

What sayeth thee now as we stand up Umpti's undying skeleton
in his corner whilst we ponder the mysteries of God's universe?

Old Umpti was always a crowd-pleaser and still is as he shows off
his unique, undying smile with his glass-mirror-image pearly whites!

This maketh the circumstances of his immortality very intriguing, as
Old Umpti stares now at Mother Earth from a timeless infinity!

Whether it be in Timbuktu, Casablanca, Rio, New York, LA or on the
Moon, Mars or in the Stars so high above—Old Umpti shall be smiling!

As we move from the shadows of our thoughts into the daylight of
our true passions and emotions—Old Umpti shall be with us too!

Yeah! Not a bad gig for someone long-dead but not at all forgotten!
When our time comes, we can rattle our bones with Old Umpti too!

March 22, 2017
(Couplet)

Visions from Beyond

the veil is crossed
spirits dance freely

human mortality passé
the soul now blossoms

angels guide us all
no more secrets here

enlightenment pervades
we are one with eternity

time is endless
awareness sublime

mankind remains
in God's thoughts

His divine message
peace, love, and hope

October 26, 2017
(Lyric)

When You Truly Love Someone

When you truly love someone . . .
Do so with all your heart!
Do so with real passion,
Do so with true emotion,
Do so with your warmest smile,
Do so with palpable pleasing thoughts,
Do so with an aura of poetic enchantment,
And do it always for love!
And be not ever afraid of doing this,
Whilst seeking divine help from
The Angels high in Heaven above!

I beseech thee, in this vein, always to remember . . .
Some memorable thoughts taken from Shakespeare's
Sonnet 116, from the year of 1609:

"True love is everlasting."
"True love is an ever-fixed mark,"
"That looks on tempests and is never shaken;"
"True love's worth cannot be measured."

With such graceful thoughts here from Shakespeare,
Need I say more?
Amen.

December 1, 2017
(Didactic)

With One's Life

There are always choices to be made and certain realities to square within the confines, conflicts, and limitations of human existence.

It is given and understood that human beings shall never be perfect, despite their religious overtures and genuflections to Almighty God.

And, it is worth noting that human beings may fall pray, at times, to the vanities of life even in situations where they seek to do better.

Nobody is perfect, but it is both noble and grand to see and witness when a person rises to the need to help others who are less fortunate.

The most challenging aspect may be for any person to put himself or herself in harm's way when an instance of direct loss of life is at issue.

Regardless, there are indeed people among all of us who do choose to positively engage in crisis situations to help others in need—all Heroes!

With one's life, the choices we all make define and shape who each of us are as we seek to find our true purpose and direction by God's grace.

What can be more noble than that?

October 30, 2017
(Didactic)

CHAPTER FIVE

Selected Poetry
(2018)

Messages of Love
Imagism
Notions of Infinity
and
Metaphysics
Mythology
and
Personal Courage

A Heavenly Spirit

A heavenly spirit from God's own heart,
Knew thy soul's love from its very start.
With thy soul's return to Heaven's heart,
God's own love of you shall never depart.

December 25, 2018
(Epitaph)

A Most Courageous American President for the Ages

I thought it would be most appropriate for me to take a moment to share some of my reflections on the life and distinguished public service of the late 41st president of the United States, George Herbert Walker Bush.

First, as a retired U.S. military veteran, I am particularly grateful for President Bush's outstanding leadership, vision, and the committed stalwart support he provided to our nation's armed forces, in times of peace and in war, during his term of office from 1989 to 1993.

Second, the depth and breadth of his long years of outstanding service to the United States of America are reflected by the number and variety of the high-level leadership positions he held, not only as president, but as vice president, and as a U.S. congressman from the state of Texas, director of the Central Intelligence Agency, U.S. ambassador to the United Nations, and as the U.S. envoy to China. All of these positions he held over the years in selfless public service to America, testify powerfully to his unshakeable commitment to and belief in freedom and democracy, and the historic role that America fulfills as the indispensable leader of the free world.

Third, as a young, decorated U.S. Navy aviator in the pacific theater during World War II, and as a veteran of fifty-eight combat missions, President Bush experienced first-hand the trials and tribulations, and the challenges of wartime service punctuated with the tragic sacrifices made by U.S. military forces in the pursuit and defense of freedoms that many today take for granted.

Fourth, related to his wartime service and contributions, President Bush was part of what is known today as the "Greatest Generation." This was a special generation of Americans that included even relatives from my own family and other families all throughout the United States. They were the ones who lived through the Great Depression and met the call of duty to confront and destroy the evil forces of fascism and demagoguery that posed a direct threat to both freedom and democracy worldwide. The people from this generation were imbued with a profound sense of "love of country," and did all they could do to ensure the best results for future generations to come.

Fifth, as vice president in Ronald Reagan's administration, George Bush was the co-architect with the president in successfully formulating and implementing the diplomatic initiatives to work toward ending the Cold War with the Soviet Union. In fact, by 1989, Bush was then president, and with the fall of the Berlin Wall on November 9th of that year, he oversaw the entire process for ending the Cold War, and in eventually bringing peace and freedom to the former eastern bloc countries in Europe after the collapse and implosion of the Soviet Union on December 25, 1991. And, during this critical moment in history, President Bush was instrumental in providing help and support to the new Russian government that stood up after the dissolution of the Soviet Union.

Sixth, President Bush, in 1991, through all of his outstanding diplomatic efforts with America's key allies, led a successful wartime coalition of countries with the United States that were directly responsible during the first Gulf War in fighting and ejecting the Iraqi Army under Saddam Hussein's command from the country of Kuwait, thus freeing Kuwait from the abject tyranny of Iraq. President Bush worked tirelessly in assembling this remarkable and highly successful coalition of countries in direct coordination with the United Nations.

With all of this said, I firmly believe that George Herbert Walker Bush will go down in history as one of America's great presidents. He believed in the spirit of true bipartisanship during his long service, and was never afraid to reach across the aisle to work with the political opposition in finding reasonable and meaningful solutions to many problems facing American society, as well as other problems in the international arena that required immediate attention, with thoughtful and deliberate bipartisan support by the Congress.

President Bush, just like the late Senator John McCain, was a devout "Atlanticist" and a fervent supporter of NATO and other international treaties that have been essential in helping the United States positively shape and influence events and actions in the world in the continuous pursuit of the maintenance of freedom and democracy.

President Bush also fully understood and recognized the real significance of "American Exceptionalism" in the international community, and the critical role that America has played, and must continue playing as the all-important bulwark of freedom in the world.

Finally, President Bush was a truly extraordinary leader in every aspect of what he accomplished in all of the positions he held while serving in the U.S. Government. He forcefully rejected the politics of fear, bigotry, and prejudice in American society. He was well-known for his deep and abiding faith in God, and for the profound love he had for his family. He possessed a sincere love of country and believed in selfless service, and in helping to make America that shining beacon of freedom and democracy in the world.

May God Bless.
Rest in Peace.

George Herbert Walker Bush is a most courageous American president for the ages.

December 6, 2018
(Narrative Tribute)

A Most Holy Vision Speaks in Mystical Tomes

Enchanted colorful images shine ever-brightly from
a wild cosmic fire appearing high in the evening sky.

As people gaze upon these unusually radiant images
there is, at once, a universal sense of calm and peace.

Poets worldwide observing this most unique heavenly
occurrence seize their pens to record all that they see.

As they begin to write what they see, it seems as though
their ink's like a magical blood flowing through their pens.

As this sacred blood flows freely, the poets write with a
palpable sense that an amazing grace moment is at hand.

The true essence of this divine moment starts as the poets
witness the appearance of God's Angels in the evening sky.

The poets seek to understand these unbelievable events in
real-time as they appear arrayed against the evening sky.

There's an angelic message that now speaks fervently through
the wondrous magic of the poets' pens—pensive and voiceless.

This holy missive canorously echoes visions from past lives,
whilst presenting highlights that speak vividly to future events.

With the past as prologue and the present now in real-time,
the angels' missive of mankind's future on Earth is positive.

As poets and other writers observe and record their notes, it's
clear the cosmic fire is not the "End of Time" fire and brimstone.

Rather, it's God's way through his angels to capture mankind's
attention and to refocus humanity's efforts in service to others.

The holy missive makes clear that the path to redemption and forgiveness lies within our own power as we seek to find God.

And that the angels shall always be with us as our souls ascend heavenward one day on trails of cosmic dust to be one with God.

November 26, 2018
(Couplet)

A Pocket Full of Stardust and Dreams

Stardust and dreams are the essence of human magic,
as God has blessed us to see beyond all that is tragic.

Stardust and its magic allow us to dream wide and deep,
as we fire our imaginations on what in life we must seek.

A pocket full of stardust and dreams blended now as one
is the real cosmic multiplier of greater human imagination.

The power of love is magical and helps us now to define
who we are in this life as we seek out God's help in kind.

The power of love in this wondrous alchemy of stardust and
dreams shall be with us always when we ascend to Heaven.

And, in Heaven's temple one day as our souls have gathered
to meet God, He shall inquire about our stardust and dreams!

November 10, 2018
(Couplet)

A Reverie of Childhood

A true sacred place and time of innocence where all things simple, fun, and happy touched deeply my heart and soul.

For things that seemed real, at first glance, but full of some surprises later that many of us were too young to understand.

A time where there was an instant camaraderie between and among us kids as we played games and chased each other.

Finding out in first grade that I was the only "left-handed" kid in my class, and having to adjust to being "different" from the others.

Developing an uncanny sense and interest in other languages beyond English when I was already overwhelmed with English.

December 7, 2018
(Couplet)

A Russian Mystic Outré

Mystical-Strannik
Grigori Rasputin
A charlatan to many
A prophet to some.

His hypnotic effect
Incomprehensible
His eyes uncanny
A saint to none.

July 18, 2018
(Double Dactyl)

A Spider's Web

a true engineering marvel
a mastery of tensile strength
flexible, firm, unrelenting

icky, sticky, viscous
this web most certainly is
all the better to trap prey
and cocoon them for later
for a tasty snack or dinner

its occupant ...
a predator supreme
a master acrobat
in the vaunted
historical tradition of
Darwin's bark spider
(*Caerostris darwini*)
a true web mastery
to behold

the web's silken strands
give the spider
the wherewithal
to navigate its web
quite freely
swinging
to and fro
hither and thither
whilst
watching and waiting
for the moment
to seize and kill
its prey

Gary Bateman

a spider's web
a true engineering marvel
a mastery of tensile strength
flexible, firm, unrelenting
icky, sticky, viscous
precision perfect

August 19, 2018
(Imagism)

A True American Hero for the Ages

I thought it would be most appropriate to take a moment to reflect on the life and public service of the late U.S. senator, retired U.S. naval officer and aviator, and military war hero from the state of Arizona, John Sidney McCain III, who is, for me, a "True American Hero for the Ages."

Since I am a retired U.S. military veteran as well, there are, for me, certain qualities and attributes that clearly define, distinguish, and portray the essence of what made Senator McCain's life, service, and commitment to the nation he loved and selflessly served—so special and important.

Throughout his sixty-three years of military, political, and public service, Senator McCain embodied and personified the calling of Duty, Honor, and Country. His leadership and character, and love of country have been beyond reproach. And, beyond the churlishness of American politics, both past and present, he always believed in putting the country first and foremost as reflected by his many noted actions and unwavering support in the defense of democracy and good governance in the United States of America and worldwide.

During the Vietnam War, the time McCain spent as an American prisoner of war in the infamous "Hanoi Hilton" during 1967-1973, speaks volumes to his personal bravery and courage in the face of horrific torture, abuse, and terrible treatment—and to his personal belief and commitment in standing together in solidarity with all of his fellow POWs.

Senator McCain believed in the spirit of true bipartisanship during his long service and time in both the U.S. House of Representatives, and later in the U.S. Senate. This was very important to him, and was a significant aspect of how he conducted himself as a congressman, and as a senator throughout his long and storied political career.

Reaching across the aisle and working with the political opposition on many occasions was one of Senator McCain's hallmark virtues in seeking to find realistic and meaningful solutions to many problems in American society, and in helping to address the continuous challenges facing America and her allies in the realm of foreign affairs.

Senator McCain was results-oriented, and fervently believed in getting things done. He was a devout Atlanticist and supporter of NATO and other international treaties that are significant to America. He recognized the critical importance of "American Exceptionalism" in the international community, and clearly saw America as that quintessential bulwark of freedom in the world.

Doing the right thing was always important to Senator McCain regardless of the challenge or task at hand. He also stressed the urgency in rejecting the politics of fear, bigotry, and division in our country, and in our society writ large. Seeking out and speaking to the "Better Angels of Our Nature" was another notion and attribute he felt that all Americans should strive for and fully embrace in their interactions with one another.

Finally, I will always remember Senator McCain for the innate sense of humor that he oft displayed in public forums, and for his unabashed love of country that he constantly reflected in many of his speeches, and in all of the positive deeds he accomplished during his lifetime.

May God Bless.
Rest in Peace.

September 1, 2018
(Narrative Tribute)

About Fear

Fear is a horrid emotion that makes one attentive at once,
whilst shocking the heart to beat hard—fast and faster!

It causes an ill-feeling and a sense of terrible foreboding,
which can instantly provoke some unintended responses.

Fear has its own unique spirit that can paralyze us cold,
whilst clouding our judgment and inciting a raw rage.

It has that lurking quality in the shadows of the mind,
that can spark moments of terror and abject uncertainty.

Fear possesses a ghastly aura that shows no mercy and
can engulf and literally devour the depths of one's soul.

The only solution, if indeed there is one, is to resist fear's
evil to the uttermost before your soul is destroyed forever!

November 28, 2018
(Couplet)

About That Certain Thing Called Nonsense

Nonsense is that certain symbolic communication form
that oft pervades our human space with its absurdity!

All of us from time-to-time have had to deal with some
people who revel and rave in it to provoke a response.

Making sense and communicating in an intelligent fashion,
reflects a spirit of human decency that's so needed at times.

"Nonsense!" used as an exclamatory pronouncement inheres
a necessary tone of disagreement to stop boorish behavior.

"Nonsense" in a whimsical use can tickle one's funny bone,
whilst creating, at times, a much-needed spirit of amusement!

And so, "Nonsense" as part of our grand human condition,
may not be all bad, except when some choose to be naughty!

Nonsense is an important part of life because it brings us to
a certain view, which should be of no surprise: *C'est la vie!*

December 9, 2018
(Couplet)

An Old Copper Vase – A First View

a rustic object
with
a worn-weathered look
symbolizing
both
an artistic beauty
and
a metaphorical grandeur

when filled
with a few
red or yellow roses

it resonates
a certain emotion
and
it presents
and
it paints
an indelible
image and memory
that
cannot be forgotten

this is made
all the more
compelling
by
its rough-rustic nature
and
its physical view
from afar
which is
at once—

defining and dominating
and is
captivating and absolute.

September 30, 2018
(Imagism)

An Old Copper Vase – A Second View

an old copper vase
a witness of age
saw a lot
during times—
but all new to me.

the grace of the
experienced one
shall share it
with everybody
who is
willing to listen.

so
the old
and
the new
are
coming together
in a
new-found way
never expected
to find everything
that is needed
on their
individual path.

grace and openness
shall help
on the way.

September 30, 2018
(Imagism)

Author's Note: A Collaborated Poem
with Ingrid Krukenberg-Bateman.

Angels Speak of His True Love

By God's intent, Angels speak of His true love,
For mankind and nature here on Mother Earth.
They help us find our path to Heaven above,
Whilst playing a role in our mystic rebirth.
Angels talk to us, and show us God's true love;
They guide our souls on ascension far from Earth,
To Our Holy Father who redeems us pure,
From which no one can ever seek to abjure!

August 5, 2018
(Ottava Rima)

Ars Poetica

Horace circa 19 BC gave some sound advice to
poets on the art of writing poetry and drama

The following thoughts may echo in our minds,
most likely, the intent of what he may have meant . . .

A poem may excite and delight readers with its
imagery, meaning, metaphors, and so much more

A poem may speak of "home" and what it means
to each of us as we grow up and reach adulthood

A poem may excite one's imagination to learn
of people, places, events, and things in our world

A poem may speak to one's emotions—
love, lust, hate, happiness, sadness, and more

A poem may speak to palpability—
touching, feeling, embracing, kissing, and more

A poem may address courage—
to stand for something meaningful against all odds

A poem may address a weakness—
cowardice, avarice, and even a temptation

A poem may address humility—
in realizing that being humble can be a strength too

A poem may address faith—
believing in yourself and others, and a cosmic destiny

A poem may address morality—
as good and evil, right and wrong are with us always

A poem may address objects and images—
that tickle one's poetic imagination and certitude

January 10, 2018
(Couplet)

Being Nowhere

A bizarre place to be, especially when
you didn't know you would be there.

The metaphysical implication of your
situation does seem incredible to others.

If this is the case, nowhere is that space,
that your mortal being and soul must fill.

Space and time in the human endeavor are
rife with inexplicable exceptions for sure.

Finding yourself in this eerie realm of nowhere,
by simple logic, bodes that you're somewhere.

If you did something naughty in another life,
then perhaps nowhere is your karmic strife.

If this isn't the case, then by cosmic fate, you've
unknowingly found yourself in another dimension.

Methinks that praying to God should be of help;
He knows that nowhere is somewhere out there!

August 8, 2018
(Couplet)

Bewitchment

Charms, spells, good and bad—
Abracadabra the word!
Be careful always...
The eye of the beholder...
Hocus-Pocus says it all!

October 31, 2018
(Tanka)

Caitiff

A word to know well—
Someone who's contemptible!
A coward for sure . . .
Infamous and obnoxious . . .
A miscreant immoral!

July 16, 2018
(Tanka)

Champagne in Heaven

The "Old Bubbly" I hope one day in Heaven to see!
And why, pray tell, should I not ever wish this to be?
Methinks that God would smile at this artful prospect,
Yet, such an occurrence may make His Angels suspect!
If His Angels protest, I shall plead my wish to God's action,
Whilst spoiling not to argue my case with all due passion!
I am quite sure my plea may ruffle proper saintly tradition,
Yet, I shall ask God's indulgence and seek not His perdition!
I know God granted an Irish soul's plea for nips of Irish dew,
And so, I am sure He'll allow my "Bubbly" in Heaven's pew!
If my request meets with Almighty God's just and fair favor,
I'll ask Him to join me in a few stout nips of dew of Irish flavor!

January 9, 2018
(Canzone)

Author's Note: *Deus est qui regit omnia! Amen! Amen!*

Charon – The Eternal Ferryman

The mythical ferryman extraordinaire of such keen gaze,
Who braves the Styx and Acheron in the deepest of haze.

Charon is a most sordid God who relishes his work as the
"Ferryman of Hades," carrying new souls to their oblivion.

With an obolus as payment and a flash of his fiery-fierce eyes,
Charon performs his morbid task with a frightening alacrity!

With his winged-demon appearance and horrifying demeanor,
He terrifies all newly deceased souls who face his vile being!

The world of the dead is the final destination for those who
Depart from the dark, dreary shores of the Styx and Acheron.

The deft 'n cruel skull-crushing force of Charon's ferryman's pole,
Ensures that all lost souls in his charge never question his orders!

Charon's fealty and devotion to Hades are absolute in his actions as
He secures the paramountcy of the world of the dead from the living.

The fleeting and finite nature of our mortal coil ensures that we shall
One day ascend heavenward or descend into a state of total perdition.

Without any doubt, if it be perdition, Charon shall be there to greet us
With the grim gaze of his fiery-fierce eyes as he carries us to our doom!

Don't forget your *obolus*—or else!
Without this silver coin the wild wrath of Charon shall be upon you!

January 21, 2018
(Couplet)

Cherish Your Life Always

Cherish your life and never the strife,
as you face with grace all you must do.

This may be challenging at times for sure,
yet it is part of who we are in this life's run.

Life is God's gift to all of us no doubt,
as we each seek to find ourselves in life.

Each and every one of us in our lives are
gifted with a God-given purpose and self.

It is just a question of how each of us seek
and desire to find our true purpose and self.

Tintinnabulation is an incredibly unique word
for sounding all of what we feel and hear aloud.

This celebrated jingling of metaphoric bells
announces our purpose, passion, and feelings.

The "always" part of the formative four-word title
above speaks to the magic of life to be cherished.

Without our aspirations, our musings, our thoughts,
then who the hell are we in this life and hope to be?

I believe now that Almighty God already knows this
question, do we? Answers shall come later. Amen.

November 30, 2018
(Couplet)

Dark Shadows

A grim place where
you dare not go
in your dreams

for "spirits" there
know all about
your anguish
and
your fears

as the sum of all
bad things
you have
done and hidden
from others in life

and
it is there
in this realm of the
uncanny and evil

those
dark spots
indelibly marking
your soul—
shall receive their
due measure

and so—
hold your tears
face your fears
accept your fate

for "spirits" there
shall judge thy fate
and they ...

shall not wait
nor...
shall they care

pray you wake
now
to end this dream

Luciferin flies
now swarm and swirl
 above and around
illuminating a path
in these deep—
Dark Shadows

awake now...
awake now...
awake now...
The Dark One Comes!
his judgment
shall be...

swift
and
without
any
mercy

this is your last chance...
awake now!

March 22, 2018
(Free Verse)

Deepest Memories and Thoughts

A little child
with big wet tears

An early love
a crushed heart

Feelings of utter loneliness
other people's cruelty

Jagged-broken glass
a big toe bleeding profusely

Crying in the dark
as shadows close in

Childhood fight
a broken-bloody nose—the "Bully Boy" lost

A person's deception foisted on others
fools are born—never give suckers an even break

A cousin in his adolescence dies suddenly
his body—soulless, bloodless, inexpressive, stone-cold

Praying to God on this tragedy
His answer—Silence, Why?

Human Nature
expect the unexpected

Unexpected Kindness
a stranger's gift or a good deed

That First Kiss
still blushing today

Your Dreams
never lose sight of them

Long-dead parents and grandparents
always in my heart and my soul

Life and Death
the finite boundaries of our mortal world

Eternity beckons to us all
have no fear—embrace it

On meeting God one day— Oh, that's who you are!
Mirabile Visu! Mirabile Dictu!

My Wife, My Love, My Life
—an eternal blessing for sure!

May 1, 2018
(Lyric)

Despicable

A descriptive word—
That's always hitting its mark!
Attacks and hurts us . . .
Hateful, wicked, and cruel . . .
Degrades the human spirit!

June 23, 2018
(Tanka)

Don't Talk About It – Write About It!

As a writer and a poet, sometimes people ask me how I do, what I do, every day as I research themes and topics for poems or prose works that I want to write about and develop for potential publication in the future.

The "how I do" and the "what I do" with regard to my everyday writing on any given theme or group of themes are predicated on the active notion that I don't, as a rule, talk idly about people, topics or themes per se, rather I go ahead and focus exactly on a certain theme or subject of interest, and then I begin to write about it.

What's the magic formula for doing all of this research and active committed work associated with professional writing? The answer can be summarized in two words: Hard Work! If one is not willing to engage and to put the effort and work into any certain writing endeavor, a true quality writing product won't be the result.

I write because I enjoy writing very much. Poetry is the one literary undertaking that I like to do the most. I find often that writing poetry has helped me to focus, and then to write on given ideas, topics or themes more succinctly. When a person sees a book of poetry that has, for example, 200 poems listed in it, just think of each poem, in essence, as its very own story.

Concerning the infamous "Writer's Block" syndrome, all I can say is that a writer or any aspiring writer just needs to keep working away at their various writing efforts and never give up. Having the requisite skills and talent to be an effective and interesting writer, poet, or novelist are a given. Yet, one also needs a high degree of raw moxie and a measure of commitment and steadfastness too, in order to see any writing venture or product to its end point, and especially toward eventual publication.

My final closing thought concerning the writing of poetry and prose, and any other literary endeavors, in general, is: Don't Talk About It — Write About It!

December 31, 2018
(Narrative)

Dreams of Moonbeams

Wondrously ethereal images always
magically abound in the dream world.

One particular image I had as a child
were dreams of moonbeams at night.

This certain majestic image and its impact
have followed me throughout my entire life.

These bright beams of light have enchanted me
always—bespeaking a brilliant aura of possibilities.

With them and the sight of a bright-lustrous Moon
on a dark night—all seemed, at once, so picture-perfect.

It was, as if, Almighty God tasked his angels nightly to
paint these moonbeams between the Moon and the Earth.

Or so, this all seemed clear to me during my childhood
as I dreamed often, and gazed so deeply at the Moon.

Dreams of these moonbeams are part of what an endless
wonderment and a truly majestic imagination are all about.

Artists may depict the images of these moonbeams in their
painted-portraits, but only Poets may depict them in words.

I dare say, whether moonbeams are illustrated in paintings
or in words, an eternal heavenly blessing they are for sure!

August 28, 2018
(Lyric)

Empyrean Rapture

Radiance sublime
God's true plan

Stars bright
Heavenly light

Angels sing paeans
In God's name

Souls ascend
Now to arrive

On cosmic dust
Trails to infinity

April 14, 2018
(Lyric)

Evil, Guns, Cowardice, Stupidity, and Fear

is anybody out there?
does anyone really care?

seventeen innocent souls departed this earth
unexpectedly and tragically so whilst leaving
grieving loved ones, classmates, and friends
to wade through another mass-murder event

is anybody out there?
does anyone really care?

many clownish and dud politicians in Washington, DC
including the vacuous person parading there as president
cleave themselves to a vaunted aura of self-righteousness
whilst singling out mental illness as the only true cause

is anybody out there?
does anyone really care?

the evil intentions and actions of a deranged person played
their horrific roles in sending these innocents through death's
door at Marjory Stoneman Douglas High School on that fatal day
as did guns, political cowardice, stupidity, and fear of the NRA

is anybody out there?
does anyone really care?

and so, it is guns, guns, guns, guns, and even more guns
proliferate American society today as many in Congress
oppose common-sense gun legislation and more stringent
background checks whilst lapping up money from the NRA

is anybody out there?
does anyone really care?

standing with those families who are aggrieved in such tragedies
and embracing the memories of those who have so sadly perished
requires compassion, moral consciousness, love, and political courage
to do the right thing and not to succumb to greed and abject stupidity

is anybody out there?
does anyone really care?

yes, many good people are out there
and many of them do really care

it is now time for Congress and this president to wake up,
to grow some backbone, and to do the right thing to ensure
that tragedies like this one never occur again!

I am out there
and I do really care—do you?

enough is enough!
this madness must stop now!
support and stand by the students!

amen … amen … amen … amen

February 18, 2018
(Political Verse)

Author's Note: This poem is dedicated to all of the students, faculty, and staff at the Marjory Stoneman Douglas High School in Parkland, Florida—in memory of those brave students and faculty members who perished on that tragic day of February 14, 2018.

Fear Not

Fear not what

the future brings you—

focus now

on your hope

and desire for a better

lifetime circumstance.

December 2, 2018
(Shadorma)

Finding Yourself

Take your time

turning deep within

while you search

in your heart

for what truly reflects now

the person you are

August 9, 2018
(Shadorma)

First Love's Indelible Memory Pure

Deep in my memory there's a pure vision of a real first love,
long-forgotten and now conjured up as a present-day image.

This rare, soulful reflection harkens back to another time long
ago to cherished moments of discovery and youthful innocence.

The slow and perpetual ravages of time now dim and affect all
of these memories except those replete with passion and emotion.

Other images now enter my mind of things that might have been,
and of things that could have been and yet, in the end, never were.

Perhaps like many others, very seldom do I ever dwell on such
memories buried deeply in my mind and spiritual consciousness.

With such old and fading memories, also come those moments
of inexplicable pain, confusion, and an aching sense of real loss.

Now, as I awaken from this image-laden daydream of the past,
I realize the different path and direction I took was the right one.

If there be a lesson to all of this, it's to always know yourself,
and never be afraid of what love's pain brings your way in life.

You can overcome it especially when you realize the role that fate
and destiny play in this whole process as you mature and move on.

The past ghosts of love's pain are just that—they lie in your past,
that's where they should remain as you seek true love in your life.

December 3, 2018
(Couplet)

Forever Love

Forever

A love unending—

spirits one

true passion

sacred always in God's eyes

for eternity

December 10, 2018
(Shadorma)

Forlorn Love – A Red Rose Dead

Love oft finds its symbolic meaning in
the beauty and grandeur of the red rose.

This symbolic meaning reflects as well
the true meaning of love shared by two.

The magic and real passion of love itself
forms the chemistry that bonds two lovers.

The wondrous nature of love fires emotions as
it touches the depth of the human soul replete.

The innate beauty of a red rose is an image that
compels star-crossed lovers so smitten by love.

Alas, when a romantic love over time becomes a
forlorn love, its red rose image withers and dies.

December 12, 2018
(Lyric)

From the Great Abe Lincoln to that Lying Ape Trump

Oh God!! What a way to begin a political verse poem!! Abe Lincoln placed in print in any proximity to the Ape Trump is as sinful and sad as it is despicable. I pray that the ghost of Lincoln shall forgive me in due course when he sees what I have to say about the current grand and the oh, so glorious political huckster, none other than the Big Ape Trump himself. Oh No!! Oh God!!

When I really think about it, I could write volumes of celebratory verses about "Good Old Abraham Lincoln." President Lincoln's historic contributions to the United States bespeak all that's good and positive with his efforts to end the American Civil War and the practice of slavery, and to preserve the Union by defeating the Confederate forces and bringing the southern states back into the Union.

President Lincoln was truly the right man, in the right place, and at the right time. His literal sainthood and fine reputation as one of America's greatest presidents of all time is beyond any doubt or question. And, I say, why not?? His many actions and efforts in this regard were phenomenal, and were all part of his canonization in American society as the "Great Emancipator."

Yet, when it comes to the current charlatan "Donald J. Trump" it is clear that he wormed his way into the White House by hook and crook in 2016, whilst defaming the hallowed traditions of our cherished institutions, and the various important roles they play in the positive outreach and furtherance of our society as one that's free and open, and one that respects the fundamental rights of all citizens, and the rule of law. This is not what President Trump is about at all, rather his mantra relishes chaos, derision, character assassinations, and questionable political activities, and abject chicanery that tear at the fabric of our constitutional democracy, and tarnish and defame America's image and standing in the world community. And so, that Lying Ape Trump really ain't a great leader at all!! Not at all!!

By way of binarily concluding, I proffer the following comparative juxtaposition of these two diametrically opposed personalities: I say, to Abe Lincoln, Yes—for sure!! And, I say to Ape Trump—No Way!! May God Help Us All!!

Amen.

December 20, 2018
(Political Verse)

Frowsy

A slovenly state—
That's always musty and stale!
Seek not this image . . .
Only a positive one . . .
That's where you shall want to be!

November 24, 2018
(Tanka)

God's Heartfelt Passion

God's true gift to us as
we feel His love daily

Angels speak to us of
His passion in our dreams

His passion and love are
limitless and everlasting

Our souls mirror always
His emotions and feelings

His heartfelt passion defines
who each of us really are

As we seek our destiny on
His cosmic trails of infinity

April 25, 2018
(Lyric)

Going Somewhere

Somewhere is a truly bizarre place to be,
if you didn't know how you got there.

Somewhere qualifies as another special
metaphysical indeterminate like nowhere.

Generally, we're all going somewhere as
part of the greater space-time continuum.

In our earthly mortal world, daily points of
destination are readily known to each of us.

This is part of that tangible-known world
that each of us as human beings conform to.

One's inner psyche, on the metaphysical plane,
may experience something entirely different.

What was once a "tangible-known" on this Earth,
may be that "intangible-unknown" of somewhere.

Space and time define us all in our human world,
whilst the terra firma of Earth is our palpable surety.

After dreaming deeply one night, who knows, maybe
your soul might become resident in that somewhere!

Perhaps your new presence in this realm of somewhere,
like being in nowhere, is your preordained karmic strife.

If this isn't the case, then by a cosmic fate, you've now
unknowingly found yourself in another dimension.

If this be so, then praying to God might be of help, since
He knows that somewhere is out there in the Great Beyond!

September 7, 2018
(Couplet)

Happiness

A positive state—
A true goal for everyone!
Seek now and always...
Never be afraid to try...
It shall make a difference!

November 20, 2018
(Tanka)

Hate's Fury

It's horrid

prompts the worst action—

vile anger

blood boils hot

a true mindless impulse that

wounds the soul deepest

November 15, 2018
(Shadorma)

Heavenly Hallucinations of Love's Divine Destiny

A wondrous spirit of true love now softly murmurs its echo
On the wings of God's angels, as they ascend heavenward.

This and more occurs as radiant cultured pearls begin dancing
Their magical-mystical dance deliciously in the oceans deep.

With this, the bright-blue-mirrored waves of the oceans move
In a melodious tempo of love with the pearls as they dance.

Caressing the heavenly sparkles rippling deep in the oceans' waves,
An enchanted diamond-cut glass now trembles and shatters loudly!

At this moment, a mermaid of angelic pulchritude takes her divine
Throne as the mystical dance continues throughout the late night.

Crystal chimes begin sounding pure with a fire and fury of emotions
Within our hearts, as they excite our passions palpably and exquisitely!

The candlelight's effulgent reflection in this moment transfixes me true,
By your warm and loving touch and the magic of your presence with me.

Coloring and scenting the air surpasses all others as the breathless and
Honeycombed eminence of your being touches the depths of my soul!

July 21, 2018
(Couplet)

Author's Note: A Collaborated Poem with Liam McDaid.

Heaven's Music

This music has such wondrous cosmic tones
Beyond the range of all human hearing.
Sometimes as one enters the deepest of sleep,
Angels may share special hints of these tones
With some mortals chosen only by God.
At the moment of holy ascension,
Each soul crosses over into the light of
God's world, and it's at that magic moment,
When the souls begin hearing this music,
That they know their heavenly destiny's at hand.

December 15, 2018
(Blank Verse)

Human Desire

As two touch

emotions run wild—

lovers bond

passions soar

seeking a loving oneness

touching souls deeply

October 14, 2018
(Shadorma)

In Love's Time

Love's that moment in God's eternal time,
That is ever progressive in real-time.

Love's that fiery emotion from the past,
Always to be part of a future fast.

Love's time defines the history we make,
And reflects the divine bliss we both take.

Love is life's wondrous moments to cherish,
For God knows that all mortals shall perish.

Love's a divine emotion in God's time,
That poets may set in iambic rhyme!

Mortals shan't ever fear love in love's time.
Our cosmic souls shall find it in God's time!

Give me your hand for this is our love's time.
Our souls shall sing as "one" in cosmic rhyme!

August 4, 2018
(Heroic Couplet)

In My Heart and Soul

In my heart and soul thou shall always be,
Full of life, passion, and a real love for me.
By equal measure I give thee my love forever,
Knowing that God's love shall desert us never.
Our freeborn spirits reflect a true cosmic pleasure,
With God's promise of an eternal love to treasure.
What more could we as mortals hope to aspire to?

May 20, 2018
(Verse)

In Vino Veritas, But Whiskey is Better

In wine there is certainly such real truth to be found,
And in whiskey there is even more of it to go around!

Wine may make one truly sagacious, whilst whiskey
Elevates one to a level known as "For Members Only!"

As modern-day bards seek true meaning in their daily
Thoughts—whiskey is man's key to his baser instincts.

The soul doth prosper even better when fueled so truest
By the cryptic, elixir-like qualities of wine and whiskey!

And doth pray tell, I say now this must be so, and why not?
Well, both elixirs do help to free man's deepest inner spirit!

Wine is that exquisite medium for introspective reflection,
Whilst whiskey excites one's self for immediate attention!

Let it be said though that wine and whiskey do complement
One another in man's quest for real truth in this crazy world!

Amen! Amen! Amen! Amen! Amen!
What more can one say? *C'est la vie!*

January 7, 2018
(Couplet)

Infinity Beckons

Your soul knows

just before you do

that your time

has come now

as holy angels appear

for your ascension

October 20, 2018
(Shadorma)

Jackaroozapoo – You Don't Say?

Someone or even something conceived or made that's associated with pure utter nonsense can be indeed quite real and tangible to those who choose to believe in this particular type of reality and swear by its innate veracity, and its certain supernatural attributes and qualities in being able to shape ultimately the life and fortunes of others who cry out loudly to be really heard and respectfully listened to.

One must learn to swim so swiftly and deeply through all of the quizzical blather in this world of what we all tend to think and call simply as "This Life," whilst realizing in the end that divine revelation may indeed be the very revolution and the strategic impetus that mankind needs and must have to find its collective soul and its true relationship to Almighty God.

It's better, of course, that mankind stays within the grace and glory of God, rather than choose the terrible fury and the wretched spirit of debauchery and the true evil that the Devil revels in as he constantly seeks to tempt and deceive each and every one of us away from the all-merciful Kingdom of God, where His Light, Love, Happiness and Compassion truly reign supreme in His Name.

If "Old Hob" should, for whatever reason, choose to come your way in this life, I say, to you to be bold, forthright, fear him not, and be sure to tell him: Jackaroozapoo — You Don't Say? This is a uniquely coded way of telling Old Hob, "Nonsense — You Don't Say?" And tell him also, "In the Lord God's Name," "I pray now that it is time for you to leave this Earth of ours Oh Evil-Dark Spirit, and to take with you all of your deception, defamation, shameful acts, and debauchery post-haste back to Hell from whence you came! And then, as I smile, and say once again: "In the Lord God's Name." And, always fear not, and be both brave and resolute in all that you do in this life, and this is exactly, as the French say... *comme il faut*. Amen! Amen!

And never forget this emphatic question: "Jackaroozapoo — You Don't Say?" And now, Old Hob, with this you be sure to have a really terrible day! And, the only other thing I shall finally say is: Goodbye and Good Riddance Forever!

October 14, 2018
(Narrative)

Author's Note: I really like the narrative of this poem and the uplifting message it leaves with the reader. "Jackaroozapoo," by the way, is the key word for this particular poem. And, it is a word I actually made up myself in the English language to capture the readers' attention relevant to this theme. I do hope that the *"Official English Lexicographers"* have a sense of humor about this. I do!

King Lear's Voice

Nothing out of nothing
William Shakespeare
A king of true tragedy
No unconditional love.

No, never, and nothing
Machiavellian
His descent into madness
Dead to Heaven above.

October 10, 2018
(Double Dactyl)

Life Cradles Us to Our Grave

Life is a gift bestowed on each and every human being by the divine direction of the Almighty Lord God with the birth of each child in every society and culture worldwide here on Earth.

This cradle idea of life speaks to a greater ethereal concept and a cosmic metaphor, whereby each of us are born into this mortal world in God's own image in a protective state that falls under the love and guidance of our parents and guardians.

As each of us grow up and mature over the years, the spiritual nature and divine aspects of our mortal existence should be understood and recognized as the true godly gifts they are, and they should always be viewed as such by all of us.

At the end of our individual life-run, the grave does indeed await each of us as our souls and spirits depart this earthly embrace of ours to return in a state of grace, goodness, and devout humility to the heavenly kingdom of Almighty God.

Amen.

December 24, 2018
(Verse)

Lolita's Conceit

Obsession defined
Vladimir Nabokov
An accursed passion
Love's true abomination.

Literary allusion
Tintinnabulation
Sounding moral oblivion
God's sure condemnation.

August 18, 2018
(Double Dactyl)

Louise Imogen Guiney – Poetess and Writer

Louise Imogen Guiney sought a certain poetry of perfection that rang true with a real radiance in her poetry, that also bespoke a passion and feeling for its lyrical nature as it was amply reflected with an aura of spontaneity, a noted élan, and a sense of a mystical moral verve. Guiney fashioned much of her work around traditional poetic themes with a distinct concern for both style and content.

Guiney's profound religious orientation and desire for this spirited feeling, along with her notion of a certain perfection was defined and embellished by her underlying concern with the Catholic tradition in literature, and by her masterful view and concept that brought the notions of *heroic gallantry* and *moral rectitude* to the forefront of her scholarship with regard to her poetry and her various literary and historical studies.

The entirety of Guiney's work and the mystic nature of her poetic and literary endeavors imbued her with a type of an early modernist touch similar to that of T. S. Eliot, whose influence was twenty years into the future, as he helped to bring the *modernist movement* to fruition with the help of Ezra Pound and other poets.

All of these experiential forces, at hand, helped Guiney to achieve her unique nature and brilliance over time as a fine New England poetess of letters and scholarship, and her poetry was all-inclusive of a grand and glorious vision of English poetic traditions par excellence.

December 22, 2018
(Narrative)

Author's Note: Certain poems from Louise Imogen Guiney have been reprinted in 2020. However, the complete and definitive anthology of her poetry: *Louise Imogen Guiney – Her Life and Works 1861-1920* was masterfully assembled by the author-writer E. M. Tenison in 1922, and it was, in 1923, published by Macmillan and Company, Limited in London. Tenison had indicated in a "personal note" that Guiney had read this book in complete draft form before her untimely death in 1920. This book is a collector's item.

Love Always

commit yourself
with all your heart
to love always
that very special person
who has captured yours

and has become
your friend
your confidant
your soulmate
your everything
in this earthly life
and beyond

fate and destiny
await you both
at life's end—
and the Angels
shall be there
to guide you into
God's eternal light

February 18, 2018
(Free Verse)

Love is that Eternal Magic in Your Eyes

Love is that eternal magic in your eyes,
That excites my heart with the truest emotion,
And it says your love's my real heavenly prize.

Destiny plays its role in our mutual devotion,
As the angels affirm our love by God's delight;
That excites my heart with the truest emotion.

The passion of our love feels now forever right,
And we embrace with the sweetest deep kiss,
As the angels affirm our love by God's delight.

A rhapsody defines our moments of true bliss,
Whilst we search for our own empyrean desire,
And we embrace with the sweetest deep kiss.

Our feelings are blessed by His divine inspire.
Love's power is eternal in God's cosmic view,
Whilst we search for our own empyrean desire.

The angels speak to us now gentle and true;
Love's power is eternal in God's cosmic view.
Love is that eternal magic in your eyes,
And it says your love's my real heavenly prize.

July 27, 2018
(Terzanelle)

Love's Dilemma

Happy one minute
Sad the next
Speaks volumes
To the constant
Ebb and Tide
Of what's called
Love's Dilemma.

When two people
Meet and fall
Deeply in love
Passions abound
Emotions afire
Whilst they bask
In true desire.

Love's power
Can heal
Can hurt
It's magic
May enchant
May mesmerize
And surprise!

Love's passion
Excites us
Teases us
Reveals us
Stirs emotions
Makes us
Feel whole.

The bargain is
It takes two
To tango
To love

To want
To have
To hold.

And always
To be bold
To love—

Unconditionally
With your mind
With your heart
With your soul!

June 8, 2018
(Accentual Meter)

Love's End

It's tragic

stabs the heart deeply—

spirit lost

passion gone

without any true purpose

heartbreak unending

September 24, 2018
(Shadorma)

Love's Magic

Heaven sent

with an angel's kiss—

star-struck now

with passion

all-around you with glee that—

our love's forever

November 29, 2018
(Shadorma)

Love's Power

It's wondrous

enchants you entire—

passions hot

your heart beats

wildly with a true desire

for the one you love

September 19, 2018
(Shadorma)

Love's Rapture

That insatiable and forever moment
To capture and hold, deep and dear
In thy heart and soul, whilst savoring
Its enchanted and palpable emotions
For the rest of thy life on this Earth.

Love is fleeting for sure as this aspect
Is a definite part of its eternal DNA in
Mankind's three-dimensional world of
Finite capabilities and true experiences
Where relationships can last a lifetime
Or be suddenly torn asunder in terrible
Moments of hot anger and sad betrayal
When a couple breaks up and all is lost.

Love in its truest sense of delectation is—
That giddy feeling when two people first meet
That instant when they gaze into each other's eyes
That aura when the air smells of fresh red roses
That hot rush of emotion as they first embrace
That sensual moment when they kiss deeply
That special confidence that all is now possible
That ethereal moment as two souls become one.

Love's rapture is that unique divine rhapsody
Heavenly sent by Almighty God Himself.

In the end, love's rapture is what gives all of us
That special sense of affirmation and shared worth
As human beings made in God's image.

Amen.

March 24, 2018
(Free Verse)

Love's Spirit Enchants Our Souls Entire

Love's an emotion infusing both of us holy pure,
Whilst touching us with that spirit of the divine.
Love becomes one with us as we seek to assure,
And accept its spirit as it enchants our souls sublime.

We exalt in love's spirit by God's own cosmic desire,
Accepting its presence as it speaks to our mortal soul.
God defines its true mystic purpose to us now entire,
As we join hands as one in fulfilling our sacred role.

Our destiny comes from love's true majesty and certitude,
As its spirit touches us in life and death, and in holy eternity.
The angels oft speak to us of love's radiant pure pulchritude,
As its spirit prepares our souls for their final cosmic journey.

We both share in love's true spirit and glory, now and forever,
And know this my darling—my love shall not leave you ever!

November 9, 2018
(Shakespearean Sonnet)

Love's Spirit Speaks to Us

Love's spirit speaks to us with deepest emotion,
Giving us all that touch of God's true love divine,
Whilst helping us find the words and the rhyme,
To express His love eternal with holy devotion!
God helps us seek our depth of love and passion,
In how we find and relate to one another over time,
Whilst sharing, special palpable moments in kind,
As we celebrate our love by God's intent and action!

Love's spirit speaks to us in words radiant and pure,
As we find those emotive bonds that make us one,
And as we share our true feelings with hope and fun!
Love's spirit tells us we mustn't love's bond abjure,
For our love by God's word is sacred by His decree,
And that bespeaks His love for us with all cosmic glee!

September 8, 2018
(Petrarchan Sonnet)

Luciferin Flies

Swarms of them form now—
An evil portent for sure!
Shades of illusion . . .
An evil that's palpable . . .
Now's your last chance to escape!

November 2, 2018
(Tanka)

Lucky in Love's Embrace

You once told me my dearest love that we
were so very lucky to be in love's embrace.
And you intimated that our love came from
deep within both of us by God's own grace.

Now as the years of our lives together have
gently passed like sand through God's own
hourglass, I know now for sure that our love
reflects forever the essence of love's embrace.

October 20, 2018
(Quatrain)

Magnanimous

Noble character—
With a greatness of spirit!
Never vindictive...
Generous and forgiving...
High-minded and always just!

December 22, 2018
(Tanka)

Mankind's Spiritual Evolution and Beyond

Suffering the real anguish of a hellish curse from an evil sorcerer or a witch may be more than just a certain medieval occurrence from the centuries past.

Magical charms, enchantment, and a sense of true fascination can be certain attributes to the actual inducement of the act of bewitchment from a human perspective.

The problematic part of all of this comes to the fore when the so-called practitioners of the "Black Arts" choose to use the art of witchcraft in a blatant manner to inflict harm on others, and to alter the ultimate fate and destiny of any person that they might come in contact with.

The innate supernatural power of an act of black magic in this particular sense, subsumes an aura of devilish overtones that are often associated with those who traffic in evil actions and who truly wish to do harm unto others.

A spiritualist may exercise his or her various forms of "abracadabra" to make a supposed contact with others who have passed on beyond our earthly dimension.

This means that the eye of the beholder is often left to ponder the veracity of such actions through the lens of fakery and hocus-pocus or the reality that certain charms and spells may have an actual salutary effect and are not at all bogus.

With all of this said, one should never discount the true essence of mankind's spiritual and societal evolution over the past centuries from the religious teachings of Christianity and other religions as part of a holy quest to bring mankind closer to Heaven and Almighty God.

The spiritual choices that face mankind in today's modern world are still inexorably tied and anchored to the aspects of human evolution from the time that our ancestors had first appeared here on Earth in God's very own image.

Historically, theology has been a principal part of mankind's development as our ancestors sought to find and define their personal relationship to God and to the greater cosmos that all of us as human beings are a part of.

Mankind's ongoing story on this planet that we call "Earth" and know, as our home, continues as a "work-in-progress" as each of us seek to find our way to God through prayer, faith, and a spiritual understanding of the endless cosmos that we are all a part of.

December 10, 2018
(Narrative)

Martians Who Walk Among Us

Didn't you know that Martians walk among us today?
And why, pray tell, would you doubt this in any way?
In fact, some Earthlings may not be really Earth born.
If this truth were known, it could bring them only scorn!
Methinks that God knows the real truth of this prospect,
And would never admit this as it could make Him suspect!
A real sense of humor is needed to consider the truth of this,
As I'm sure one's mental state would be in doubt with this.
Yet, for a moment, suspend your proclivity toward disbelief,
And ponder what a Martian might say to win your true belief.
It's natural for humans to be such a doubting, questioning lot;
For Martians who walk among us—it's all a real human plot!

April 1, 2018
(Canzone)

Author's Note: Happy April Fool's Day!

me and you

yes, we are "me and you," a couple
whose mutual love and sweet spirit
and affection for one another dates
back to other lifetimes before in the
recent and deep past.

whether we are "me and you" or
"you and me," it really makes no
matter and no difference at all.

what counts now and what is so very
important, from past to present and
from present to future, is that we will
remain always the best of friends ever,
whilst sharing the truest measure and
devotion of real passion, feeling, and
love that transcends the magic prism
of our earthly time and existence, and
which bespeaks a continued union of
our souls into the afterlife beyond the
here and now.

two lives and two souls bound by
a steadfast, immortal belief in the
power and grandeur of real love
and respect for one another in this
life and beyond in God's Kingdom.

yes, it is truly "me and you," as one,
fulfilling the promise and the destiny
of our love, our hopes, and our dreams
until the end of time.

amen.

December 24, 2018
(Verse)

Mimesis Master

Reality's mirror
Erich Auerbach
Manifest vision
Literature's reality true.

Stylistic panache
Presignification
Mingling literary styles
Elegant in reality's view.

April 8, 2018
(Double Dactyl)

My Broken Heart Shall Never Now Last Forever

My broken heart shall never now last forever,
As your true love captured my heart and soul,
And darling our love is my heavenly treasure.

Our life and love are truly a wondrous pleasure,
As our souls form as one by God's cosmic role.
My broken heart shall never now last forever.

Our true passion is beyond all infinite measure,
As our life and love form a bond that's so bold,
And darling our love is my heavenly treasure.

Our shared desire is limitless forever and ever,
And our love's heartfelt emotion is one to extol.
My broken heart shall never now last forever.

Our love and your beauty are my real pleasure,
Their worth exceeds all of Earth's natural gold,
And darling our love is my heavenly treasure.

We share a life and love by God's own endeavor,
And in His view as two loving spirits of one soul.
My broken heart shall never now last forever,
And darling our love is my heavenly treasure.

November 18, 2018
(Villanelle)

My Heart's Spirit and Love

My heart's spirit and love you truly art,
Full of love and passion now and forever;
I feel thy presence now deep in my heart,
And pray that our love shall leave us never.

September 2, 2018
(Epigram)

Nefarious Spirit

The Human Creature is not exempt
As the nefarious spirit lives within.

Even the saintliest of us all have
A touch of the nefarious within.

My secret is that I am with you always—
When you're awake, asleep, and dreaming.

I am your alter ego at times and even
That dark shadow in the room beyond.

When you gaze into your morning mirror—
I am there too as only a faintly bare existence.

Don't look too hard and too deeply into the mirror—
For I shall disappoint, become invisible, and disappear.

In your evil-thinking moments of real anger and rage,
I shall haunt others for you at your behest and desire.

But I shall haunt you and surely play on your emotions,
If you're wrong about the others, no matter who they be.

Being an uncanny spirit of action, sorrow, and chaos—
I can act on a moment's notice and bring pain to bear.

I live in the deepest, darkest chasm of your inner psyche.
Be sure to use me wisely, whilst you show all due care!

March 8, 2018
(Couplet)

Nightmares Shall Follow Us

Buried so deep within the clustered cobwebs of the mind,
Lurks certain synaptic images of things both ugly and evil.

These mental clustered cobwebs do accumulate over time,
And with them their synaptic images grow in proportion.

These images contain reflections of our daily life experiences,
And may form negative visions of people, things, and events.

These are the nightmares that follow us in life's finite run.
They can be evil and frightening, devouring all things good.

They can even develop a synergy of their own from a wealth
Of painful and traumatic experiences deep within the psyche.

Deep in the shadows of the mind, one person's night terror,
May be another person's incubus—who can say for sure?

The psychic boundary separating reality and fantasy in our
Dreams may blur, at times, yet nightmares shall follow us.

March 4, 2018
(Couplet)

On Being Soulful

Spiritual moments
on being soulful
find their certain
metaphysical aspects
when one seeks
a deeper meaning
and a real sense
of true joy,
by connecting
with one's soul
that lies at the
very core of all
human beings
and their
individual existence
on this
physical entity,
we all call
and know, as—
Our Mortal Earth,
Our Mother Earth.

Thinking about
and truly
understanding the
special elements,
and the wholly
transcendental nature
of one's self-ego,
whilst mastering
the spiritual art
of self-reflection,
whereby—
one finds
His or Her
true ethereal sense

and begins
to see
Mortal Life
entirely unfettered,
and without any
human falsities
and obvious

facades of deceit—
that speak directly
to the
essence of
balance and harmony,
and the
true cosmic
passion and purpose
of the
spirit of soulfulness.

It's this
that brings
all of us
in the end
closer to
God's Kingdom
and to
Almighty God Himself.

Amen.

December 22, 2018
(Verse)

On My Way to Work

As usual, I was on my way to work. As I was driving along, I was already busy thinking about problems and my situation at work—restarting all over again at the very point I had left off at work last evening before going home.

Suddenly and most surprisingly, I started to notice just how wondrously beautiful this morning was—with its sunbeams radiantly shining over the countryside, the fresh air, and trees covered all over with blossoms.

With all this enchanted pleasantry, I began to wonder: What is really the difference between a tree along the road and us—as humans? The tree needs water, nutrients, sunlight and fresh air; a place to live, atoms and molecules—and, at the end, there are not really any basic differences at all since trees and humans are both living organisms here on Earth subject to the same basic support provided on God's behalf by Mother Nature.

Yet, there is one really big difference: We (humans) allow the never-ending, inner-circus-cinema moments of our mental doubts to screw up our entire day! So much for the vaunted and overrated "mental superiority" of human beings, eh? Really?

As I finally reach my workplace now, still with a smile on my face, I begin searching for a place to park my car. At that very moment, there was another car starting to leave so I could take its spot. It was a car from another company located in our city. And then, to my utter amazement, I just happened to notice a special logo on the side of that car with the company owner's last name: "Peace."

I was really surprised at this simple course of events leading up to this very special moment. Yet, at the same time, I was totally at ease with a complete sense of peace with my true inner self.

Still feeling being one with nature as God's own creation, I then suddenly realized the lesson I was taught this morning of a simple workday: If you want to experience peace you have to cut out first those never-ending, inner-circus-cinema moments of mental anguish. Only then, can you be at ease to appreciate this special moment on this day, and you feel you are part of nature and creation—and are in harmony and peace.

I was very much touched, and told myself: Whenever you are feeling stressed, busy and alone, remember this very morning—and close out the mind-chatter and just focus on nature—there you can always be one with nature, and therein lies real peace and harmony.

May 6, 2018
(Narrative)

Author's Note: A Collaborated Poem with Ingrid Krukenberg-Bateman.

Only a Mensch

Yes, a mensch

only shall I be

with frailties

abounding

and with a most noble love

for you—forever

October 14, 2018
(Shadorma)

Our Dreams from Times Before

Dreams that come to us from times before,
Oft tease our minds inciting images galore.

Speaking to us psyche-deep, in our deep-sleep,
They nudge us gently to take that ethereal leap!

Dreams may surely incite past emotions very sad,
Causing us wicked thoughts that are mad and bad!

These dreams may also bring us even to Heaven's gate,
Ensuring we see what glorious images there so await!

Angels may come to us in our dreams from times before,
Telling us of God's love as our souls now find His door.

Our souls shall find that eternity-true beyond God's door;
What a wonder awaits us in our dreams from times before!

July 14, 2018
(Couplet)

Our Final Dance with Death

One way or another in this life each of us shall end up,
In that final dance of our life—that dance with Death.

Some shall experience this dance routine earlier in life,
Whilst others shall follow later in the course of a life's run.

Hope, faith, courage, and a spirit of love may help each of us
To cope with the expected final eventualities from this dance.

It's oft easier to wax philosophically about someone else's
Circumstances with Death's spectre rather than our very own.

Ultimately, one's faith in Almighty God is the eternal power
Far beyond our death that beckons all of us to His Kingdom.

And so, this final dance with Death is our transition from the
Mortal Coil as our souls ascend skyward into God's Kingdom.

Deus est qui regit omnia—and we are one with Him in the end.
Deus miseratur, Deus vobiscum—Amen! Amen! Amen! Amen!

September 12, 2018
(Couplet)

Paronomasia

Rhetoric usage—
A pun, a true play on words!
Shades of confusion . . .
Ditto sounds, other meanings . . .
Phonetic pun poetic!

July 28, 2018
(Tanka)

Persephone's Flower

Asphodel flowers are said to blanket complete the expanse of the Elysian Fields with their white, pink, and yellow colors.

These asphodel flowers in their multicolored clusters bespeak an ancient time of power and consequence in the Underworld.

In the depths of the Underworld, Hades knew very well the true pulchritude and power underlying the fields of asphodel there.

The asphodel, by legend, is Persephone's sacred flower that both captivated and mesmerized her with its lily-like presence.

Persephone was particularly drawn to the magical beauty and the lure of the Narcissus with its dominate deep-yellow hue.

With all this said, no wonder Hades kidnapped Persephone and spirited her away to the Underworld to be His chosen Queen.

And with her new presence as the Goddess of the Underworld, Persephone, in time, became the Goddess of Spring and Nature.

Persephone's story is interesting even in today's world since she became known as the personification of vegetation here on Earth.

And so, next time you spy a look at some fields of asphodel here on Earth, you shall be aware of the mythical legend they portend.

October 14, 2018
(Couplet)

Phasmophobia

Fear of ghosts—Boo! Boo!
Don't be afraid, they're spirits!
From Land of the Dead...
Talking only at nighttime...
And so, what's the fuss about?

October 31, 2018
(Tanka)

Poetry and the Occult

The human psyche and its thirst for both inward
and outward reflection finds its medium in poetry.

The source of poetry's metaphorical power and its
wonderment exist in the realm of the supernatural.

Poetry oft reflects many arcane notions of the mysterious
as it thrusts mankind into the reality of the ethereal world.

The precepts of the everyday world of mankind may be
inherently challenged, at times, by the aura of the unknown.

Mankind's historic pathway to true enlightenment brings
each of us closer to God as we seek His divine attention.

The mystical evolution of our individual soul bodies
helps us to understand who we are in relation to God.

The most essential aspect of all of this is for mankind
to have true faith always in the power of the Almighty.

Mankind must never fall prey to fear, temptation, and
darkness which personify the Devil's earthly presence.

The past, present, and future speak to our soul's essence,
And poetry's one impetus to awaken us to our divine role!

October 13, 2018
(Couplet)

Reflections in the Mirror

A mirror may reflect more than any mortal can really see,
Whilst revealing timely images past, present, and yet to be.

The real depth and true imagination of our human mind,
May affect what we see as either finite or infinite in kind.

Such varied images form a painter's palette of dreams,
That poets may put words to beyond all human schemes.

Seeing and dreaming of such images give all poets a pause,
As though we are all now little kids adrift in the Land of Oz.

These images give poets a portal beyond all space and time,
To the realm of the metaphysical with much to set in rhyme.

This portal to the Fifth Dimension gives us all a taste of infinity,
And speaks to the images we see as part of a true cosmic divinity.

A mirror may reflect more than any mortal can ever expect to see,
Whilst revealing cosmic images of all past, present, and yet to be.

The task falls then to our poets to record the images seen over time,
And with Almighty God's help—to set all in perfect cosmic rhyme!

May 16, 2018
(Couplet)

Sadness

Emotional pain—
A soulful melancholy
A sense of deep hurt…
Avoid when it's possible…
An epiphany for change!

November 25, 2018
(Tanka)

Sailing Away Under a Silver Moon Forever

As the morning slowly awakens, I see how those beautiful eyes
Of yours warmly shine bright and share thy palpable feelings of
Enchanted moments of our true love and unbridled fiery emotions.

Making love to me in the depths of your sweet dreams proves to be
Quite interesting, as angels fly by and giggle softly at this prospect.
Yet, as we touch, caress, and kiss deeply—your dreams are so real.

A sweet passion burns inside your loving beauty as we fall in love,
And I know you are that special one I have longed for my entire life.
The pulchritude of your radiant presence and spirit bedazzles me now.

As we adorn one treasured pearl filling our hearts with its deep pleasure,
Our minds now connect as one, visualizing eternal dances of a true love
That echo on and reflect the depth of our lives and our mutual passion.

Sailing away under a silver moon forever is where we need to be as two
Sultry lovers and like-spirits who have eaten that sweet forbidden fruit,
And to know we shall both scale infinite heights one day into eternity.

April 29, 2018
(Tercet)

Author's Note: A Collaborated Poem with Liam McDaid.

Soul Essence

Release comes with death.
The mortal host is no more.

A faint and sad cackle is heard,
As all illusions come to an end.

The bare body lies in a stiff repose.
What once was, is now no more.

Tears are shed in a mortal milieu,
As the soul begins its ascension.

The flowers in decoration serve
As a human memory of the past.

Tender emotions now permeate the air,
As the flowers' sweet smell is realized.

The moon shines bright in the dark sky,
As the soul now meets its cosmic destiny.

March 30, 2018
(Lyric)

Soul Ghosts

close to our
inner-core self

they are there now
nestled beyond reach

still living as part of
our past, present, future

they never forget
nor should we

they can't forgive
but maybe we can

part of the fifth dimension
they can come at anytime

to haunt us
to talk to us

to like us
to love us

to sleep with us
to dream with us

beyond the mortal coil
they are always there

they are us
we are them

yes, may god love
yes, may god bless

amen
amen

January 7, 2018
(Lyric)

Souls of the Dead

Souls of those who have passed on

are keenly aware of our mortal coil,

for they once were part of this earthly

world that many of us now nonchalantly

take for granted since—just as sure as the

sun rises in the morning and sets in the

evening—this makes us all creatures of

habit reflective of our innate finite nature

and a possessive incurious proclivity toward

things ethereal and oft lacking a true sense

of the cosmic imagination and certitude that

God wishes for us over time to seek out as

part of our divine destiny that awaits us in

eternity far beyond this mortal world—for

the souls of the dead know this already.

July 26, 2018
(Verse)

Stardust, Love and Dreams

Stardust is what our love and dreams are made of in this mortal life of ours, from birth through childhood and until our final breath. All three of them blend together as one and bespeak a heavenly wonder that we should all marvel at with their magical and loving presence in our lives, as they reflect that divine touch of Almighty God, and the holy presence of His angels as they smile now and touch our hearts and souls blessed by God's own eternal love and His grace forever. Amen.

October 14, 2018
(Verse)

Strife

Actionable word—
Reflecting human passions
Out of all control . . .
Stupidity reigns supreme . . .
Mankind's tragedy and shame!

May 22, 2018
(Tanka)

Synchronicity and its Prophecy

By its very nature, Synchronicity and its relationship to the outside world and human consciousness are laden with poetic overtones whereby the dream world and situational objectivity may both coincide and collide simultaneously. The metaphoric implications of this particular phenomenon have a relationship to the world of poetry and may influence, at times, how poets ponder and interpret conscious and unconscious imagery that reflect the mortal world we live in today, as well as any related historical antecedents from years and centuries past.

Dr. Carl Jung, as the creator of synchronicity, tied its application to the dream world in another dimension which opened the door to how philosophers, poets, pundits, and writers today could gain a more profound and personal relationship to the human experience writ large.

Relevant to the world of poetry, past and present, Jung's notion of synchronicity has brought the world of spiritual awareness and consciousness together as they pertain to how human beings actually live together and interact with one another. Dr. Jung saw the "deliverance of the self" as the epitome or embodiment of spiritual awareness of the human condition and how people live in human society.

My purpose with this narrative essay has been to give the reader (and any aspiring poets) a basic conceptual view of synchronicity, and its related relevance beyond the scientific community to the fields of literature, poetry, and creative writing in general.

October 20, 2018
(Narrative Essay)

Author's Note: Synchronicity (or *Synchronizität* in the German) is a pioneering concept first introduced by the famous Swiss analytical psychologist Dr. Carl Gustav Jung. His seminal work, among others, on this fascinating subject is: *Synchronicity: An Acausal Connecting Principle, Princeton University Press (1960).*

Täuschung

A very powerful German feminine noun that's replete in certain life situations with shades of of deception, delusion, and illusion—which, in turn, depend on certain circumstances and life experiences which seek the situational power and force that speaks to and shapes the very nature of projected and expected outcomes in another person's favor or even another group's true intention and advantage as a move is made for one to invariably "strike while the iron is hot," whilst ensuring that "all of the other pearls of no value," are conveniently cast out to the "pigs" who are the true losers and shall never possess the real spoils at hand. If you have ever been lied to, fooled, or deceived, then I am afraid you are in the sad company of many others in life who have been similarly affronted in a life's run. If this should be the case, I proffer to you, to never forget the word *Tauschung* and its real, teachable meaning in this instance. It's worth thinking about. After all, I might also add, that the famous comedian, W.C. Fields, had once so poignantly posited the following very famous expression: "Never Give a Sucker an Even Break." Need I say more? I rest my case. Amen! Amen!

October 14, 2018
(Didactic)

Tender Emotions

Tender Emotions are very special and are nurtured and blossom
Deep within each person's heart by the divine touch of Almighty
God with His direct and true intention and most holy inspiration.

It is up to every person as a mortal being on this Earth to seek out
Their own destiny whilst embracing the true purpose of this life
With the God-inspired goal of becoming spiritually one with their
Immortal Soul.

It is essential that each of us in this mortal life find and realize
This higher level of understanding and its ethereal importance in
The sacred preparation for that special moment one day when one's
Soul finally ascends to that most heavenly world in that eternal and
Infinite cosmic place known as The Great Beyond.

Tender Emotions are what defines us as human beings and makes
Each of us so special in God's eyes and in His own image, whilst
Imbuing each of us with His sense of hope, love, and true compassion
For one another, and the God-given inspiration to pursue our cherished
Dreams as we each live our lives to their fullest measure in this magical
Mortal World we all call "Earth."

Amen. Amen.

Deus miseratur. Deus vobiscum.

April 28, 2018
(Free Verse)

Tenebrae – The World's Shadow

A very old, odd man approaches me out of nowhere
with his face contorted, fearful, and noticeably sad.

A strange person truly he is with . . .
deep-set wrinkles that profusely cover his entire face.

I notice immediately that this rather
unusual man has coal-black eyes—eerie they are.

He begins to talk to me haltingly,
telling me where he comes from . . .

A place of utter darkness known as
"The World's Shadow," he says.

Shocked, I am, naturally as this "man" has now
entered my private space spewing all this stuff.

I am immediately suspicious, of course, being
the normal and rational man as I believe I am.

With the grotesque facial appearance of this very strange man,
I am transfixed by his deeply-wrinkled face and coal-black eyes.

They send icy-cold shivers up and down my spine as they
bespeak a real, true sense of a palpable fear and foreboding.

What the Hell?? What the Hell?? I thought . . .
Why in God's creation is this strange man here?

Apparently reading the words in my mind . . . he says,
"I come from the Earth's future."

With that, the very word that popped into my mind was
"Presentiment" . . . a sense of absolute anxiety and fear.

I could see, sense, and feel that this very old man was a Lazarus-sort of character with his sores and all, and his black eyes and a dark demeanor. Despite the shock effect of his appearance, there seemed to be a certain aspect of this very old man that stirred a sense of sympathy deep within my heart and soul.

His stark and demonstrative appearance bespoke a sort of character who was perhaps once very holy and had bathed and basked in God's holy light of promise and redemption.

This very old man, this prophet, if you will, told me he was sent to warn the people of today's world of the force and power associated with the coming darkness of "The World's Shadow," and what may befall mankind, if mankind is not vigilant and ready to combat the true spiritual evil that now awaits the human race and its final fate and destiny.

The prophet went on to speak of the coming days of darkness that shall envelop mankind, beginning with the arrival of the Dark Angels of Satan, Gorgons, Witches, Warlocks, Ghouls and Goblins. It looks like mankind may end up facing a wrath of an unspeakable fury and ferocity!

Before leaving my presence, the prophet told me that in the end it's really all up to mankind regarding what shall happen, and what the ultimate destiny of the world, as we all know it today, shall be.

The prophet said, "Mankind's best course is to stay in the true radiance and holy redemption of God's heavenly light." And then, he added, "If mankind does otherwise and falls prey to the powers of Satan and his dark machinations, the future shall be one of utter darkness and misery." And so, it is really up to mankind to make the decision of what path to take—to follow the radiant light of Almighty God or to choose the utter chaos and darkness of Satan. It's mankind's decision to make in the end. We have no choice and we must get it right!

Amen.

October 14, 2018
(Lyric)

That Ancient Darkside of All-Hallows' Eve Past

As in the fabled medieval times of centuries in the deep past,
It's time once again to celebrate the hidden ugly horror that
Seeks to infest and devour all human souls in this new century.

Be warned that false-faced beggars shall knock at each door,
And unbeknownst to the common people that they shall meet
On this All-Hallows' Eve—all shall not be well and normal!

With their bloodstained masks these real Ghosts, Ghouls and
Goblins shall shout out "Trick or Treat" as a fiend's true cover
For something that's sordid, unclean, ungodly, and macabre.

Looking for a clever sweet surprise for the unsuspecting souls,
These devilish minions begin gathering and dancing wildly to
"The Dark Spirit of the Pale Hallowed Moon" on this night!

Shawled with the darkness of souls and their living nightmares,
Ghastly silver phantoms now seek to scare the living-death out
Of every innocent person they encounter on this darkest eve.

Houses are marked by an eerie orange-pumpkin-light escaping
Into the dancing-dark shadows that hold all night-life precious,
As these phantoms move freely in the frigid breath of this night!

Creating a palpable angst they begin shaking the tree branches as
Horrid and terrifying spirits of true evil and witchcraft escape into
The cold-dark ether caught up in the vile magic of Lucifer himself.

Fortunately, they are tricked by the sound of an old tune playing a
Heavenly paean for knowing "What's Right From What's Wrong,"
And warning them that the wrath of Almighty God awaits them!

In the end, the absolute power and holy majesty of Almighty God
Served as the saving grace to this foul situation which threatened
The innocent souls who were ensnared by these unholy phantoms.

And so, if thou doth question the probity of what hath been related to
You in this sacred narrative, then thou shall risk forfeit of your soul,
As these evil phantoms lurk always in the shadows and never forget!

October 19, 2018
(Tercet)

Author's Note: A Collaborated Poem with Liam McDaid.

That Heart on Your Sleeve

It is very sad to see a situation where a person or any
person ends up wearing his or her heart on their sleeve.

In the end, the expression, "wearing that heart of yours on
your sleeve" does seem to be a big ditto in human society.

When love and emotions come into conflict it can be quite
easy for someone, man or woman, to have their heart broken.

Unfortunately, this is always a possibility of sorts when two
people meet and they end up falling "head over heels" in love.

Feelings of utter loneliness and the cruelty of another person
may end up destroying a relationship that once had promise.

It takes "two to tango" in any love relationship and especially
in a marriage where people in love must learn to live together.

Some couples are successful and some others are not, but that's
the real situation in any relationship involving love and emotions.

Beware of anyone who should tell you differently about any state
of affairs concerning "that heart on your sleeve." Be cautious!!

Life is short in human terms, but a real love between two people
in an ethereal and eternal sense could last forever. Good Luck!!

And, in the end, only Almighty God knows all of this for sure.
I certainly hope so!! Amen.

December 5, 2018
(Lyric)

That Thief in the Night

Who do you think I am thinking about with this poetic theme?

One very good guess could be "Death," and if you thought that, then you would be one-hundred percent right!

The reality of Death and its existential personification in the long history of mankind is indeed most well-established.

The idea of Death, and its natural result and corresponding effect on the human race is very sad—yet very compelling from a mortality standpoint.

Death is always associated with darkness, sadness, and in many cases with a disbelief that things like this just don't make sense, and why do they happen?

Death, as in Life, is in the natural order of things that affect our individual mortality.

For a life that ends suddenly or too soon, it is natural for all of us to view such a sad event with a degree of askance and to ask why?

This result gives rise to the notion that Death is "That Thief in the Night" that can strike any of us at any time with short or no notice.

What can we do as human beings when we are faced with such a natural and inevitable result? The answer, from my perspective, is to embrace and to live your life always to the fullest extent possible by the holy grace and true blessing of Almighty God.

Be not afraid, have faith, and always seek to find and fulfill your God-given destiny.

Amen.

November 25, 2018
(Narrative)

The Ancient Mariner's Fate

Eternally doomed adrift
Samuel Taylor Coleridge
The Mariner repeats his
Story over and over now.

A sad soul in true agony
Incomprehensible
His heart now dry as dust
To his fate he must bow.

December 3, 2018
(Double Dactyl)

The Body Finds its Rest

After a long life
Of all kinds of experiences
You are thinking about the end.
You are at the bottom of
All life, of all experiences
and of all expectations
so the only worry, which is left
is to find a place
where all is taken care of
and the body can
rest after a life
of both burden and joy
of enjoying the world
in all earthly measures.
You need one person
To take care at the end
When it comes...
To fulfill and end
The life of a lifetime.
The one person
you can trust
to honor the person
in this body.
And when the body
Is taken care of...
The horror of this life on Earth
Until its natural end...
So the soul can now go on
To other realms
In freedom, joy, and peace.
The body lays honored
In the ground, at the bottom of the sea
Or flying-floating in ashes over
The surface of the Earth
In freedom, joy, and peace.
So be it.

June 10, 2018
(Verse)

Author's Note: A Collaborated Poem
with Ingrid Krukenberg-Bateman.

The Circus Fat Man

This unusual man is truly a real sight to see as
"The Circus Fat Man" for a local Cajun circus.

He takes a sense of definite pride in being known
by this distinctive moniker, whilst always smiling!

When talking to groups of circus attendees, at once,
he announces his title with a twinkle in both eyes!

He makes sure they know he's a spokesman for his
circus and that he comes from LOOU-ZEE-ANNA!

Coming from the southern bayou region of this state,
he's truly legendary as the genuine "strong man" he is.

That's really his true secret, which by his blubbered
appearance and presence doesn't seem at all possible.

That is, until he starts lifting and curling a series of
progressively back-breaking weights done by Olympians.

The Fat Man is known also for his unique ability to pull
immensely heavy Caterpillar equipment with no problem.

At the end of his circus introduction spiel, whilst always
smiling, he knows what the circus attendees want to see.

Moving with him out to a very large open area, the circus
attendees, with wide eyes, see the weighted objects he uses.

And don't forget the Caterpillar equipment—it's there too!
With bright lights blaring into the dark evening sky, all is ready!

As the Fat Man goes through his various demos, the crowd now
grows in size, truly mesmerized by the sight of his real muscles!

As the weights increase and the difficulty of each demo multiplies, the crowd both gasps and sighs as they witness each of his events!

For his final act, The Fat Man prepares to lift a weighted object above his head that has never been attempted by anyone at all.

With a hushed silence, he starts his lift, whilst moaning and groaning at the truly immense weight of his chosen object.

Inch by inch, he lifts the impossible weight with his head now tilted toward the vast infinity of the star-lit, deep-dark night sky.

The circus crowd gasps momentarily, and then, is silent, as they bear witness now to this stupendously executed Herculean event.

The Fat Man now appears in a perfectly-flexed musculature as the real Circus Strong Man that he truly is and has always been.

With the mesmerized circus crowd looking on with amazement, The Fat Man, with legs locked, achieves his final lift sequence.

Holding his final lift for a period of very long seconds, he looks as if he bears the whole weight of the world on his bulging shoulders.

The Fat Man knows that he is truly an Olympian without any equal as he looks intensely at the utter vastness of the deep-dark night sky!

November 4, 2018
(Couplet)

The Clock

dial bright-white
imposed with
bold-black numbers

scored sounding
repetitive

like 1-2, 1-2, 1-2
or
tick-tock, tick-tock, tick-tock

dial colors
contrasted

tick-tock sounds
perfect precision.

August 16, 2018
(Imagism)

The Cosmos

Eternity pure—
Beyond mortal awareness!
A true cosmic realm . . .
Mystic and spiritual . . .
Souls arrive there in God's hands!

June 23, 2018
(Tanka)

The Curse of the Dead Sea

Dark ghosts traveling through the chilled air mist
where rare rough rivers, eddied and revolved, in
twists around into a violent, furious funnel offshore,
as this turbulent salt sea of iniquity opens up its storied,
salted bowels with its turgid moving fluids drowning
into a space of predestined bedded death—for all who
unknowingly venture into the embrace of the Dead Sea.

Be aware that Poseidon, as the ancient god of the sea,
may not be there in time to spare thy life that be in the
fatal grip of this salted deadly destiny, and its jeopardy,
as it's written in the "riddle of sands" that remain blowing
as this earthly desert speaks to thee, spiced by the coldest
of raindrops carried on winds held deep within, as dark
clouds escape with their droplets running down into the
mountain "waters of life" that feed and form an evil river
that pulsates through the deep veins of existence, as drums
inside heartbeats play to a harmonious harp filled with a
mystic music dancing to visions of a salted angel who lives
deep within the Dead Sea.

Falling throughout the depths of time in the history of this
ancient sea of sure death, are grains of sand and pure white
salt which hold misted gems that speak to each and every
human footprint, leaving an imprinted, indelible image true,
behind the frame left crowned in the deep well of a forlorn,
shimmering pond that presciently knows that this ancient
Dead Sea, with its "salt of the sand" shall explain to you,
in kind, of the dangers that lurks within the waters of its
salted, deadly grip, if you choose unwisely to venture in
knowingly or unknowingly.

For Poseidon shall not be there in this "modern age" to save thee and thy immortal soul!

Amen.

December 16, 2018
(Narrative)

Author's Note: A Collaborated Poem with Liam McDaid.

The Darkness of Cold Oceans Dwelling Deepest

Into the utter darkness of cold oceans dwelling deepest,
there is far beyond any glimmer of hope an outer limit
that defines a dark realm of the true supernatural reality
existing beyond any iota of human understanding on Earth.

In this dark realm lies a catacombic-womb of dead souls
bled white from the inside-out-turning of sand-blasted
nightmares of pure evil that envelop into a desert storm,
whereby living-dead apparitions appear in the shadows.

In this Procrustean bed there lies these horribly-tortured souls
who are like fossils of a past strife-torn life—a past without
any mercy since the unloved ghosts who exist there sense a
palpable pain erupting deep within every second of eternity!

This achingly slow-death falls into a sentence as forgiveness
now is impossible and a weathered-weakness of bowels spiced
from this seabed's loving memory appear as a bright-white pearl,
and the golden sun rises and sets as rats spread the Black Death!

August 15, 2018
(Quatrain)

Author's Note: A Collaborated Poem with Liam McDaid.

The Devil Cometh Tonight

The fright of this unholy night
says the Devil cometh tonight
to capture my soul
before I grow old,
it is told
on this night.

God, save my soul on this dark night,
by your true grace make it all right,
save my holy soul
so I may grow old,
being bold
this dark night.

November 13, 2018
(Clogyrnach)

The Ghosts in Those Dark Woods

The wind blows quite hard and icy-cold from those foreboding dark and dense woods that lie ahead of us as the last vestiges of the warm daylight disappear now, and as a truly sinister darkness on this night begins to envelope all of us whilst presenting us with a dreadful, tragic sense of impending doom and evil.

There was supposed to be such a big, bright Full Moon in the sky on this night! It did appear briefly, in fact, but was not at all bright, and certainly not luminescent enough to provide any real degree of positive visual radiance for us. Rather, what appeared was only—a dull, sad, and truly depressing visage of a hazy-cold and pale-white orb that was ritualistically arrayed high in the night sky as if it were to bespeak and imply a special omen or warning to us.

And yet, now with even a more studied second glance—that sad, sullen, and pale-white Moon that lurks high in the night sky looks even more ominous than any of us could've ever possibly imagined. Its peculiar image has left us bereft of any reflective light. A definite sense of true evil and ill-foreboding shadows touch all six of us now in our group as we walk toward the dark woods ahead of us. To me, I seem to be the only one in our group who truly senses, with the peculiar and suggestive sight of the pale-white Moon on our horizon now, that a supernatural specter of evil is actively seeking to pervade our immediate space as we continue with our collective journey to the dark woods.

So much for this evening adventure being a really "fun hike," and for us to end up being afraid of the dark just like a small group of little kids. And, six miles for us doesn't really seem a long distance to walk especially since all of the guys in our group are athletes and run a lot. And yet, I still get the troubled feeling that our hike out to the dark woods on this evening may have more in store for us than we could've ever imagined! It would've been better and much quicker, if we could've taken the SUV we had available for making this trip out to the dark woods, but we were warned by local residents in the area that the old country road going toward the dark woods was in a state of advanced disrepair; it was full of deep potholes and not readily available for any passable vehicular traffic given the very rough terrain and all of the thick brush that grew in, on, and around the road itself. "Walking" was the only real mode of travel we all could reasonably do to get to our destination.

The open land terrain beyond the old country road was equally challenging and could only be successfully navigated by riding horseback. No horses on this short notice were available to us, and traveling there by helicopter was not an option for us as well. And so, walking to the dark woods was the only real option open to us!

And then, for some reason, another disturbing thought had just crossed my mind based on what some of the local residents of this area had mentioned to us in passing. We were told, that is, "warned" that the dark elements of the Spiritual Unknown that are reputed to haunt the dark woods at night may actually appear without any warning! This was something that had really stuck in my mind as a deadly premonition for sure, as we had later started our walk toward the dark woods on this chilly, mid-September evening in good old rural Montana. We were constantly debating and discussing any and all options open to us for traveling to this unusual destination.

As it turns out, I'm the superstitious one in our group who often tends to worry about these things that the others don't. And being the guy who happens to be the unofficial navigator-map reader of our group, I just noticed, with some additional curiosity, a unique brown-hatched "area symbol" on our map now that shows the location of the dark woods. This particular symbol actually looks like an ugly spot of cancer! At least that's the mental impression and feeling that I'm left with as I gaze further at this map area symbol. Strange it is—indeed!

A definite omen, I thought, but something worthy of concerned awareness and attention, as if the others in our group really cared at all. In the fine print, the map refers to this special marked "restricted area" we were presently walking toward as "The Devil's Flats." All of us in our group had studied the map earlier. How did we miss this name? One would think that a peculiar name such as this one would've stood out immediately. But somehow, we all missed it. Regardless, we all now know this fact for sure as spooky as it seems to be!

Luckily for us, the old country road we had started walking on to eventually arrive at the dark woods could at least be seen in the dark of night—or so the locals told us! Oh joy! It's nice to know that we have some sort of a set way back, if we should have to leave the dark woods quickly on a moment's notice! Yet, I still had my doubts given the boulders, potholes, and thick brush in and around this old country road, especially at night!

Now, after we had started the walk out to our eventual destination at "The Devil's Flats," I noticed, especially given the rough terrain and obstacles in front of us, that in just over two hours we had made some real progress after all, with at least four miles or so behind us now in our supposed "fun hike." At this point, we all knew that we were closer now to the end point of this terrible road that we'd been traveling on with the forested plateau area of "The Devil's Flats" now appearing straight ahead right in our direct line of sight. It did take us some careful, steady walking to arrive at the point we are now at, which is right about at five miles.

We were all well-aware now of our impending closeness to finally arriving at "The Devil's Flats." In fact, we began smelling increasing traces of sulfur in the night air. Although we had, at least, a reasonable visual sight of the road during our walk with the help of our flashlights and map compass readings we had performed while walking, we began to notice that our general visual acuity at a greater distance was hampered by the challenging nature of the bleak darkness that had started to envelope the terrain and the immediate horizon in front of us. And, it was obvious, as we walked on, that the lack of any sufficient moonlight on this dark night played a negative factor, and slowed us down, at times, as we pushed onward to the "Flats."

Within another hour thereabouts, we slowly began stepping off the road now or what was left of this very old road, and headed on toward the dark woods as they now appeared visually to us in the immediate distance. What we all saw was a starkly dark and menacing silhouette of trees, rocks, and brush about a thousand feet ahead of us.

Our initial plan, as we had all discussed earlier, was to camp overnight near a faint clearing area we had just found in close proximity to the dark woods. Luckily for us, the stifling sulfur smell we had encountered earlier during our walk had largely dissipated and was no longer strong at all now. In fact, it seemed that all of us had gotten used to it. We then, had finally decided we would begin our final walk into the woods first thing during the early morning hours. This would give all six of us, at this late hour, at least some much-needed rest, if only for a few hours, and just enough to refresh us from this very long and arduous walk. And some rest and a break were exactly what we needed now before attempting our planned exploration of this densely wooded plateau area very first thing at the crack of dawn.

We all realized and knew that this was something that we would need to do during the hours of daylight, especially since this famous geographic plateau area we would be exploring was at least a mile or more in circumference. At least that's what our map had indicated to us.

Just then, as we had all begun stepping off the road that we'd been walking on, we noticed that the road itself had abruptly ended anyway, and then, we all began feeling the freezing rush of very cold wind! And there we were with only our hiking clothes on, and wearing only light jackets! Since we visited this area during mid-September, the daytime hours were still moderately warm and we were not expecting such a robust drop in the ambient temperature during the nighttime. *(Diary Entry Note: Make sure to bring warmer clothing and jackets, if we should ever have to come back to this area again in the future—especially during both the Autumn and Winter months!!)*

We continued forward with our walk now with the unexpected freezing rush of a very cold wind nipping at our heels and freezing our faces. Yet, having been on other hiking expeditions, our group took all of this in stride being the adventurous sort of hikers we are.

Concurrently, we then began hearing, what sounded like some faint voices emanating from the "Dark Woods" themselves that were now directly ahead us. These particular voices had a certain pronounced and eerie nature about them for sure! These faint voices gave all of us a palpable feeling and a sense of something that was of a macabre nature. It presented us with an instantaneous shock that something truly evil now awaited us in those dark woods ahead. These faint voices, in an imagistic sense, presented us with a strange type of mental image likened to the tortured feeling and utter despair of old haunted souls who are not at rest, nor at peace.

With this immediate occurrence, I then clearly remembered the stern and pointed warning we received from some of the town locals in the old bucolic village of "Hobbs Center" now located about six miles back in a southerly direction on this old dilapidated, unused road in this bleak and desolately rugged western region of Montana. The locals told us about the rock flats in this area and its deeply-dense forest, but never called it by its actual name: "The Devil's Flats." They just referred to it as "The Old Forested Plateau," or just "The Plateau" that's populated with some supposedly "bottomless" sulfur tar pits, and that this elevated plateau area, according to local historical legend, had been a former Indian burial place used during the nineteenth-century, and perhaps even earlier than that. Some of the locals had emphasized to us that no one ever goes out "The Plateau" due to rugged terrain there and the seemingly abrupt changes in the weather surrounding that particular area.

As it turns out, from what we had learned earlier about this austere country region, there had been a former local Indian tribe, known as *"The Matupaba"* that had lived near this plateau area at one time. Given the dense forested area of this elevated plateau and the line of sight it afforded to the Indian tribe, that made it easier for the Indians to repel anyone who chose to attack them. The Matupaba tribe used this plateau as a staging ground for planning and executing attacks on white settlers who had begun populating the new village area close by that later become known as "Hobbs Center" during the 1840s. This Matupaba tribe deeply worshipped this area, but later vacated it when they supposedly discovered that the flats had been apparently possessed and haunted by the malefic influence of "The Great Evil Spirit of the White Man," or the "Evil One," as Indian legend has it.

This "Evil One," known historically to the White Man as the Devil, Satan, or Lucifer was, in fact, the true tenet spirit of this bleak surrounding plateau area known as "The Devil's Flats." No wonder the local native Indian tribe had vacated this haunted area with all due haste and fear! The Indian tribe had lived for several years in and around The Devil's Flats long before the white settlers had begun populating this area, and later built the current village town of Hobbs Center. The Matupaba Indians, in fact, blamed the haunting of the "Flats" on the inimical influence and the hostile, malevolent behavior that the white settlers had adopted and invoked toward their local tribes from the 1840s and on. It seems the problems started later on when the White Man and their families began settling in this regional area of Montana. Over time, after a number of unexplained occurrences and tragedies, a true spirit of evil and an aura of unmitigated malignancy became the predominate story lines among the Indians and the white frontier settlers who struggled to live in the vicinity of "Flats."

Well, that's the story and legend about the ghosts in those dark woods that lie now straight ahead of us as we all prepare to bed down for the rest of this cold, dark night before embarking on our exploratory jaunt of this area right at daybreak. But remember, I'm the superstitious one in our group, and my friends, as the adventurous lot that they are, see me as always overreacting to any circumstances that I end up being sensitive about. Well, it is, after all, only a one-day visit to this dense forested area that will begin very soon tomorrow morning at dawn. But then, eerily, I just remembered and realized that we all had just arrived at "those dark woods" during the dark-dead of the night! Another one of my so-called "omens," I guess, right before I began nodding off and falling into a deep sleep.

My final thought . . . just as a cloud of much-needed sleep started to overcome me, was my hope that all six of us in our group would awaken the next morning in good order, fresh—fully alert, and ready to do our planned-exploration and investigation of "The Devil's Flats," that is, unless the ghosts in those dark woods just ahead of us had other nefarious nocturnal plans in store for us! I then, faintly murmured . . . May God and His Holy Angels in Heaven protect us and save us from this evil! Amen!

September 15, 2018
(Narrative Story)

Author's Note: I wrote this story originally, in my first draft, as a poetic verse that over time morphed into a full-fledged, fictional-fantasy-horror narrative story of sorts based on certain "myths" concerning various Indian tribes that once populated the western region of the United States before the coming dominance, plunder, and tribal decimation brought on by the White Man who settled in this area during the early nineteenth-century. In this particular narrative, "The Devil's Flats" is a very dense, and dark forested area surrounding an elevated plateau replete with rugged rock formations and bottomless sulfur tar pits. Located in the bleak western region of Montana, these rock flats were once an ancient American Indian burial place that the resident Indian tribe there had eventually vacated when they discovered that the flats were possessed and haunted by the malicious influence of "The Great Evil Spirit" or "The Evil One," known historically to the White Man as the Devil, Satan, or Lucifer. Today, the local townspeople from the small country village of "Hobbs Center," live a relatively quiet and peaceful existence about six miles away from that dark, dense forest that's on and surrounds the plateau at The Devil's Flats. The locals still claim there are "Ghosts" and "Evil Spirits" in those dark woods. Very few, if any of the locals, have ever ventured close to these woods, that is, with the exception of some unsuspecting tourists who may have unknowingly ended up in this remote area. It is said that a number of the tourists or outsiders over the years who had foolishly made their backpacking treks to visit "The Devil's Flats," had virtually all disappeared with the exception of a few survivors who managed to stumble out from the woods, barely alive, and driven to a state of total insanity with their lives ruined and changed forever! This is a place of true evil that no one should ever contemplate visiting. There's a very good chance that you will disappear forever! "Good Luck" is all I can say, if you should ever choose to visit "The Devil's Flats." I'm quite sure that Old Hob would have it no other way! *Deus miseratur! Deus tecum!*

The Grimace of the Human Race

Oh, Human Race, when shall thee ever learn? The age-old stain of sin and selfishness remains omnipresent with us in this modern age, just as it was in centuries past, dating to mankind's first-ever presence upon this Earth... yes, Our Earth, I say, dating back to mankind's first awkward presence, pre-historic and all, on this, our magnificent celestial orb, *"Our Home Sweet Home"* if you will, by the hand and the divine beneficence of Almighty God Himself.

Should we not strive to do our very best in all that we do, rather than trudging along, wallowing, for some, in a state of perpetual self-pity and doing sad, evil things to one another instead of seeking to do our best, sharing love and showing respect for one another as we seek to find the *"Better Angels of Our Nature"* in all we do individually and together? To this I say, Why Not? What do we have to lose? Think about it.

The *"Four Horsemen of the Apocalypse"* which take the the form of War, Famine, Pestilence, and Death manifest themselves historically and readily in our modern age today a la Tyranny, Poverty, Disease, and War itself. These evils deserve a stern reckoning from all of the collective societies on Our Earth if all of us can ever hope to find real solutions to the abject suffering, shame, and pain that they inflict daily, at will, on many of the people who comprise the societies of our so-called modern world of today. Only when mankind chooses to stand firm and decisively against the many ills wrought by the insidious nature of these *"Four Horsemen,"* can we ever hope to find true peace and happiness on Earth.

Therefore, our undeniable existential challenge in rising to this herculean task, in a truly metaphorical sense, shall be to change over time *"The Grimace of the Human Race"* into *"The Grace of the Human Race."* This is something that's truly worth fighting for, if mankind can ever hope to bring about a real and everlasting peace to the world we live in today. Our ultimate survival today truly depends upon it!

May God Bless. Amen.

August 20, 2018
(Didactic)

The Journey to the Cosmic Beyond

Life
God's divine spark heralds our mortal presence on this Earth,
Whilst angels sing their mystic paeans to our cosmic rebirth.
The soul's constant transformation transcends all mortality,
As it brings each of us closer to God's vision of immortality.
Life should be lived by all with due passion and sincere love,
As we mortals reflect on Life's true meaning in Heaven above.
This mortal coil defines our self-existence in this human strife!

Death
Death bringeth a spiritual transition at the end of our mortal days,
And its reality frees our souls to find their destiny in many ways.
After death, our souls can now seek out their cosmic connections,
And return to God's Kingdom to share their earth-life reflections.
Death itself should never be feared but embraced at the end of life,
For our souls shall find their spiritual freedom and opportunities rife.
With death comes a new beginning as our souls ascend into eternity!

Hell
This spiritual possibility exists for those souls with big debts to pay,
As earthly sins come home to roost, and Lucifer shall have his way!
Redemption's possible for some souls with minor mortal infractions,
Whilst others reside here forever as Dante smiles at their sad reactions!
His Inferno is truly horrid for those who enter in shall forfeit all hope,
As Lucifer turns a literary portrayal into a reality as all souls must cope!
Hell's that darkest cosmic state of mind where things macabre rule all!

Heaven
One's holy place in the realm of the "Pearly Gates" is the true intention
Of souls who proffer their goodness but reckon not with God's objection!
Others shall ascend here for good deeds done to help those in real need,
Whilst others with hidden warts and all shall be revealed for their greed!
Despite mortal flaws, Heaven's the place for many who strive their best
In God's eyes, realizing the reality of who they are at end of their quest!
God's judgment may oft be merciful, yet must never be taken for granted!

Cosmic Beyond

Life, Death, Hell, and Heaven from the view of Mother Earth are refined
By how mortals interpret biblical scripture with holy deliverance in mind.
Yet, as souls make their way to God's heavenly realm they may surely see,
More from God's infinite creation of the universe and who they are to be!
God's wish may be for us to discover, learn and experience as we move on,
With the spiritual love and appreciation of His creations in the Cosmic Beyond!
The Cosmic Beyond knows no astral borders—it is limitless, and it is eternity!

June 17, 2018
(Canzone)

Author's Note: A Collaborated Poem with Ingrid Krukenberg-Bateman.

The Kiss of a Christmas Elf

An elf, as one of Santa's little Helpers,
is bringing presents to a family on Christmas Eve.
A little girl is sleeping close to the Christmas Tree
and to the chimney, too, so she will not miss Santa's Visit tonight!
Cookies and Milk are well prepared.
The elf is taking his task very seriously,
and is making sure,
that nobody will see him doing his job.
But when the elf was placing
the last present under the Christmas Tree,
the little girl woke up, rubbing her eyes and whispered:
"Santa—is it YOU?"
"No," said the elf, "but I am one of HIS Helpers."
Then the little girl gave him a big smile,
and rushed over to him and gave him a big hug, and said:
"Thank you soooo much, that you came tonight!
I was waiting soooo long for a sign from Santa—
and now HE sent YOU!
I am soooo happy!"
The elf was surprised, he did not expect
that the little girl was totally happy with an elf
instead of Santa Claus himself,
but he was so deeply touched—
by seeing this pure joy on that little girl's face.
So he smiled and gave her a big hug, too,
and placed a little kiss on her cheek
leaving a tiny glimmer of fairy dust there.
But tonight was Christmas Night,
with so much "Magic" and "Wonder" in the air!
And a kiss from an elf,
given in pure love and joy,
has magic in itself,
but on Christmas Eve—
it has a very special magic,
and an aura of enchantment too!
And so, that little girl

got a special gift on this Christmas Eve:
From now on, whenever she smiles,
and is looking at someone with pure joy,
there is a "real magic" in her smile,
and it lets each person around her
remember the message of Christmas Eve—
To bring love and light
To everyone on Earth: Hallelujah!
And Santa Claus later smiled at his little helper and said:
"Well done, my little elf, well done!"

December 19, 2018
(Narrative)

Author's Note: A Collaborated Poemwith Ingrid Krukenberg-Bateman.

The Last Dance of the Autumn Leaves

The summer goes
And autumn comes around the corner.
The green of the leaves
Turns now into yellow, orange, and red.
The first soft winds
Let them move
Into the melody of autumn
Until the first storm
Will take them
And lead them
Up and down
For their very last dance
Until they finally
Move down to earth
Where they find
Their final rest
Under their tree of all seasons.

November 4, 2018
(Verse)

Author's Note: A Collaborated Poem
with Ingrid Krukenberg-Bateman.

The Last Red Rose of Autumn – First Portrait

The last red rose of Autumn signifies a real
heartfelt farewell to all of us, as the coming
changeover to the icy-cold Winter season
begins to make its frigid presence known
all around as the faint glimmer of Autumn
slowly and inevitably says its goodbye to us.

The last red rose of Autumn is very special,
in its magical and enchanting radiant-red hue,
and in the divine spirit it conjures for all of us
to see its wondrous image and truest beauty,
whilst we marvel at the majestic nature of its
richly redolent aroma that captivates our senses.

The last red rose of Autumn now sheds a big tear
since she must depart with the coming of Winter.

Goodbye.

November 24, 2018
(Free Verse)

Author's Note: A Collaborated Poem
with Ingrid Krukenberg-Bateman.

The Last Red Rose of Autumn – Second Portrait

The promise of Mother Nature
to come back
after a deep Winter's sleep
under thick white covers
green leaves
colorful blossoms
humming bees
singing birds
in between
newborn red roses
full redolence and true beauty.

November 24, 2018
(Free Verse)

Author's Note: A Collaborated Poem
with Ingrid Krukenberg-Bateman.

The Little Children are Crying

Of recent sad occurrence—
At the southern border of the USA
In prescribed DHS detention centers,
Little refugee children are crying
For their mothers and fathers—
From whom they had been cruelly taken
And caged like mere animals,
Full of tears, fears, and horrifying sadness
All at the capricious and unchristian whim
And quoted-biblical-certitude of the
Pied Piper's chief law enforcement officer,
The U.S. Attorney General,
And known by his Pied Piper-given moniker as
"Mr. Magoo," hailing all the way from Alabama!

Mr. Magoo's wondrous quote from
The Holy Bible
Unfortunately—
Is the same one historically cited
In previous years
As a vaunted justification for
"Slavery in America." Really?? Eh??

Maybe Mr. Magoo will be awarded
With a seat one day on the
U.S. Supreme Court—eh??
For his vast juridical knowledge and prowess,
And command of the Holy Bible—eh??
Anything is possible in the realm of
The Pied Piper.

And all the while during this time—
The little children are still crying
And remain caged on the
Southern border,
And separated from their parents,

As the Pied Piper
And his merry-prankster advisers
Continue their pathetically-fine
Tuned and crafted
Rhetoric of ranting and raving
About helpless people in their time of greatest need
Who wish to seek asylum in the United States.

Yes, unfortunately we've all been here before.
The Pied Piper and his Gang
Thrive religiously on playing the "Blame Game,"
That is, blaming others for these immigration policies,
Whilst continuously lying and denying,
And distorting the facts to suit their ultimate goals and aims.

This is all very sad to see and to write about.
It really is!!
Just take a moment to think about this.

And it's also quite disgusting and very un-American
To see little children and older children—
Ripped from the very arms of their mothers and fathers.

Where is the compassion, mercy, and sympathy??
Where is the human decency??
Where is the individual dignity??

We as a people are better than this—
Or at least we should be!!

The whole world is watching.
Shall we continue to be a vibrant democracy—
Or shall we welcome in a new reign of illiberal democracy??

Regardless, the little children are crying
And remained caged along with older children
Whilst being separated from their parents.

And during this whole time...
Lady Liberty in the New York Harbor
Cries for these children and the others too,
Whilst bowing her head in shame!!

We can and must do better than this!!

God Bless the United States of America.

June 19, 2018
(Political Verse)

The Magic of Love's First Moment

It's a very special time when suddenly you can't eat,
And your thoughts and emotions are not all rational.

Your emotions 'n heart are set afire and so is your blood,
As nothing makes sense—then everything makes sense!

You have all the words you want to say to your new love,
Yet you find no words pass from your lips to affirm all!

One of life's mysterious surprises—yet one so very real;
One of life's grand and puzzling Gordian Knots so true!

Emotions, feelings, hopes, fears—each with its singularity;
All clashing together all at once and providing no clarity!

Yes, this is that initial feeling and moment of truest passion,
When one's blood warms to red-hot and emotions run amok!

The magic of love's first moment is a marvel for all to behold;
It reflects love's complexity and its precious nature to be retold!

February 2, 2018
(Couplet)

The Magical Epiphany of an Old Rusted Can

whilst out hiking one day in a countryside area that
was quite desolate and remote from any nearby city,
I discovered, amazingly, an Old Rusted Can that
was at least four-liter-sized and was partially-buried
in a long dried-out riverbed in the middle of nowhere

this Old Rusted Can protruded out upright at about a
thirty-degree, right-slanted angle with some sharp and
jagged-edges located all along the top of its circular lip

its striking physical presence and the way in which it
was positioned, still partially-filled with dried riverbed
sediment, for me, bespoke some sort of an old artifact
of sorts, yet it was the only object like it, right in the
middle of this long dried-out riverbed

its unique silhouette was, at once, quite discernable at
a distance on the horizon as it casted a very curious and
most soulful shadow under the limitless canopy of the
late-morning sunlight

although it was very rusted, this Old Can actually
reflected radiant light rays at various times when it
was touched by the rays of the bright sunlight as it
ascended to its customary cosmic dominance in the
late-morning sky

it also had five certain hole punctures located front
and back, in its upper-area, from whence the bright
sunlight reckoned a kaleidoscopic effect of sorts as
the sunlight touched and passed through these unique
apertures that were arrayed on this Old Rusted Can

inelegant as this Old Rusted Can was—this unexpected
and most unusual light-show lasted for several minutes
until the darkened clouds overhead blocked out all of
the bright sunlight for the rest of the morning

yet, I just couldn't help but feel the true divine presence
of Almighty God Himself—as I had fervently focused on
every aspect and precise detail of this radiant and very
unusual light-show which presented a magical aura of
empyrean enchantment

and whilst I continued my deep gaze at this Old Rusted
Can, I was simultaneously and singularly transfixed by
the utter majesty and true joy of the holy epiphany it had
presented to me. I thought for a moment... God does
indeed relate to us, at times, in very mysterious ways!
God is everywhere!

Amen! Amen!

August 21, 2018
(Imagism)

The Metaphor of Time

Time's metaphor reflects the essence of a constant
and continuous progression into an endless cosmic
void of infinity itself, far beyond mankind's world
of a defined, finite reality and expectation.

The concept of eternity in this finite construct begs, at
once, much more than a sense of realistic credulity and
understanding. It considers cosmic aspects which often
transcend any earthly notions of a Prufrockian sense of
a melancholic desire that oft pervades the greater human
endeavor and circumstance.

Eternity is more than any mere snapshot of ongoing and
progressive actions, and any projected events frozen in a
defined and finite prism of time.

What about immediate actions like:
a rustling of trees and leaves in the wind,
the sounds of human voices near and far away,
the sounds of birds chirping loudly and softly,
the birthing sounds of baby animals in the forest.

Do we just observe and witness such events passively?
-or-
Do we listen for the progression of sounds and cries?
-or-
Do we just sit in moments of observed silence?
-or-
Does it matter in the end at all?

Indeed, there is much to think about in our world of this
finite reality where illusions abound as well.

This is perhaps why the notion of an endless infinity appeals
to and captivates the finite world of human beings, where the
notions of both cosmic fate and destiny, in an ethereal sense,

play a compelling role worthy of significant interest and a continuous pursuit of awareness and enlightenment.

Only time will tell! Only Almighty God knows for sure!

Tempus fugit ... for a good reason!
Tempus omnia revelat ... always in the end!

November 10, 2018
(Didactic)

The Mind's Cornfield

Dreaming deeply on this dark, dank, frigid-cold night,
My spirit-body walks freely in this place of solitude—
The Mind's Cornfield, where fantasy and reality are one.

In this place, free from mortal constraints and strife,
One can see and speak to spirits of those now dead,
And to those whose souls wander around aimlessly.

These spirits know of my still-mortal connection to
The earthly plane and are sometimes confused by my
Wandering presence with them in this vast cornfield.

I believe these spirits sense a form of hidden conflict
In my own spiritual body manifested perhaps by a
Tragic event impacting my soul from a former life.

I have learned over time there are others like me who
Are still mortally connected to our human world, but
Who choose now to walk about in this place of solitude.

Questions abound: Why does this netherworld exist?
What is its true purpose? Will the wandering spirits
Move on? Will they find the peace they are seeking?

And with this—I wake up again and find myself centric
In this mortal world of human creatures who are made
In the very keen, like-image of Almighty God Himself.

I can't help but feel a psychic-style influence with this
Image of a mental cornfield in the chasm of one's mind.
The soul's bond to the ethereal world may well be the key.

Situations like this call for a real mystical awareness of
How one thinks, what one sees, and what one perceives—
In this finite mortal world that defines us as Human Beings.

July 29, 2018
(Tercet)

The Moon

This mysterious mystical orb should be worthy of everyone's attention as it,
Heightens what each of us may think of the moon in today's mortal world.
Elevated heavens-high in the dark-night sky it bespeaks a supernatural nous.

Many mortals in centuries past have sought out the Moon's vaticinal power,
Open to those who truly seek to understand the source of its power and the
Optic essence of its existence as it touches the depths of mankind's very soul,
Never to disappoint, rather to excite mankind's quest to understand the cosmos.

October 20, 2018
(Acrostic)

The People from Those Shithole Countries

The people from "those" Shithole countries, eh??
Really?? Really?? You don't say?? I didn't know that!!

This is a recent stream of consciousness comment, which constitutes a new low in the American political discourse, courtesy of, none other than "America's Infamous Circus-Show Master" to whom I have referred to in a past poem from 2017 as "The Pied Piper from New York City."

Again, this individual refuses to conduct himself with the highest standards of civility, decency, manners, comportment, and intellectual curiosity expected from any person who holds or would endeavor to hold the highest political office of the land.

The Pied Piper's off-the-cuff comment in this instance about "those people" certainly does not represent nor does it portray "The Better Angels of Our Nature" as historically and originally posited by President Abraham Lincoln.

In effect and intent, the Pied Piper's deplorable comment, shared in a discussion with other political leaders who were there to hear it and witness it, is one that speaks volumes to several words which amply describe it, to wit: despicable, disgusting, racist, demagogic, idiotic, evil, and just plain stupid! A very poor comment, indeed, from the supposed "Leader of the Free World."

The Pied Piper has again besmirched the dignity and honor of the high office he holds, and has given America another unwanted and unnecessary "Black Eye," with his unfortunate comment, which only further tarnishes America's historically symbolic reputation as the land of freedom and democracy as a traditional immigrant nation.

With his recent comment here about "Those Shithole Countries," along with his incessant attacks on freedom of speech and press, libel laws, federal courts, the U.S. Congress, and the Justice Department— we are witnessing a very sad episode and saga of American democracy.

His childish actions continue to cheapen and weaken America's essential relationships with its key allies and its strategically-important international alliances. And, they help to create a narrative among nations of the world that America is becoming a "rogue-state" that no longer wishes to be the indispensable leader of the free world. A very sad tragedy for sure!

I recommend that the Pied Piper put on his current paltry reading list, that is, if he has one, some important documents and books that are well worth reading and understanding, to wit: The American Declaration of Independence, the U.S. Constitution and Bill of Rights, Abraham Lincoln's "Gettysburg Address," Alexis de Tocqueville's "Democracy in America," Thomas Paine's "Common Sense" and "Declaration of the Rights of Man," and Dr. Martin Luther King Jr.'s famous speech, "I Have a Dream." Maybe someday he will actually read at least one of these prized selections, and perhaps, he will actually learn something. Although, I sincerely doubt that shall ever be the case! His abysmal track record in this regard amply speaks for itself—incredible as it is stupid!

The people from "those" Shithole countries, eh??

A real intellectual and racially-unbiased comment from the Pied Piper!

Ha! Ha! Ha! I'm only kidding!

May God Bless, Save, and Help the United States of America!

Amen! Amen! Amen!

January 13, 2018
(Political Verse)

The Pilgrim's Ghost of a Thousand Heavenly Dreams

Looking through a magical dewdrop we now see an enchanted
Chandelier, liquid-sparkling pure, where a mystical quicksilver
Mirrors a living-moonlight reflection of a thousand radiant stars.

These stars are heavenly focus points that reflect the true celestial
Magnificence of Almighty God's prescient intention, whereby all
Cosmic music forms a clockwork of tick-tocks of a certain vision.

This vision streams and sounds throughout the cosmos entire on
Starbeams with the dimension, power, and force of Almighty God,
Whilst casting a glorious panoply of light illuminating the darkness.

The reach of God's eternal light into this deep-dark void of the cosmos
Is known as "The Pilgrim's Ghost of a Thousand Heavenly Dreams."
It has an undeniable metaphorical place in mankind's collective psyche.

This ethereal, eternal ghost by God's own direction on our mortal Earth,
Allows for mankind's curious interest in exploring the deepest-darkest
Crevasses of the oceans and the silent, sacred-secrets of the cosmos itself.

This ethereal, eternal ghost resident in mankind's consciousness fuels now
Man's desire, divinely-inspired, to see ourselves as a mirror-image of God,
As we fulfill God's desire that our souls shall ascend one day to Heaven.

October 10, 2018
(Tercet)

Author's Note: A Collaborated Poem with Liam McDaid.

The Sacred Heart

The Sacred Heart
Shines radiantly
With all colors
Which are not known
On the earthly plane.
Its radiant warmth
Is beyond all dimensions
And cannot be described
By any earthly measure.
Its size and mystical reach
Are beyond the person,
And when you are open—
You can feel it, too.
Let your own heart
Grow beyond any measure
So you can touch
The Soul of Others.
The only connection
Between souls on Earth
Is the Sacred Heart,
And this beyond all measure.

November 25, 2018
(Verse)

Author's Note: A Collaborated Poem
with Ingrid Krukenberg-Bateman.

The Silence of the Butterfly

The Soul of the Butterfly was already
there in the Caterpillar and in the Egg.

In the Egg, the Soul enjoyed
the time of being well protected,
to have the time to develop
everything necessary
before entering the world.

As the Caterpillar, the Soul enjoyed
climbing up the plants
until the green leaves
were now in reach...
the Caterpillar enjoyed chewing
on those luscious leaves
until finally...
all of the tasty juice
came out of them.

The Caterpillar saw the Butterfly
drinking the sweet nectar
out of the flower blossoms.

But did not understand
why the Butterfly...
after his transformation,
forgot all about those tasty green leaves.

And the Butterfly, then remembered...
his own thoughts—
when he drank the nectar for the
very first time
and the
perfect sweetness
of it,
which let him forget, at once,

those green leaves that were so tasty . . .
yet now . . . are nothing but bitter leaves.

Only now does the Butterfly realize
each of his forms of existence—
enjoying his natural way of being . . .
the way food is eaten,
the way of movement,

the way of taking part,
in Nature's most magical
and wonderful creation.

And the Butterfly enjoyed
this moment of pure bliss.

After this experience,
the Butterfly fell into a pure silence—
and it turned out
to be the most
enchanted moment of the day
with that sweet smell of
a rose close by
a cool breeze of the evening
and the flush of pink colors
in the sky

June 12, 2018
(Imagism)

Author's Note: This special Imagism poem was authored by Ingrid Krukenberg-Bateman.

The Strawberry Moon

This moon rises up ever slowly among the clouds,
As it begins its ritual journey of peeking slyly out,
Appearing for all to see in that far-distant horizon.

This wondrous eidetic image is a Strawberry Moon
That's so softly-red with a magical touch of orange,
And so very rare to see—yet so special to gaze upon.

As this enchanted moon continues its skyward ascent,
It begins to kiss the Earth goodbye whilst following its
Heavenly path in the sky to be amongst the radiant stars.

This glorious moon now follows its celestial path into
The Dark Beyond as its strawberry tint passes away,
And its ancient, brilliant-bright luminescence returns.

Oh, Strawberry Moon—our pride of the month of June,
Shall you tell us more when you come back to us, of what
We shall see in the Dark Beyond, in the Sky of Nowhere?

And perhaps we can expect in your next journey to us,
Another special kiss by you—a welcome kiss telling us
That a reunion awaits us all on the eternal path of light!

July 6, 2018
(Tercet)

Author's Note: A Collaborated Poem with Ingrid Krukenberg-Bateman.

The Wedding Clock's Wish

The Wedding Bells
Are ringing,

The little Bluebird
Is singing,

When the marriage band
Is knotted.

Happy times for
The married couple
Are wished for,

And lying ahead—
The clock will be
Silent proof of that.

May 21, 2018
(Free Verse)

Author's Note: A Collaborated Poem with Ingrid Krukenberg-Bateman. We both wrote this poem for two friends of ours who had recently married here in Germany.

Thinking Out of the Box

Ah, yes! It is! Another one of life's great challenges!
Thinking Out of the Box should never be taken lightly.

Being human beings, it is well worth remembering
that we are all in this thing we call "Life" together.

Does this mean the challenges that each of us face
are easy? No! Life just doesn't work that way.

There will always be personal and professional
challenges, and tasks and people to test our mettle.

Thinking Out of the Box does require, at times, to go
beyond notions, ideas or concepts that are obsolete.

This is where the proverbial "rub" comes in with
human nature, for people tend to resist new things.

It's part of human nature for people, at times, to
resist change and become set in their attitudes.

Thinking Out of the Box, in this sense, is not new
at all. It's part of seeking to improve life's situations.

Thinking Out of the Box definitely has a personal
and a professional meaning to us in our life's run.

Otherwise, what kind of a world would we expect to
live in, if all becomes obsolete and there is no change?

November 20, 2018
(Didactic)

Thoughts On Infinity

Infinity comprises that endless empyrean reach of a
True continuous nature far beyond mankind's ability
To truly comprehend and appreciate the sheer magic
Of the real enchantment and beauty of Almighty God's
Kingdom of everlasting peace, love, and devotion.

Infinity is beyond all time, space, matter, and destination.
It is bounded by a mystical aura of a true divine cosmic
Perfection created by the heavenly design and intention
Of God Himself as He has made His revelatory overtures
To each of us for our eventual spiritual transformation.

Infinity oft bespeaks stark images of an endless cosmic vortex,
Punctuated by planets, stars, black holes, comets, and star dust;
When it realistically may be more of a perfected state of a true
Self-awareness and an accentuated level of consciousness that
Transcends mankind's finite level of reality and understanding.

One day when each of us reach the end of our mortal coil on
Earth, we shall, in turn, make that final storied leap into the
Heavens as our souls begin their cosmic ascension into God's
Kingdom, and shall arrive at their ultimate state of holy bliss
Into the embrace and eternal love of Almighty God Himself.

August 29, 2018
(Quintain)

Triskaidekaphobia

And so, you have "Triskaidekaphobia" on your mind. Indeed, fear of the Number "13" does have a real and a certain palpable feel and meaning for people who harbor this particular phobia and carry it with them in their lives. With triskaidekaphobia, superstitions abound regardless of any rational explanations that are proffered in western societies. The history of mankind is rife with superstitions and old wives' tales dating back through the centuries as human societies grew and evolved over time and became more or less sophisticated by their own enculturation processes.

Nevertheless, next time you're on an elevator you may notice that a button for a "Thirteenth Floor," doesn't exist, and that Floor 12 progresses to Floor 14. And, with a "Floor 13" being non-existent, this may give a person, a pause for a moment, with a certain mental flavor of the phantasmal aura about everything that surrounds a "Floor 13" existing and being listed on the elevator's button-panel selections—let alone even being mentioned at all.

Sometimes the slack in this oddity of the floor numbers may be deflected with a listing for the "Mezzanine" that is an intermediate second floor that's open to the ground floor by a stairwell. It's also worth mentioning that many old hotels in the past that still exist today were built with the inclusion of a "Thirteenth Floor."

What to do? Do nothing. "Triskaidekaphobia" will exist regardless, and this phobia, among many others, will help to keep psychiatrists employed, occupied, and busy with all of their various professional endeavors.

When in doubt, just remember that the "Loch Ness Monster," a la "Nessie," does, in fact, really exist. And, never push that button for that "Thirteenth Floor," or else . . . !! HA!! HA!!

November 29, 2018
(Narrative)

Turning Inside Out

To be able to dream is really
something that's so human

At times though dreams may
become something else unexpected

Despite any individual privilege
or just plain good old fortune

We sometimes find out that our
dreams may become our nightmares

This sometime-reality reflects a type
of volte-face circumstance

Which oft flies in the face of one's personal
hopes, dreams, and aspirations

When a type of an about-face situation like this
occurs—one's life has perhaps turned inside out

And, it may even result further in turning a person's
life completely upside down, ushering in fear and despair

And this is never a good thing at all since—
living in this hyper-modern age of ours is difficult enough

Thought, mediation, prayer, counsel, and good friends
may give each of us that certain way forward we need

When something turns inside out for you—
never despair nor take counsel of your fears

Find solace and strength in God's divine message
of eternal peace, love, hope, and a shared humanity

You actually may be surprised just how much all of
us have in common as human beings in this world

October 30, 2018
(Lyric)

Twilight Whispers

Our whispers during twilight,
highlight a mystical moment
of owl-light during our special
walk together in this lush forest.

This moment captures for us a
period of true tranquility where
issues, problems, and other earthly
worries carry no weight, no penalty.

Holding hands now, we walk slowly,
whilst gently speaking to one another
in whisper-like tones bespeaking a
mythical rhythm that's now one with
our souls and the spirits of this forest.

October 5, 2018
(Free Verse)

Two Words – A Glimpse

Dream
Scheme

Beam
Team

Shout
Pout

Duel
Shot

Life
Death

Brain
Drain

Stupid
Cupid

Dumb
Numb

Rum
Thumb

Prosecute
Electrocute

Einstein
Infinity

Immigrant
Us

Atom
Bomb

Strength
Weakness

Love
Hurt

Fate
Destiny

God
Cosmos

Lucifer
Lost

Passion
Torpid

Feelings
Flatline

Politician
Huckster

Glorious
Despicable

Moon
Mars

Space
Race

Beguile
Style

Truth
Lie

Cake
Pie

Bicycle
Tricycle

Car
Jar

Balloon
Burst

First
Last

Lust
Like

Fist
Fight

Right
Write

Left
Deft

Genius
Idiot

Manners
Rude

Give
Take

Rate
Deflate

Washington
Jefferson

Hamilton
Burr

Trump
Nixon

Hitler
Wotan

Karloff
Lugosi

Frankenstein
Dracula

Foot
Feet

Think
Blink

Popcorn
Unicorn

Coffin
Fly

Fish
Fry

Good
Bad

Think
Drink

Smile
Scowl

Teeth
Towel

Grimace
Ace

Lash
Bash

Date
Hate

Hurry
Wait

Freeze
Animate

Brave
Wave

Holocaust
Heydrich

Fool
Drool

Slob
Blob

Dead
Undead

Alive
Thrive

Evolution
Revolution

Vampire
Umpire

Wire
Dire

Flour
Flower

Alien
Robot

Klaatu
Gort

Tower
Power

Rush
Hour

Talk
Walk

Hysterical
Empirical

July 8, 2018
(Short-Form Free Verse)

Two Words – First Glimpse Redux

Thumb
Finger

Hand
Foot

Toe
Toes

Blunder
Thunder

Seam
Beam

Stupidity
Contagious

Intelligence
Desired

Planets
Stars

Venus
Mars

Milky
Way

Iambic
Rhyme

Real
Divine

Curve
Time

Nose
Ears

Sticks
Styx

Bald
Hairy

Baloney
Piffle

Top
Bottom

Trump
Mussolini

Charlatan
Fascist

Sun
Mercury

Cosmic
Certitude

Mad
Man

She
Monster

Eyes
Flies

Turd
Bird

Money
Desire

Fruit
Empire

Pain
Pane

Brain
Drain

Red
Blue

Tie
Shoe

Gun
Bullet

Fun
Bun

Wind
Rain

All
Same

Drugs
Thugs

Atwill
Actor

Lamarr
Actress

Snot
Plot

Rasputin
Putin

Monk
Dictator

Zombie
Walking

Run
Bum

Much
Talk

Franklin
Adams

Madison
Monroe

History
Record

Fake
News

Some
Say

Bale
Hay

Reflections in the Mirror | 563

Right
Way

Not
Today

Toe
Jam

Computer
Scam

Earthen
Dam

Heaven
Hell

Magic
Spell

Athena
Bubo

Perseus
Andromeda

Poseidon
Kraken

Action
Motion

Yes
No

Yup
Nope

Submarine
Scope

Bismarck
Battleship

Gloom
Doom

Titanic
Tomb

Job
Rob

Bank
Banc

Anne
Frank

Humpty
Dumpty

Big
Egg

Stand
Tall

Rick
Ugarte

July 22, 2018
(Short-Form Free Verse)

Two Words – Second Glimpse Redux

Push
Pull

Donut
Hole

Toilet
Bowl

Laundry
Fold

Sing
Song

Ping
Pong

Mao
Zedong

Fly
Eater

Cloud
Nine

Moon
Shine

Vinegar
Brine

Wild
One

No
Pun

Arm
Leg

Black
Plague

Circle
Square

Head
Hair

Sonic
Whistle

Broom
Thistle

Pretty
Face

Human
Race

Alien
Space

Mountain
Road

Horned
Toad

Meteor
Rock

Mister
Spock

Start
Dart

Go
Flow

Pol
Pot

Hope
Not

Green
Brown

Smile
Frown

City
Town

River
Creek

Circus
Freak

Stuffy
Nose

Big
Toes

Bogart
Bacall

Free
Fall

Standing
Tall

Music
Note

Castle
Moat

Witch
Hag

Laundry
Bag

Robber
Rubber

Space
Discover

Race
Car

Bucket
Tar

Fruit
Jar

Phrenology
Psychology

Logo
Pogo

Wine
Beer

Whine
Jeer

Weather
Clear

Beach
Chair

People
Stare

Garden
Hose

Bloody
Rose

Genius
Knows

Alaskan
Snow

Car
Far

Road
Tar

Proud
Hound

Ground
Round

Upside
Downside

Aladdin
Jafar

Genie
Wish

Table
Fish

Wash
Dish

Slobber
Swish

Babble
Gabble

Clark
Gable

Atlantic
Cable

Stool
Pool

Fad
Lad

September 3, 2018
(Short-Form Free Verse)

Two Words – Third Glimpse Redux

Wax
Wane

Big
Train

Hood
Wood

Tooth
Booth

Gosh
Posh

Purple
Pink

Kitchen
Sink

Ice
Rink

Nays
Ways

Moon
Shine

Twine
Thine

Wild
One

Hun
Pun

Smart
Enough

Not
Tough

Prince
Wince

Ping
Pong

Bong
Dong

Real
Thing

Voice
Hoarse

Winning
Horse

Grasshopper
Stridulate

Cosmic
Force

Too
Much

Not
Enough

Poll
Toll

Pool
Tool

Duel
Fool

Bread
Roll

Place
Race

Brawl
Tall

Ace
Chase

Bath
Wrath

Back
Rub

Bone
Daddy

Phone
Mommy

Bingo
Bango

Exciting
Tango

Fango
Jango

Play
Piano

Porky
Pig

Dance
Jig

Hour
Tower

Flower
Power

Witch
Hazel

Nose
Nasal

Eye
Brow

Black
Cow

Bow
Wow

Fat
Man

Diet
Plan

Circus
Politics

Dirty
Sure

Facts
Blur

Sham
Shame

Many
Blame

Propel
Excel

Pain
Contain

All
Same

Total
Insane

Pica
Print

Time
Went

Odor
Vent

Pint
Tint

Rile
Pile

Gomer
Pyle

Vex
Hex

Hey
Tex

Tyrannosaurus
Rex

Flex
Perplex

Flick
Fleck

Bird
Peck

Oh
Heck

Card
Deck

Slick
Wick

November 2, 2018
(Short-Lined Free Verse)

Two Words – Fourth Glimpse Redux

Superman
Krypton

Elton
John

China
Dish

China
Country

Booth
Assassin

Bold
Gold

Pimple
Prick

World
Crisis

Eye
Ear

Rain
Dear

Pluto
Far

Popeye
Sailor

Bugs Bunny

Daffy Duck

Robin Hood

Friar Tuck

Little John

Hells Bells

Orson Welles

John Boy

Ships Ahoy

Country Western

Fly Eye

Comic Meaning

Cow Patty

Horse
Dung

Bells
Rung

Cool
Drool

Double
Speak

Equal
Weak

Not
Unique

Mercury
Jupiter

Brew
Beer

Deuce
Tennis

Wrath
Fear

Double
Talk

Hone
Bone

Mood
Rude

Zebra
Stripes

Depress
Digest

With
Pith

Dark
Park

Cork
Pork

Trance
Sleep

Pour
Pitcher

Witch
Finder

Finger
Toe

Rake
Grass

Shovel
Snow

Dairy
Milk

Holler
Collar

Bat
Ball

Sweet
Tooth

Babe
Ruth

Old
Man

Fish
Wish

Gorgon
Medusa

Few
Pew

Stop
Drop

Hood
Hide

Alchemy
Chemistry

Boil
Toil

Black
Oil

Dime
Nickel

Sour
Dour

On
Off

Rilke
Poet

Home
Run

Plant
Ground

Blue
Jay

Bunch
Hay

Breed
Seed

Brush
Pad

Mom
Pop

Movie
Flop

Go
Now

Holy
Cow

Blink
Wink

Sync
Sink

Pole
Whole

Hole
Dole

Wold
Told

Frown
Crown

Ping
Ding

Whig
Whine

Wine
Sublime

Lime
Blind

Kiss
Hiss

December 15, 2018
(Short-Lined Free Verse)

Vincent Willem van Gogh

Vincent van Gogh—a genius artist *par excellence*
As most famously he was known to all,
Whilst mired deep in shades of a frenzied, frantic confusion
Slices off his left ear he does—faster than he could slice a pear!

December 15, 2018
(Clerihew)

Whatever We is We are

Whatever We is We are . . . and have no doubt of this ever.

Whatever We is We are is something that should never be denied. Why? Why Not?

Whatever We is We are speaks with a devout degree of both a singularity and plurality in our human world with its simplicity, complexity, and contradictions in both truth and honesty that shape and define each of us, by fate and destiny, in the course of our lives.

Whatever We is We are suggests to each of us to tell who we really are without all of the metaphoric hype and subterfuge, and the common notions of jiggery-pokery that, at times, does pervade and corrupt human nature even in the best of us, no matter how grand and great our intentions and actions may be.

Whatever We is We are . . . and have no doubt of this ever.

November 24, 2018
(Didactic)

When It's Time to Pay The Piper

When it's time to pay that infamous character known as "The Piper" and then, to face "The Viper" at the end of one's life, it shall behoove thee to make sure that thou hast all of the necessary pleadings and exculpatory notions and the reasonings at hand, in the hope of a divine intervention from the angels in Heaven, since "The Viper" by legend hast that noxious-nasty strike and sting in the Devil's own tradition, and both shall bring thee swiftly to the front of Death's Door whereby, Death's immediate and compelling grip is at once flash-quick and flash-fatal, which is not at all merciful in the end. One's immortal soul may be at risk too!

If thy exculpatory and most humble pleadings do meet, perchance Heaven's angelic standards, then thy immortal soul shall be safe and sound in Almighty God's Kingdom.

Deus miseratur. Deus vobiscum.

Amen. Amen.

December 10, 2018
(Narrative)

Whiskey Lips So Sublime

Whiskey Lips step now over the line of true fire-water,
As a warm-burning brings forward one glowing sign.
The golden mead of sweet mountain dew appears now,
As each golden drop sighs its moment of escape and as
The alcohol signals and sparks the wildest of spirits in
One's own true self!

This moment of sublime ecstasy excites and sparks your
Deepest inner-spirit and you begin to slur and sing loudly,
As your mind begins to reel from the drunken delight of
Your very own intoxicating breaths—noble, yet stupid,
As you become drunken forever under each psychic sip
You take from the deepest pool in the very depths now
Of your eternal soul!

Your very eyes now glaze over a breathless message
You have found in the cheapest of whiskey bottles.
Saying a divine prayer to Almighty God Himself,
You open the bottle cork now and take notice that a
Little genie pops out of nowhere and begins to take all
Three of your mythic wishes granted together into one!

With that, this little genie shall begin dancing and singing
An ancient Irish whiskey song in your presence into the
Wee hours of the morning until you both pass out and fall
Into a drunken stupor with your whiskey lips so sublime!

July 23, 2018
(Free Verse)

Author's Note: A Collaborated Poem with Liam McDaid.

Wild Roses in Ice

At the
very edge
of a
frozen pond
during
the
ice-cold
Winter
deep
in an
old
country
forest—
unbelievably
I gaze upon
three
wild roses
frozen
in a
block
of ice
as part
of the
larger
ice flow.

These
roses
at the
pond's
very edge
are
rosy-red
radiant
beautiful
and even

redolent
although
encased
they are
in the
frozen
ice.

These
rosy-red
roses
appear
to be
perfectly
set
in a
straight
order—
horizontally
just like . . .
1-2-3.

A
wondrously
enchanting
sight from
Mother Nature
for sure—
bringing
a big
smile
to my
face
whilst
capturing
my thoughts
and
stirring

my emotions
and
touching now
the
very core
of
my being
and
my heart
and
my soul
forever!

November 12, 2018
(Short-Lined Free Verse)

CHAPTER SIX

Special German Lyric Poem
(2019)

"The Light of the Moths"
(Das Licht der Nachfalter)

The Light of the Moths

Even the moths want to go into the light.
But they must be careful:
If they want to go into the light of the sun,
they burn very fast.
Because the moths need the moonlight
And not the light of the sun—
This is their true nature.
Some of the moths forget this and just burn.

Ingrid Krukenberg-Bateman
August 13, 2019 (Lyric)

Original German Version of this Lyric Poem:

Das Licht der Nachfalter

Auch die Nachtfalter wollen ins Licht
Aber sie mussen auf passen:
Wenn sie in das Licht der Sonne wollen,
verbrennen sie schnell.
Denn die Nachtfalter benotigen das Mondlicht
Und nicht das Licht der Sonne –
Das ist ihre wahre Natur.
Manche vergessen das und verbrennen.

Ingrid Krukenberg-Bateman
13. August 2019

Book Author's Note: This is a very special heartfelt poem written by my wife, Ingrid, first in the original German, and then it was translated by her later into the English version. This poem, in both language versions, has a very compelling and deeply poignant metaphorical meaning that the reader should find most interesting.

Milton Keynes UK
Ingram Content Group UK Ltd.
UKHW040141170224
437973UK00001B/174